DATE DUE

~~OC 9 '96~~	~~AP 6 '00~~		
~~MR 6 '97~~	~~⌀~~		
AP 7 '97	~~JY 10 '00~~		
~~MY 29 '97~~	NO 6 '00		
OC 6 '97	NO 28 '00		
~~DE 19 '97~~	FE 8 '01		
~~MR 16 '98~~	~~MY 31 '01~~		
~~MY 13 '98~~	~~JE 11 '01~~		
~~JY 9 '98~~ DE 4 '01			
~~JY 30 '98~~	~~MY 13 '02~~		
~~NO 17 '98~~	~~SE 18 '02~~		
~~MY 11 '99~~	DE 6 '06		
MY 24 '99	~~JE 6 '07~~		
~~NO 22 '99~~			

DEMCO 38-296

Language Minority Students
in the Mainstream Classroom

BILINGUAL EDUCATION AND BILINGUALISM

Series Editor
Professor Colin Baker, *University of Wales, Bangor.*

Other Books in the Series
Building Bridges: Multilingual Resources for Children
    MULTILINGUAL RESOURCES FOR CHILDREN PROJECT
Curriculum Related Assessment
    TONY CLINE and NORAH FREDERICKSON (eds)
Foundations of Bilingual Education and Bilingualism
    COLIN BAKER
A Parents' and Teachers' Guide to Bilingualism
    COLIN BAKER
Policy and Practice in Bilingual Education
    O. GARCÍA and C. BAKER (eds)
Multicultural Child Care
    P. VEDDER, E. BOUWER and T. PELS
Teaching Science to Language Minority Students
    JUDITH W. ROSENTHAL
Working with Bilingual Children
    M.K. VERMA, K.P. CORRIGAN and S. FIRTH (eds)

Other Books of Interest
The Good Language Learner
    N. NAIMAN, M. FRÖHLICH, H.H. STERN and A. TODESCO
Language Diversity Surveys as Agents of Change
    JOE NICHOLAS
Making Multicultural Education Work
    STEPHEN MAY
Three Generations – Two Languages – One Family
    LI WEI
The World in a Classroom
    V. EDWARDS and A. REDFERN

Please contact us for the latest book information:
Multilingual Matters Ltd, Frankfurt Lodge, Clevedon Hall,
Victoria Road, Clevedon, Avon, England, BS21 7SJ.

BILINGUAL EDUCATION AND BILINGUALISM 7
Series Editor: Colin Baker

Language Minority Students in the Mainstream Classroom

Angela L. Carrasquillo and Vivian Rodríguez

Multilingual Matters Ltd
Clevedon • Philadelphia • Adelaide

Riverside Community College
Library
4800 Magnolia Avenue
Riverside, California 92506

APR '96

LC 3731 .C3428 1996

Carrasquillo, Angela.

Language minority students
in the mainstream classroom

Library of Congress Cataloging in Publication Data

Carrasquillo, Angela
Language Minority Students in the Mainstream Classroom/
Angela L. Carrasquillo and Vivian Rodríguez.
(Bilingual Education and Bilingualism: 7)
Includes bibliographical references and indexes.
1. Minority students–Education–United States. 2. Mainstreaming in education–United States.
3. English language–Study and teaching–United States–Foreign speakers.
I. Rodríguez, Vivian. II. Title. III. Series.
LC3731.C3428   1995
371.97'00973–dc20   95-31222

British Library Cataloguing in Publication Data

A CIP catalogue record for this book is available from the British Library.

ISBN 1-85359-298-6 (hbk)
ISBN 1-85359-297-8 (pbk)

Multilingual Matters Ltd

UK: Frankfurt Lodge, Clevedon Hall, Victoria Road, Clevedon, Avon BS21 7SJ.
USA: 1900 Frost Road, Suite 101, Bristol, PA 19007, USA.
Australia: P.O. Box 6025, 83 Gilles Street, Adelaide, SA 5000, Australia.

Copyright © 1996 Angela L. Carrasquillo and Vivian Rodríguez.

All rights reserved. No part of this work may be reproduced in any form or by any means without
permission in writing from the publisher.

Printed and bound in Great Britain by WBC Book Manufacturers Ltd.

49, 50, 66, 161

Contents

Acknowledgments

The idea for this introductory book came about as a result of our being challenged to prepare a course on Second Language Acquisition and Learning for students in the Fordham University Initial Teacher Preparation Program. These college students were enrolled in an elementary school teacher preparation program and were receiving training to work in mainstream classrooms. As part of their academic program, these college students take one course in second language acquisition and learning in preparation for working with language minority students, especially those who may not have adequate English skills but who are receiving most of their instruction in mainstream classrooms. After devoting many hours to the preparation of the syllabus for this course and to the identification of several sources for instruction, we came to the conclusion that a text addressing language minority students in the mainstream classroom was not available. Seeing this as an unmet educational need, especially in the area of teacher training, we initiated the preparation of such a text. This need, coupled with our own experiences in working with teachers in mainstream classrooms, motivated us to begin planning the scope and sequence of this book.

We thank those students who opened our eyes and minds to the preparation and writing of this publication. We thank those individuals who indirectly contributed to the content of the book: undergraduate and graduate students at Fordham University, teachers working with culturally and linguistically diverse students in New York City and Elizabeth, New Jersey, bilingual and ESL teacher trainers, school principals, and, especially, language minority students and their parents.

We also thank those individuals who helped us in the preparation of this book. We thank Ruth Abrams, a second language practitioner who read the manuscript and provided us with the practitioner perspective and a second language appropriateness, and Dr Catherine Biggins, who helped the authors with the proof reading phase. Thanks are also due to Lourdes and Ben Willems, who prepared the final format of the book; and Lissette García, the secretary of the TESOL and Bilingual Teacher Education Programs, who contributed on a daily basis to the completion of this book, especially making sure Multilingual Matters received the several faxes that we sent them, and receiving and distributing those faxes that were sent back to us. We thank Multilingual Matters, especially Mike Grover and the editorial consultant, Colin Baker, for their guidance and suggestions throughout the entire process of planning and writing this book.

The support and encouragement of our spouses, Ceferino Carrasquillo and Luis Rodríguez, were invaluable in making this book become a reality.

Angela L. Carrasquillo
Vivian Rodríguez

Introduction

This book begins to address the need facing many educators in the United States and other countries in the English-speaking world, how to teach students whose primary language is not English. The purpose of this book is to make mainstream educators aware that language minority students, especially the limited English proficient (LEP), need special attention: appropriate assessment, appropriate language environment, a challenging curriculum, and a creative delivery of instruction relevant to their *English language development* as well as their performance in *subject matter content* and *skills*. The book has been written from the perspective of helping educators in the mainstream classroom to integrate language and content areas into classrooms where there are language minority students who are not totally proficient in the English language.

Schools impose many language demands on all students, requiring them to use and think about language in ways unlike those of many LEP students' homes. These demands involve the conventions of reading and writing as well as the verbal and non-verbal conventions of the interactions in which communication takes place in the classroom. Lack of understanding of the communicative conventions that apply in the classroom may be an important factor in the poor school achievement of many language minority students. Limited English proficient students not only need to know the content of the correct answer but also how to present that answer in a way that will be socially acceptable to the teacher and the school community in general. As Jordan & Joesting (1983) say:

> 'It seems reasonable to conclude that minority children, whatever their first language may be, often enter school with two strikes against them. Unlike the majority culture children, they must learn not only academic content but a new set of communicative conventions at the same time' (p. 217).

At the classroom level, modifications are needed in the content and the manner teachers organize and deliver instruction to students and the way teachers assess language content learning. For this reason, all the chapters of this book give constant attention to the following general language principles:

- *Vocabulary and technical terms* associated with the subject matter content (mathematics, social studies, and science) need to be consciously addressed in planning and delivering instruction.
- *Language functions* need to be carefully integrated into the curriculum for effective academic communication. These language functions include, but are not exclusive to informing, explaining, summarizing, rephrasing, classifying, and evaluating.
- Each curriculum area has *language structures and discourse features* that are different and may impede LEP students' performance at high levels of cognitive functioning.
- There are *different language skills* emphasized in the classroom for *different academic functions* that may not yet be mastered by LEP students. Among these are included listening comprehension for academic explanations, reading for information, speaking for oral presentations, writing for presentation of written, or oral reports.

In structuring the book, difficult decisions had to be made in terms of appropriate terminology used throughout the book as well as assessment of the type of message to be presented to the reader. Related to the purpose of writing this book, the authors want to emphasize that it was neither the attempt nor the intention on the part of the authors to give the impression that language minority/limited English proficient students can be successfully educated in mainstream classrooms. On the contrary, the message is that, if mainstreaming instruction is the only instructional option for these students, careful attention and instructional planning need to be exercised to allow for integrating the acquisition of content knowledge and related skills with the development of English language skills.

In writing the book, we struggled with two terms: *limited English proficient* (LEP) students and *mainstream classrooms*. Authorities in the fields of bilingual education and second language learning have identified the disadvantages of using these two terms or labels (Chamot & O'Malley, 1994; Enright & McCloskey, 1988). Chamot & O'Malley (1994), among others, do not like the term 'LEP' because it has a negative connotation. They say: '...but we (and others) find it to be a negative and even pejorative term because of its emphasis on what students are unable to do rather than on what they are learning to do' (p. 83). We agree with Chamot & O'Malley. However, we have found that the other two terms used to refer to these students, *English language learners* and *language minority students* are not specifically related to students who come from non-English speaking backgrounds and who demonstrate limitations in the understanding, speaking, reading and writing of the English language. After consulting with several experts in the field, we have decided to use both terms (language minority students and limited English proficient students) throughout the book. Also, in specific sections of the text we referred to these students as 'second language' or 'English as a second language' learners to infer that, although they are learning in an all English school environment, they bring to the school experience language competencies in a language other than English.

For the title of the book we preferred the term *language minority students* because the book addresses the linguistic, cognitive, and academic instructional needs of all students for whom English is a second or third language. For convenience and clarity purposes, titles of individual chapters use the term 'LEP' to emphasize the idea that the main purpose of the book is the integration of language and content in grade level classrooms where limited English proficient students may be enrolled. In many instances in the text, we use both terms, 'LEP students' and 'language minority students' interchangeably.

At this point, we would also like to note that these terms are not employed universally. An example of alternate terminology can be found in the United Kingdom. Recent British government and academic literature have referred to LEP students as 'pupils for whom English is an additional language'. This appears to be a relatively neutral term even positive, toward language minority students. However, like all similar terminology for language minorities, the term eventually becomes an euphemism for those ethnic minorities with less power and status in society.

Not everyone agrees with the concept of the *mainstream classroom*. Authorities, such as Enright & McCloskey (1988), prefer the term *grade-level classroom* to refer to classrooms designed for native-English-speaking students. In these classrooms, the school curriculum has not been modified for non-native speakers of English and the assumption is that all participants are native English speakers. Although we like the term used by Enright & McCloskey (1988), we decided to use the term 'mainstream classroom' for clarity and convenience purposes. In the United States, when reference is made to the 'mainstream classroom' as it relates to language minority students, educators clearly understand that the instruction delivered in these classrooms is primarily planned for native English speaking students.

The term 'American Society' used throughout this book refers to the cultural traits and values of the middle class, which are strongly influenced by the Western European tradition. While American institutions, such as government, schools, business, and social welfare are rooted in this tradition; many other aspects of American life have been greatly influenced by changing demographics, which have incorporated diverse cultural groups into the United States population.

ORGANIZATION OF THE BOOK

The book is divided into ten chapters. In an attempt to make the content of the book relevant to a variety of educators, we have integrated theory and practice throughout the book, especially in the content areas. The focus in all the chapters is on how to make content relevant and understandable to these students, who may not have the English language experiences, background, and proficiency.

Chapter 1, *Limited English Proficient Students in the Mainstream Classroom*, presents the theory upon which this book is based: the theory that LEP students are presently enrolled in mainstream educational settings, and educators influence academic and language development by providing appropriate learning contexts and instruction. The chapter defines the concept of mainstreaming as it is used in the field of second language teaching, and outlines educational instructional practices and decisions to consider in mainstreaming language minority students.

Chapter 2, *Limited English Proficient Students: Who Are They?*, provides an overview of the linguistic, academic, and cognitive factors to be considered in identifying characteristics of language minority students who are labeled as 'limited English proficient'. This chapter recommends that mainstream educators identify, through appropriate assessment, the students' strengths and weaknesses in a variety of ways in order to provide appropriate learning environments and relevant delivery of instruction.

Chapter 3, *Cultural and Linguistic Diversity in the Classroom*, provides a framework for understanding language minority students in the United States. Students, teachers, administrators, and community members, who have the opportunity to participate in interculturally sensitive schools and classrooms, find that their world is expanded and opened to many new options and alternatives. Mainstream classrooms enroll a variety of ethnic groups manifesting diverse cultures, languages, and cognitive styles.

Chapter 4, *Alternatives to Mainstreaming*, describes Bilingual and English as a Second Language Programs as alternative instructional programs to mainstreaming. Language and culture are integral components of the instructional process in Bilingual and ESL classrooms and, as such, they provide important foundations upon which cognitive and affective development are based. These programs provide academic and language contexts that facilitate the learning of the English language, as well as growth in content area knowledge and processes.

Chapter 5, *The Integrated Development of Oral and Written Language*, provides a rationale for the integration of the four modes of language: listening, speaking, reading, and writing. The thesis of the chapter is that language minority students best learn by using an integrated and experience-based approach to language acquisition.

Chapter 6, *Instructional Strategies for LEP Students' Oral and Written English Language Development*, examines instructional strategies which focus on meaning and support the reading comprehension and writing development of language minority students. As students work with challenging levels of background knowledge, vocabulary, and language proficiency, they become successful learners.

Chapter 7, *Integrating Language and Social Studies Learning*, outlines strategies of integrating Social Studies content and language development. Teachers need to provide an interactive approach to learning in which vocabulary development and background knowledge are built into the Social Studies curriculum.

Chapter 8, *Integrating Language and Science Learning*, poses the theory that the acquisition of science knowledge and processes may be affected by the level of language proficiency of the students. The chapter offers both conceptual and practical guidelines for integrating the processes and concepts with language instruction at the appropriate language level of the students.

Chapter 9, *Integrating Language and Mathematics Learning*, outlines conditions that enhance the achievement of LEP students in mathematics classrooms. A list of strategies for LEP students to learn concepts and skills in mathematics are outlined. Educators, who are able to mix language development with mathematics content, provide highly motivating lessons.

Chapter 10, *The Role of Teachers in the Development of Linguistic, Cognitive, and Academic Skills of LEP Students*, addresses the important component that the role of the teacher plays in helping language minority students to adjust and to learn in the mainstream classroom. Working with students whose language and cultural heritage is different from that of the school can be challenging to mainstream educators, especially teachers. Openness to students' language strengths (although not in English) and their background can result in a mutual learning experience, which enhances understanding and communication.

We realize that there are many issues which remain to be addressed and resolved in actual practice. We encourage others to continue to investigate and write on language minority students in the mainstream classroom to develop effective instructional and assessment practices for English as a Second Language students. As the numbers of these students increase, educators, especially teachers, will need to meet the challenges presented to us by these students. Our hope is that this book will contribute to meeting those challenges.

CHAPTER 1

Limited English Proficient Students in the Mainstream Classroom

Introduction

Mainstreaming LEP Students: A Definition

Guiding Principles for Mainstream Classrooms
A Word of Caution

Issues in Mainstreaming Limited English Proficient Students

Conclusion

CHAPTER 1

Limited English Proficient Students in the Mainstream Classroom

INTRODUCTION

The large wave of immigration and the high fertility rates among linguistically and culturally diverse groups in the United States continue to increase the number of limited English proficient (LEP) students in schools throughout the country. Thousands of people from Latin America, Southeast Asia, Eastern Europe, and other non-English speaking countries have been entering the United States. These immigrants, refugees, international students, and second generation immigrants, together with native born non-English speaking Americans, all have a need to learn English and be successful members of the 'mainstream' American society. The challenges to the schools presented by the influx of these students concern language specialists as well as regular classroom educators.

The types of instructional services provided by school districts to LEP students vary greatly and are dependent on several factors. These factors may be related to the size of the linguistically diverse population in the particular school or district, the resources available locally, or merely community/school district decisions as to the use of English only for instruction for all learners regardless of their English competence or proficiency (Carrasquillo, 1994; DeGeorge, 1988; Hamayan, 1990). The most satisfactory instructional approach to meet the immediate needs of LEP students would be to place them in special language programs. But the reality is that only a small group of LEP students receive instructional and language support through special language programs such as bilingual education, English as a second language, or compensatory education for basic instruction in reading and mathematics for poor and low income elementary school children and preschool education. The needs of many other LEP students remain unmet (New Levine, 1993; Rigg &

Allen, 1989; Spangenberg-Urbschat & Pritchard, 1994). Many LEP students do not receive any specialized language services, and are assigned to regular classrooms where they are mainstreamed with English speaking students, in spite of their limitations in understanding instruction presented in English. This means that LEP students may be taught by regular classroom teachers who may or may not have the support of a language specialist. Consequently, the majority of LEP students receive most, if not all, of their instruction from classroom teachers, many of whom have had no specialized training in this area (Spangenberg-Urbschat & Pritchard, 1994).

Mainstreaming LEP students needs careful planning and the provision of organized instructional and programmatic steps. Most authorities who have written on mainstreaming students have cautioned that the choice of instructional programs for LEP students must be considered carefully or these students will not succeed in the mainstream classroom. Because mainstreaming LEP students requires profound planning and development of appropriate procedures, programs, and instruction, this chapter presents a general overview of pedagogical issues to consider in mainstreaming limited or non-English speakers. It provides information which will help regular classroom educators to be more effective participants in the education of linguistically and culturally diverse students.

MAINSTREAMING LEP STUDENTS: A DEFINITION

The United States' national educational objectives for school students, 'Goals 2000', foresees a restructured educational system in the United States that will hold all students to high common standards of world-class achievement. The idea behind the implementation of new academic standards is that the result will bring better teaching, more learning, and more success for all students. The concept of 'all students' includes the 2.31 million children classified as limited-English proficient in the United States in 1992 (United States Department of Education, 1993a, 1993b). This new conceptualization requires that educators carefully find ways of meeting the needs of this significant group of students in accomplishing the content standards of subject matter areas such as mathematics, science, social studies, English language skills, and English reading. Although it is true that a significant group of LEP students' academic and linguistic needs are met through specialized programs such as ESL and bilingual education, there is another group who do not receive this type of specialized instruction, and they are integrated with English proficient students in the regular classroom. In many cases, teachers are not aware of the LEP students' linguistic levels, cultural diversity, and learning styles, and these teachers just plan and deliver instruction as if everyone in the classroom has the English language sophistication to follow instruction in English. Limited English proficient students may have a more difficult task than proficient English speakers because, while proficient English speakers will only have to focus on cognitive tasks, LEP students will have to focus on cognitive and linguistic tasks at the same time. Mainstream educators need to understand that these students do not have the sufficient academic English language skills to be able to follow the subject areas curricula. Also, because

LEP students come from many different places and from different countries of origin, curricular sequences, content objectives and instructional methodologies may differ dramatically from American practices. This curricular contradiction may create some level of confusion to LEP students especially if students come to the United States at a high grade level, where the cognitive and linguistic loads are complex.

Although mainstreaming LEP students into the regular classroom has been a common educational programmatic practice in the United States (Christina, 1992; DeGeorge, 1988; Hamayan & Perlman, 1990; Riddlemoser, 1987), the term is not well defined in the current educational literature. A review of this literature reveals that, in spite of the frequent use of the term in the jargon of education and the frequency of its mention by educators and educational writers, mainstreaming means different things for different individuals. In the United States the term may refer to three different concepts:

- The inclusion of special education students in grade-level (regular) classrooms.
- The exit of students participating in language assistance programs such as ESL or bilingual education, transferring the students into grade-level classrooms where the instruction is totally in English.
- Classrooms in which the school curriculum is delivered through the medium of English and it has not been modified for non-native English speakers.

Most of the literature on mainstreaming describes (rather than defines) the steps to be followed in making decisions about mainstreaming students to the grade-level classroom. In this respect, the term is commonly used to list the types of students in mainstream classrooms rather than identifying measures to follow in determining the characteristics and organization of the instructional program. More specifically, the term 'mainstreaming' is used in the context of LEP learners to identify three broad groups of students. These are: (a) students who are removed or exited from bilingual or ESL programs, (b) students who are placed in grade-level classrooms for most of the day but receive specialized language development (usually English as a second language or basic skills development) during the school day, and (c) students who are placed in an all English classroom for the entire school day. An explanation of these three groups of mainstreamed LEP students is presented in the next three descriptive explanations (see Figures 1.1, 1.2, 1.3).

There is no agreement in terms of the numbers of years LEP students need to be learning English in order to be exited from the language assistance programs. The United States Federal Government guidelines suggest that, after three years in the program, LEP students may be ready to be mainstreamed to a grade-level classroom. However, authorities such as Collier (1992) and Cummins (1994) indicate that English proficiency may take between five to seven years.

Although one hour or less of specialized language instruction is not the best recommended instructional model, it helps students by meeting their immediate communication skills, especially at the listening and speaking level.

Figure 1.1 Mainstreaming LEP students from the bilingual and ESL programs

Mainstreaming is one of the important goals of all specialized instruction. The placement of LEP students (who are or were participating in bilingual or ESL programs) in an all-English mainstream program for all or part of the school day comes as the result of a complex process that assesses and determines if students have acquired the skills and knowledge necessary to function well in an all-English classroom.

In the United States, procedures to assess students' readiness for all English instruction vary from state to state. Some states recommend procedures and instruments, other states leave the identification of procedures and instruments to the school district. New York State, for example, requires that students score above the 40th percentile in the Language Assessment Battery Exam (a proficiency exam) before they are mainstreamed into an all-English classroom.

In some school districts appropriate instructional programs are developed for these students including: (a) identification of the language demands of the subject areas to be taught in English; (b) analysis of each subject area by content and skill area to determine that these skills match with students' prior experience with these content areas; (c) identification of prerequisite cognitive areas to allow students to benefit from instruction in each subject area; (d) analysis of each subject area for linguistic components: vocabulary, technical terms, language structure, language functions, and discourse features to determine academic language proficiency demands.

Figure 1.2 Mainstreaming LEP students with the provision for special English language development

This group includes those students who are already receiving mainstream instruction in all subject areas and receive additional English language development by a language specialist, usually an ESL or reading teacher. There are several reasons why these students are assigned to mainstream classrooms: (a) when there are not enough LEP students from a particular language background or grade to organize a bilingual class; (b) when parents want their children in an all-English classroom with the idea that this immersion will facilitate their acquisition of English; (c) the school district's policy is to mainstream all students. In most situations the school district may be required to provide some type of specialized language assistance to these students.

Most of this group of LEP students participate in specialized language programs such as pull-out ESL, or compensatory instruction in English reading and mathematics for one hour or less a day. The rest of the instructional day in the school life of these students is spent in regular classrooms with peers who are proficient in English. All instruction is in English with no linguistic assistance. LEP students are at a disadvantage because they do not have the necessary communication and academic English language skills.

Figure 1.3 Mainstreaming LEP students with all instruction in English

A large group of LEP students, upon their arrival at American schools, are initially assigned to mainstream classrooms. The reasons why these students are enrolled in an all-English classroom are the same as those listed for Group 2. Most of the time, this group of students is ignored by the school organization and the classroom teacher. However, they are required to meet the same linguistic and cognitive demands required for English proficient students. But the reality is that these students are not ready to tackle the rather difficult task of functioning in an academic setting where English is the medium of instruction. There is no special curriculum for teachers to follow and, in many instances, the teachers of these students do not know what to do with them and opt to follow the 'sink or swim' approach.

Because of the growing numbers of LEP students presently enrolled in mainstream classrooms, preparing educators to work with them is a serious educational concern (Hamayan, 1990; Rigg & Allen, 1989). Mainstream educators who have LEP students in their schools and classrooms are often at a loss as to how to reach these students. These educators do not have the training they need in order to properly address the instructional needs of these students. Mainstream classes are usually taught by teachers who have not been trained to work with limited English language learners.

The literature on mainstreaming has identified elements in which mainstreaming, if well implemented, may contribute to students' social, linguistic, and academic development (Hamayan, 1990; New Levine, 1993; Rigg & Allen, 1989, Trueba, 1987).

GUIDING PRINCIPLES FOR MAINSTREAM CLASSROOMS

We have identified four important principles that are relevant and should be considered in well-planned and developed mainstream programs for LEP students.

Principle 1:
Mainstreaming should provide a full range of educational opportunities to all students, eliminating social and racial barriers

The American society stresses the concept of equality, and knowing English has been linked as an important component in being considered an 'equal student' and an 'equal citizen' in the United States. Under the mandate of the Constitution of the United States, which requires the provision of an equal education for all students attending public schools, many educators and policy makers have recommended the practice of providing LEP students with opportunities to interact with English proficient students on a daily basis. Educators assume that teaching students English would provide them with equal educational opportunity. This interaction not only provides an environment of 'equality' among the diverse student population but it becomes the context for English language development. Since all students will learn together, racial and social tensions may be resolved or reduced in the classroom context by effective classroom teachers and other supportive personnel. Conflict resolution techniques are recommended strategies to use throughout the school day to reduce social and racial barriers.

Research on effective schools (Brophy & Good, 1974; Edmonds, 1979; Faltis, 1993) indicates that one of the characteristics of successful schools is the autonomy which the school leadership and staff possess to determine the exact means by which they address the challenge of eliminating social and racial barriers as well as increasing students' academic performance. One important variable to consider is the recommendation of maintaining high expectations for all students in the school including high expectations for the LEP student population (Collier, 1992; Lucas, Henze & Donato, 1990). Mainstream educators should be prepared to challenge LEP students in the same way that other students in the school are challenged. Educators need to see LEP students as equal to their other English proficient students in terms of cognitive and social strengths. At the same time, these educators should be sensitive to students' linguistic needs as well as cultural and ethnic differences. These differences should be seen as an enrichment factor in the classroom, rather than as deficiencies to be eradicated from students.

> *Principle 2:*
> **Mainstreaming should provide opportunities for English language learners to interact socially with English proficient peers**

The mainstream classroom provides an excellent informal context for English language development to take place. Language learners remember and use language that is meaningful; they learn through a creative construction process of putting together the bits of the language they know, and using it in purposeful interactive situations. Since the purpose of language is communication of meaning, LEP students may want to communicate with peers in the classroom, and they will use whatever means are available to them both to understand and communicate the meaning of the message. LEP students are surrounded by English proficient peers. This interaction forces the communication to be meaningful to both groups, the limited and the proficient English speaker. Opportunities are provided for real communication with English-speaking peers and adults. This process is helped by what LEP students already know about language through their first language so that they can make successful transfers to and correct generalizations in the second language.

There is the need to maximize the students' exposure to authentic language during the school day. Second language learners need a great deal of language input. Meaning is not conveyed through language alone, but with the help of concrete referents that the students can touch, hear, and see. Meaning is also conveyed through gestures, and body language, making it easier for the students to comprehend the concepts being presented (Krashen, 1981b; Terrell, 1981). When speakers have something to say of real importance or interest to the listener, they will make every effort to understand and this very effort will advance the second language acquisition process. English speakers will naturally adjust their language to the needs of limited English proficient students and they will paraphrase, explain, or demonstrate, if necessary, in order to get their meaning across. Teachers will do the same. LEP students will recognize the interest of everyone in the classroom to communicate with them, and they will make every possible effort to understand the message received. At the same time, LEP students will develop the mental freedom to communicate with their English-speaking peers and with their teachers. It is important to point out that this interaction, necessary for language acquisition, cannot happen unless the school and the classroom provide the appropriate atmosphere for its development. Administrators and teachers have a very important role to play by planning and carrying out interactive and experiential activities involving both LEP and English proficient students.

Principle 3:
Mainstreaming should provide opportunities for groups to function effectively once successful instructional strategies are employed

---

Active involvement of students is one way of ensuring learning and social development. It has been mentioned in the literature that initially mainstreamed students lack social skills and have low self-esteem of themselves (Carrasquillo & London, 1993; Hamayan, 1990). A series of instructional strategies have been recommended to improve students' social skills, self-esteem, and academic development. These strategies include: (a) highly interactive learning activities, (b) heterogeneous groups, (c) cognitively demanding tasks, and (d) cooperative learning procedures. Authorities such as Johnson, Johnson & Holubec (1988) and Slavin (1981, 1990) have indicated that cooperative learning strategies promote higher achievement, develop social skills, and put responsibility for learning on the learner.

Cooperative grouping has been shown to be an effective classroom management technique that promotes learning among heterogeneous groups of students (Bossert, 1993; Slavin, 1981; Slavin & Karweit, 1985). In cooperative learning groups students are guided to work together to accomplish a specific task or set of learning activities. The task may be as simple as suggesting that students study together or as complex as arranging differentiated rules for individuals within study groups. Because cooperative groups are heterogeneous, LEP students are mixed with English proficient students encouraging them to work in different tasks agreed upon by all members. Each student has a vital role to play in completing the task that the group is given (Cochran, 1989; Hamayan & Perlman, 1990). These strategies help all students to talk via discussion, interact with other English speakers, use effective social skills, and, to some extent, care about each other's learning. When mainstreamed LEP students are placed in heterogeneous, cooperative groups and assigned to specific roles, their achievement generally increases and their psychological health improves.

> *Principle 4*:
> **Mainstreaming should provide opportunities for all teachers to consider the language demands of all the students in the classroom**

Mainstream classrooms reflect a variety of linguistic backgrounds as well as a variety of language development among students. Not all students, even those that are labeled as 'English proficient' show the same level of English proficiency. Classrooms that have LEP students reflect a broader variety of linguistic and cultural language differences. Teachers of mainstream classrooms have to be aware of these linguistic and cultural differences and plan accordingly to provide instructional experiences that take into consideration all these levels (Faltis, 1993). By making teachers aware of all the linguistic levels in a given classroom, they will be more careful in planning instruction to meet the cognitive and linguistic demands of all the students in the classroom.

A Word of Caution

Extreme caution needs to be taken to identify steps for mainstreaming LEP students. If these steps are not carefully followed it may result in LEP students being inadvertently placed in instructional situations where the linguistic demands require an English proficiency level these students have not yet achieved (DeGeorge, 1988; Tikunoff, 1985). This puts the LEP students at an unfair disadvantage in classrooms with students who are already proficient in English. Being aware of learning and linguistic levels allows schools to develop appropriate instructional sequences which provide students with the necessary opportunities for developing academic language proficiency in English without sacrificing the acquisition of subject matter. Sound instructional decisions require reliable and relevant information about students' capabilities and achievement patterns. Decisions as to whether or not language minority students are ready to be mainstreamed have often been made solely on the basis of students' oral ability. It may be beneficial to determine the status of students with respect to the demands that will be made upon them in mainstream subject area classes (Chamot & O'Malley, 1986, 1994; Cummins, 1984; DeGeorge, 1988; Hamayan, 1990). It is necessary to assess the cognitive demands that will be made of LEP students in the mainstream and the language demands of the mainstream classroom. These two steps provide the basic information and criteria for determining whether or not LEP students are ready to be mainstreamed. If they already are participating in grade-level instruction, what instructional modifications are necessary to meet their linguistic and cognitive demands?

ISSUES IN MAINSTREAMING LIMITED ENGLISH PROFICIENT STUDENTS

Schools and community school districts should only consider mainstreaming LEP students once they have explored other recommended instructional approaches (such as ESL and bilingual education) and have found that these approaches are impossible to implement in their school setting. The following questions represent issues that have been raised by educators and policy makers involved in the education of LEP students.

> **Issue Number 1:**
> **Do LEP students belong in the mainstream classroom?**

Perhaps no issue is more widely discussed in education circles than mainstreaming students to the regular classroom (Christina, 1992; Enright & McCloskey, 1988; Hamayan, 1990; New Levine, 1993). It is assumed that every student should have the opportunity to an equal education in which the curriculum standards and the expected learning outcomes are the same for all students. In dealing with limited English proficient students, the assumption is that these students will eventually become familiar with the English language and will learn through this language. Many times LEP students are mainstreamed to overcrowded classrooms without serious consideration given to their learning and special linguistic needs. Some assume that the more exposure to English the students have, the more English they will get, subsequently bringing them to a desired English language proficiency level. The reality is that this assumption is not true. Most LEP learners need a specialized instructional mode to teach them English, making sure that they do not stay behind in their academic development because of their linguistic and cultural differences.

The answer to the question of whether LEP students belong in the mainstream classroom is no. LEP students do not belong in the mainstream English classroom because they do not have the communicative and necessary academic English language skills to be able to successfully learn through English. However, the reality is that there are thousands of LEP learners who are enrolled in mainstream all-English classrooms, with teachers and administrators who have no background or experience with those types of learners. In many instances LEP students have been registered in regular classrooms without informing the classroom teacher that these students do not understand instruction in English. The teacher assumes that all students are English speakers until he/she discovers that there are students who are limited in English, or worse, that they are non-English-speakers. Many teachers' reactions have been that the problem is in the student and not in the educational system, the teacher or the school, because 'all students are supposed to know English on entrance to school'. A system, which assumes that the cause of learning, behavior and language problems must be found in the student, can represent a gross oversimplification of complex learning systems (McKay & Wong, 1988; Trueba, 1987).

Another factor that appears to be affected when LEP students are mainstreamed is their self-esteem (Hamayan, 1990, Urzua, 1980; Wong-Fillmore, 1991b). This is true, especially when they are in an educational environment where English is the only medium of instruction, and some teachers may ignore the students due to lack of ability on the part of the teacher to communicate with them. Students feel they are not part of that instructional setting, and their self-image may be negatively affected. Since self-esteem is constantly re-evaluated on the basis of new encounters or experiences, as LEP students enter school they will engage in many new social interactions that will enhance or lower their self-esteem. And since high self-esteem is positively correlated with being able to successfully meet the demands of the academic life, it stands to reason that educational systems should promote self-esteem in students. Carrasquillo & London (1993) have identified teachers' behaviors that have significant effects on self-esteem and social development on language minority students. These are:

- The amount of respectful, accepting, and concerned treatment students received from teachers.
- The provision for opportunities for the modification of experiences that accord with values and aspirations.
- The manner in which teachers respond to students' queries or remarks.

Teachers can become significant 'others' in LEP students' life experiences, in terms of the classroom climate, attitude, instruction, assessment, grades, and awards (Hoge, Smith & Hanson, 1990). Thus, how students perform at school may, indeed, become a condition of several factors, not the least of which is the nearest significant 'other', the teacher (Carrasquillo & London, 1993).

Issue Number 2:
Is mainstreaming an excuse for the elimination of special language programs?

Language programs play an important role in the academic and linguistic development of culturally diverse populations. Most of these programs are initially funded by the federal government to support additional educational resources for those students with special needs: poor students, students with disabilities, and individuals for whom English is a second language. Compensatory education (especially the federally funded Chapter 1 Program), bilingual education, special education, and migrant education are among the most popular special programs. Chapter 1 provides extra academic help for 'disadvantaged' preschool and elementary school students. Most of its financial resources are used for basic instruction in reading and mathematics for poor and low-income elementary school students, but some money is used for preschool education. Migrant education provides funds to states to provide educational services, including English language development, for students of migrant workers. The federal government also provides funds for special education of children with disabilities. Disabled children between the ages of three and twenty-one are provided with a free and appropriate public education in the least restrictive environment. Language development is one of the key elements of special education programs. Bilingual education is a popular program, largely funded by the federal government, that is intended to build a language bridge for students whose first language is not English. English as a second language is a special program to provide initial help for LEP students to develop proficiency in English. Educators, who work with LEP students, believe that all these programs, as well as others, are necessary and that they fulfill a very important need.

Educators go on further to say that, because all the children who need these programs are not being served, school districts need to allocate local funds to supplement those programs funded by the federal government. Also, when the federal government stops funding those programs, the school districts need to continue to offer them. Unfortunately, many schools provide these special language programs only when they are funded by the federal government, and, once federal funding is no longer provided, the programs disappear from the schools and the school districts. Mainstreaming should not be used as an excuse for cutting budgets and eliminating needed special programs. All these programs meet a very important need that cannot be met by assigning students to an all-English classroom.

Issue Number 3:
Does the regular classroom provide an appropriate learning environment?

An issue raised in mainstreaming LEP students is the concern of how LEP students will feel in a regular classroom and how much acceptance they will receive from the teacher and the other students (Christina, 1992; Enright & McCloskey, 1988; Hamayan 1990). The school is an institution created by society with the main purpose of providing opportunities for all students to acquire factual information, develop skills, and learn to think. Students attend school to become successful learners, that is, to increase their knowledge of facts and skills and to develop thinking strategies. The main objective of the school is the full development of each student's character and intellect, personal and social relationships, and academic achievement. Thus, the school is an institution interested in students as persons and their total and individual development. In the long run, schools perform three functions: (a) imparting knowledge and skills, (b) preparing students for the academic/working world, and (c) helping students become participant citizens of the society. In order to meet these three goals, schools must provide all students with an appropriate educational environment that is conducive to learning, and one in which every student is challenged to his/her maximum potential. An important variable in learning is the school and classroom setting. Learning and successful students are related to successful schools and successful classrooms. Milk, Mercado & Sapiens (1992) posed two fundamental questions in discussing the prerequisites for effective instruction: (a) What kind of learning environment would most successfully engage students in the learning process? (b) What kind of learning environment would be most conducive to language development for learners who possess unique linguistic and cultural characteristics? They answered these two questions by saying that the key aspect is the structural organization within the classroom in which there is a functional communication between teachers and students, and students and students. An appropriate learning environment is an influential factor in students' academic performance.

The mainstream classroom must offer the same rich, challenging, interesting curriculum to all students. The classroom should emphasize the development of problem-solving and thinking skills by engaging all students in interactive and experiential tasks. Once educators accept that LEP students have the capacity to learn English, they must involve them in meaningful, interactive language activities.

They must develop a classroom environment that is linguistically rich and success oriented, where all students are free to express themselves, to experiment, and to explore. The classroom and the school environments of LEP students need to be one in which respect for racial, ethnic, cultural, and linguistic diversity is infused throughout the school by including diversity into instruction and by reflecting it in all aspects of the classroom climate and environment. An adequate instructional setting means that the instruction provides experiences in which students' strengths are used as a medium of effective academic and social development (Carrasquillo & London, 1993). The classroom needs to be staffed by teachers who believe that all children can learn and who have autonomy to respond flexibly and adapt teaching to the different needs of the children and the families they serve. The other students in the classroom and the regular classroom teacher cannot see LEP students as 'different'. Too often 'different' has been translated into 'deficient' or 'less than'. There is a risk in sending the message to second language learners that they are not capable of doing what is expected at that grade level. The sad result is that many non-English speakers grow to believe this same myth. The environment in which children learn to use language is not different simply because there is a first or second language student doing the learning. The environment must be the same: interactive, responsive, and supportive, with encouraging human beings who believe the function or message is far more important than the form in which it is sent (Chaudron, 1988; Hoge, Smith & Hanson, 1990; Urzua, 1980). Well-planned and practiced, mainstream classroom interaction can be meaningful to LEP students; it provides interaction with native speakers of English. This increased contact also contributes to the improvement of self-concept and academic development for language minority students.

Issue Number 4:
Are mainstream classroom teachers prepared to work with LEP students?

To date, much of the classroom-based research on teaching has sought to describe effective teaching behaviors, positive learner outcomes, and teacher–student interactions that are believed to lead to successful second language learning (Chaudron, 1988; Faltis, 1993; Wong-Fillmore, 1991a). In the context of the classroom, the teacher is the primary source of encouragement and support. Teachers' perceptions of minority students affect their academic performance. Teachers who value students as individuals with unique capabilities are aware that language, be it spoken, written, or nonverbal, is a form of transaction that has a tremendous power in the learning–teaching process. Since, in many instances, the only models or English demonstrators LEP students meet on a daily basis are the teachers, the importance of their presentation of an appropriate linguistic classroom environment is crucial to students' overall performance. Research has shown that the ever-growing number of linguistically and culturally diverse minority students with varied educational needs will necessitate changes in instructional practices, and special training for teachers, especially mainstream teachers educating language minority students (Enright & McCloskey, 1988; Hamayan, 1990; New Levine, 1993; Rigg & Allen, 1989).

Researchers of teacher effectiveness have found that engaged time on task, academic emphasis in teaching, the pacing of the lesson, the content covered, the activities of instruction, and items such as grouping, monitoring, and helping during seat work are important aspects of both management and effective teaching (Brophy, 1979; Squire, 1987).

When educators in mainstream classrooms seriously plan for LEP students' development of English skills and academic subject matter content, they are providing students with access to appropriate curriculum and instruction. LEP students need to be instructed to become *participatively, interactionally* and *academically competent*. Tikunoff & Ward (1991) define these three concepts as follows:

> **Participative Competence:** Students respond appropriately to class task demands and to the procedural rules for accomplishing them.
> **Interactional Competence:** Students respond appropriately both to classroom rules of discourse and social rules of discourse, interacting appropriately with peers and adults while accomplishing class tasks.
> **Academic Competence:** Students are able to acquire new skills, assimilate new information and construct new concepts.

Therefore, teachers play an important role in LEP students' academic, linguistic, social, and cultural development (Chaudron, 1988; Hamayan, 1990). The literature on effective teachers has identified six major functions of the mainstream teacher in contributing to students' social, cognitive, and academic development. These are:

The teacher is a mediator and facilitator of learning. Teachers are mediators in the teaching–learning process, especially when students need some type of feedback to understand the language of instruction and the content of the subject areas. Clark & Peterson's (1986) comprehensive review of the research on teachers' thought processes purports that teachers are decision makers who process information and act upon those decisions within complex environments. They must perceive all learners as capable of constructing and reconstructing meaning and knowledge over time. Teachers need to provide opportunities for students to share each other's knowledge and questions as successful contributors to their own learning. The teacher functions as a key individual making instructional decisions for all students including those for whom English is not their native language. The teacher plans instructional programs that meet the students' academic and linguistic demands.

The teacher is a facilitator in the acquisition of English. Teachers establish positive classroom behaviors and, by reducing linguistic anxieties and frustrations in the classroom, contribute to students ease in their acquisition of English. When teachers make instructional decisions, they consider the appropriateness of a particular teaching strategy and the students' language skills, their academic ability, and their knowledge of the content areas (Christina, 1992; Mohan, 1986; Short, 1991). Teachers' instructional activities are directed at ensuring students' understanding, motivation, involvement, and interaction. Effective teachers continually question the appropriateness of their teaching strategies in promoting English language development; they judge their own effectiveness in relation to student responses, and therefore, they seek confirmation, through instructional processes, that students are understanding and that they are actively engaged.

Teachers take every opportunity in the classroom, lunchroom, and playground to foster the development of language. For example, teachers expand LEP students' vocabulary, syntax, and grammar by effective classroom interaction between the teacher and other students in the classroom. Since listening comprehension plays an important role in acquiring a second language, teachers provide LEP students with instructional strategies for listening comprehension. Teachers promote interpersonal as well as academic language.

The teacher is a model of a proficient English language user. Mainstream teachers have a difficult task in working with LEP students. Their role includes the teaching of English and, at the same time, making sure that students learn subject content through this new language. In accomplishing these tasks, teachers serve as linguistic models for their students by:

- Progressively developing students' comprehension and ability to interact with English-speaking students through mastery of communicative competence in English as it is used by the English-speaking population.
- Evaluating students' progress in English language learning and content and identifying their strengths and weaknesses in performance, adjusting instruction accordingly.
- Selecting appropriate teaching techniques and materials for language and content teaching.

To achieve the objectives of their teaching roles, teachers are expected to demonstrate proficiency in spoken and written English at a level commensurate with their role as a language model. The command of the language should combine qualities of accuracy and fluency. Teachers need to understand the nature of language, the nature of language variety — social, regional, and functional. Teachers should also have an understanding of the factors which contribute to the life styles of various peoples, and which determine both their uniqueness and their interrelationships in a pluralistic society. Proficient English teachers make an impact on their students by what they, as teachers, say to them. The teachers' impact is seen in the development of students' English literacy and academic content.

Teachers do not correct students' 'errors', but provide immediate correct language feedback. Teachers expand what students say through questioning or re-phrasing. These strategies give students the correct linguistic model, and send the message that the students' attempts at communicating are accepted.

The teacher is a representative of the mainstream culture. LEP students who enter American public schools for the first time quite often are unfamiliar, not only with the English language, but also with school traditions, rules, and expectations. The mission of the school is most simply described as providing students with the explicitly necessary academic, social, and civic skills for negotiation with life in the dominant mainstream society. The purposes of the school encompass not only what is taught and learned, but also the organization, patterns, and process of education in the social and cultural setting (Sleeter & Grant, 1993). Teachers contribute in many ways to students' adaptation to a new culture, or better said, to students being better participants in a culturally pluralistic society. In a culturally pluralistic society, members of diverse cultural, racial, or religious groups are free to maintain their own identity and yet simultaneously share a larger common political organization, economic system, and social structure. It is the role of mainstream teachers to help students, and, to some extent, their parents, to find ways to be part of this pluralistic society.

Many LEP students and parents do not understand the purposes of the school and, even less, the social settings of the mainstream society. In a society as complex and multi-ethnic as the United States, discovering what the mainstream culture is can prove to be a difficult task for language and cultural minority learners. In many instances teachers are the initial contact with the mainstream society, and students' initial acceptance of differences with the mainstream culture will depend on how teachers present these differences. In the case of the students who come from a cultural background that is different from the dominant culture, there is a need for developing and maintaining the social and cultural bridges between the students' home culture and that of the school (Carrasquillo & London, 1993; Hamayan, 1990; Ovando, 1989). It is the responsibility of mainstream educators to provide an environment in which students feel that their culture is respected, thereby enabling them to be willing to accept traits of the second culture.

The teacher is a mediating agent in the socialization and acculturation of the students. Teachers play roles that go beyond just imparting instruction; their role must take into account social and affective variables in their relationship with LEP students. Teachers constitute a vital element in humanizing the total educational experience of LEP students in school. In the process of instruction, teachers must be aware of the diverse ethnic and linguistic groups, personalities, and characters present among students. They must be empathic in order to understand and be sensitive to the students' sociocultural and linguistic make-up and needs (Baruth & Manning, 1992; Carrasquillo, 1994). Teachers must consider students not only as receivers of cognitive language skills, but also as whole beings with feelings, personality, prior knowledge, and other human attributes that play important roles in the acquisition of language. Teachers must go beyond general instruction to view individual differences among students as more important to the strategic teaching than their similarities. Such differences provide teachers with the opportunities to differentiate instruction and to fulfill more of the affective and social needs of individual students.

Through teachers, LEP students discover the school environment. Positive teachers' classroom social interactions promote the development of students' cultural identities by accepting, respecting, and valuing cultural and linguistic differences in the classroom and by imparting a sense of peaceful co-existence of diverse life styles, manners, language patterns, and practices (Havighurst, 1978; Sleeter & Grant, 1993). However, it is also imperative for LEP students to learn to function success-fully in mainstream cultural and linguistic groups. For example, students need to develop competence in the ability to know which behavioral patterns and cultural knowledge of other cultural groups are necessary for providing the means for more equal opportunities in society (Sleeter & Grant, 1993). Mainstream teachers help LEP students incorporate cultural traits of the American mainstream culture without losing their own ethnic and cultural identity. For example, LEP children may opt to adapt English language patterns, kinetics, value systems, and social interaction styles of the United States, thus enabling them to become bicultural.

Teachers have to build an understanding of the culture of LEP students enrolled in their classes. Regular classroom teachers, unaccustomed to instructing LEP students, may lack the sensitivity to the cultural differences that the students experience in their new surroundings. Teachers need to bridge the gap between students' cultural background and the experiences these students confront in school.

The teacher is an advocate of LEP students' needs and strengths. In working with children, teachers should always act on a foundation of human values. One of their roles is to alert all those individuals (principal, social worker, psychologist, parents) of what is best for LEP students' education. Teachers play an advocacy role in recognizing LEP students' academic needs and in identifying successful instruc-tional programs that will consider the students as a whole, including social, linguis-tic, and cognitive development (Carrasquillo, 1994; Cazden, 1986).

Sensitive mainstream teachers collaborate and consult with other teachers and educators in the school, especially with the school's administrators, by sharing information about the academic, cultural, and linguistic needs of LEP students. They are a valuable source of information about LEP students' performance in the mainstream classroom.

Social and psychological factors are of utmost importance in teaching LEP students. It is often frightening for students of any age to be placed in a new classroom. This is magnified by the new language and cultural differences LEP students confront in a new linguistic instructional setting, the classroom. A 'buddy system' is an excellent way to help LEP students to minimize their fear of a new environment and a new language (Riddlemoser, 1987), especially if the 'buddy' is from the same language background and is English-proficient.

In some instances, teachers' commitment toward LEP students will require them to go beyond the school boundaries to challenge policy makers and community practices. The teacher is the best equipped individual to present students' strengths and to describe how proposed instructional programs or practices will expand on students' strengths and will contribute to the eradication of students' deficiencies.

CONCLUSION

When students enter school, they bring all of their personal and community environmental influences. Both the school and the community must work together and cooperate in order to motivate students to learn, to support children in their learning, to instill work habits, and to reward achievement. Educators are influential in helping LEP students to establish their individuality by providing appropriate learning contexts and instruction. Teachers influence, facilitate, and help students' perceptions, behaviors, and academic performance at school and elsewhere. LEP students' interaction with their parents, teachers, and the school as a whole will form the basis for self-esteem and social development.

Mainstreaming language minority students from bilingual and ESL programs is an educational reality. Assigning LEP students to the mainstream classroom on their arrival in the United States is also a common programmatic reality. However, educators, especially those in mainstream educational settings, need to understand the linguistic and academic challenges encountered by LEP students. It is then that educators can provide all students with an appropriate learning environment and teaching strategies that are instrumental in the development of learners' linguistic and academic competencies. This awareness will help educators identify avenues to motivate and challenge these learners to get the most out of the content areas as well as their English literacy development. Well-planned mainstreaming can be the force behind exciting programs in which educational responsibilities for cultural and linguistically diverse students are shared, and cooperative relationships between educators enhanced.

CHAPTER 2

Limited English Proficient Students: Who Are They?

CHAPTER 2

Limited English Proficient Students: Who Are They?

INTRODUCTION

There is a significant number of culturally and linguistically diverse students for whom English is not their first language. They are learning English and usually they are labeled as 'English learners' or 'limited English proficient' (LEP) students. As we said in the general introduction of the book, the term 'LEP' is not an appropriate one in describing these students because this label focuses on what English language learners are unable to do rather than on what they are learning to do. The literature usually refers to these English language learners as 'language minority students' (Chamot & O'Malley, 1994; Cummins, 1989; Garcia, 1993; Ovando & Collier, 1989). However, in order to distinguish language minority students who are learning English from those that are English proficient, we have decided to use, for clarity purposes, the identification 'LEP students' throughout this chapter.

In many school districts throughout the United States, LEP students are placed in ordinary mainstream classrooms in which only English is spoken. No special provisions are made in these classrooms to help the students learn, in English, skills they need to succeed in school. LEP students, whatever their school experience, or communicative and academic abilities in their native language may be, are called upon to advance simultaneously in the stages of developing interpersonal skills, mastering subject area content and skills, and acquiring academic language proficiency for each subject area, all in their second language, which is English. Educators, and especially teachers, may ask, 'Who are these LEP students?' As individuals search for a comprehensive and cohesive definition of the culturally and linguistically diverse student, or a 'limited English proficient,' a specific definition is not found, but rather a set of linguistic and academic characteristics related to their assessment and instruction in the second language. This chapter provides an overview of these characteristics, as well as a discussion of pertinent assessment practices with implications for the provision of services to LEP students in the mainstream classroom.

THE 'LEP' POPULATION IN THE UNITED STATES

Limited English proficient students are those individuals who have a primary language other than English. In the United States, (and probably in other English-speaking countries), they are usually immigrants from other countries who have adopted the United States (or any other English-speaking country), as their second home, or they may have been born in the United States (or any other English-speaking country) and raised in a non-English environment in which their parents, guardians, or caretakers may have little understanding of English. Also, chances are they have been living in the country for only a short period of time. Another group of English learners are those who are learning English in countries where English is not the language of the country, and the school where they attend provides all the instruction through English. These students are learning content through a second language. Thus, there is a variety of English learners. And they vary, not only in terms of location and purpose for learning English, but in terms of individual differences.

Estimates of the number of LEP students in the United States have been compiled by state and federal government agencies on several occasions. The information gathered helps these agencies to determine the relationship between sources of funding and the nature of services provided. Although the data gathered are not always the most complete or accurate (some states or school districts do not always send the requested information, and if sent, it may be incomplete or inaccurate), these data provide overall information to researchers, policy makers and school personnel in making generalizations on the number of LEP students in the United States and the types of instructional services provided. We alert the reader to understand that most identified LEPs have been those locally screened and assessed. It is our suspicion that, in several instances, LEP students are not identified, that their linguistic differences have been ignored, and that they are attending classrooms under the speculation that they will succeed in an all-English curriculum (Waggoner, 1994). Schools across the country use a wide range of methods and standards for identifying students as 'limited English proficient,' for assigning them to specific services, and for exiting them from LEP status, or services. The United States Department of Education (1993a) warns us that: 'The lack of standardization across the country can affect estimates of the size and characteristics of the national LEP student population. Presumably, if the methods and standards were changed, in some large school districts, estimates of the numbers and characteristics of the LEP population might also change' (p. 15). Thus, quotas regarding numbers of LEP students in the United States provided in the following paragraphs need to be taken with caution; these are conservative numbers.

The LEP population in the United States continues to be linguistically heterogeneous with over 100 distinct language groups identified (García, 1993; Waggoner,

1994). While the number of monolingual English speakers increased by 6% in the 1980s, the number of home speakers of language other than English increased by 38% (Wagonner, 1993). As a result of shifting demographics, the United States is currently experiencing an increasing representation of limited-English-proficient students in schools, placing unprecedented demands on teachers, administrators, and educational policy makers. Particularly striking has been the rate of growth for Hispanic and Asian students. In 1990, African Americans, Hispanics, American Indians, and Asians made up 32% of the total public school enrollment in the nation, and 33% of the largest school districts had an enrollment of over 50% ethnic and language minority students (National Center for Education Statistics, 1993). Nationally, identified LEP students enrollment population has increased by 56% between 1985 and 1992 (United States Department of Education, 1993a). Spanish speakers are in the majority (75%) followed by speakers of Asian languages (12%). Although Hispanics, Asians, and Pacific Islanders form the largest segments of the non-native-school students, the number of native speakers of Arabic, Armenian, Polish, Haitian Creole, and Russian have increased considerably (United States Department of Education, 1993a). The result is a diversity of languages and cultures in the United States' classrooms. By the end of the century, language minority students will make up almost 42% of the total public school enrollment. According to a United States Department of Education report (1993a), the number of LEP students is growing; there were 2.31 million identified LEP students in public (elementary and secondary) schools in the 1991–1992 school year. Observers believe that this figure underestimates the actual number of LEP students enrolled in the public schools and suggests the number between 2 million and 3.5 million, depending on the definition of 'limited English proficient' (Lara, 1994). Increased population from Latin America, Asia and North Europe, as well as high fertility rates within these populations, are the major factors contributing to this recent demographic shift. The following data provide examples of the challenge:

- In *Anchorage, Alaska*, more than *100 languages* are spoken by students enrolled in bilingual education programs.
- In *Los Angeles, California*, the growth in the enrollment of language minority students has outstripped the growth in total district enrollment, a trend likely to continue (Wasney & Wilde, 1987). Students speak about *79 languages*. Bilingual instruction is offered in Spanish, Cantonese, Vietnamese, Korean, Filipino and Armenian. In California Public Schools, *one* out of *six* students was born outside the United States; and *one* in *three* speaks a language other than English at home (Gray, 1993).
- In *New York City*, in the academic year 1991–92 there were *133,948* identified LEP students enrolled: 101,587 in community school districts (elementary through intermediate schools, kindergarten-ninth grade); and 32,361 in high schools (grades 9–12). Bilingual instruction is offered in Spanish, Chinese, Haitian Creole, Russian, Korean, Vietnamese, French, Greek, Arabic, and Bengali (New York City Board of Education, 1993).

- In the *Washington, DC*'s school system, students speak *127 languages* and dialects (Gray, 1993).
- There were 1.4 million language-minority children and youth in *Texas*. Language minority school-ages constituted 39% (Waggoner, 1994).

The LEP population in the United States continues to grow. According to the United States Department of Education (1993b):

- The number of LEP students is growing. There were 2.31 million identified LEP students in public elementary and secondary schools in the 1991–92 school year. This is a 70% increase in the last eight years.
- The concentration of LEP students varies across districts. Approximately 43% of the nation's school districts enroll LEP students. While approximately 24% of these districts serve 9 or fewer LEP students, 8% of the districts serve a thousand or more LEP students.
- Most LEP students are young. Over two out of three LEP students are in grades K–6, 18% are in grades 7–9, and 14% are in grades 10–12.
- Almost three out of four identified LEP students speak Spanish as their native language, followed by Vietnamese, (4%) and Hmong, Cantonese, Cambodian, and Korean (2% each).
- About 2.5% of United States' LEP students speak one of 29 different Native American languages.
- Some LEP students are not immigrants or recent arrivals. Forty-one percent of LEP students in United States elementary schools were born in the United States. Of the Spanish speakers at all grade levels, 40% were born in Mexico, 7% in Puerto Rico, and 39% in the United States.

The above information serves to alert educators to recognize that almost three out of four LEP students speak Spanish as their native language. This group, as well as the Asian groups, have specific linguistic and cultural characteristics that need to be recognized and included in the content of the curriculum of the school where they are enrolled. Also, it is important to highlight the fact that about 2.5% of the nation's LEP students speak one of 29 different native American languages especially since there are very few times these languages and their respective cultures are represented in the school curriculum.

The United States Department of Education indicates that most LEP students in the nation's elementary schools were born in the United States: 41% of the LEP students in United States elementary schools were born in the United States, many of them Hispanics (United States Bureau of the Census, 1993). There are also native-born American students for whom the United States is their homeland. We need to question how these students may linguistically differ from those who were born outside the United States. Distinguishing characteristics may be that foreign-born students come to United States schools speaking only their ancestral language. Their families may be voluntary immigrants or involuntary uprooted refugees. They may reside in the United States legally or as undocumented workers. All of these students may fall anywhere on a broad continuum of language status, ranging from entirely monolingual in the non-English language to bilingual in the home language and English, to dominant in English, with only a few fragmentary skills in the ancestral language. Linguistic and academic differences between these two groups of students have not been carefully studied. We suspect that, although both groups are limited English proficient, their language background and literacy are at different levels of development. Relevant comparisons need to be made across LEP students from different perspectives, including comparisons between immigrants and native-born individuals of the same ethnic group, as well as differences in linguistic and literacy strengths and weaknesses.

The majority of the LEP population reside throughout the United States, but with a distinctive geographical clustering. Most language minority students reside in Arizona, Colorado, California, Florida, Illinois, New Jersey, New York, New Mexico, and Texas (Waggoner, 1993). All these states have high minority birthrates and high immigration rates. In Texas and California, minority student enrollment exceeds white enrollment. In these states, mandates may be in place to provide LEP students with an appropriate classroom placement (such as ESL or bilingual education). In cities such as New York City in which by 1994 there were 154,526 identified LEP students in public schools, there are several legal mandates, as well as sources of funding, to meet the linguistic and instructional needs of LEP students. These legal mandates and sources of funding are illustrated in Figure 2.1.

Other states or school districts do not have large numbers of LEP students. Also, in many situations, LEP students are included in mainstream classrooms without assessing their linguistic strengths and weaknesses.

Although there is great variation depending on the students' background and schooling opportunities, most LEP students do not achieve well academically. Limited English proficient students are at risk of failure in school. Many LEP students appear at school unprepared for the subjects usually taught to students of their age. The Council of Chief State School Officers (1992) published a report, and concluded that LEP students' success in school hinges upon gaining access to effective second language learning opportunities and to full educational programs. Although this is a problem in all grade levels, it is most pronounced among older LEP students especially those of junior and high school age from economically underdeveloped regions. Because a great deal of immigration has been caused by economic desperation (especially in Mexico and Haiti) a high proportion of immigrant students arrive in the United States with serious educational deficiencies. Families with children in high-poverty schools have lower rates of high school completion, more single-parent households, and a greater likelihood of being non-English speakers (National Clearinghouse for Bilingual Education, 1993–94). The Council of Chief State School Officers (1992) recommend that programs developed for LEP students ensure that these students continue to earn and expand their knowledge of new content and therefore do not fall behind peers whose native language is English. Consequently, the provision of English language and subject

Figure 2.1 New York City Legal Mandates and Sources of Funding

---

City and State Regulations

- **The Consent Decree of August 29, 1974:** An agreement between the Board of Education of the City of New York and Aspira of New York which specifies a particular program for students 'whose English language deficiency prevents them from effectively participating in the learning process and who can more effectively participate in Spanish.'
- **The Lau Plan of September 15, 1977:** An agreement between the New York City Board of Education and the Office of Civil Rights for students 'whose limited English language ability prevents them from effectively participating in the learning process and whose home language is other than English or Spanish.'
- **Regulations of the New York State Commissioner of Education, Part 154:** Establishes 'standards' for the use of funds made available by the Legislature to provide financial assistance to school districts having pupils of limited English proficiency. In accordance with the provisions of Part 154, each school district receiving funds shall provide a program of bilingual education or English as a second language (ESL) for pupils identified as having limited English proficiency.'

Funding Sources

- **Part 154:** It provides supplemental State education aid for LEP programs based on the number of LEP students served in each school.
- **Pupils with Compensatory Education (PCEN):** It is a State program similar to the federal Chapter 1 program providing general funds for compensatory education programs. Like Chapter 1, it may not be used to supply basic instruction but must supplement it.
- **Title VII:** It supplies competitive grants, and it is used overwhelmingly for LEP students. In addition, it is used for some developmental language programs.
- **Emergency Immigration Education Assistance (EIEA):** It is a federal program designed for immigrant students only, whether they are LEP or not. It provides funds for programs serving these students for the first of three years of their enrollment.

---

matter instruction to those students is one of the most critical challenges confronting educators today. Many LEP students bring literacy skills in their native language that can be cognitively used in the acquisition of English. Another group may have never experienced literacy development in their countries of origins. But, after they arrive to the United States, these students may be placed in mainstream classrooms in spite of not having the necessary English background to perform academically well in an all-English classroom. Culturally and linguistically speaking, everything is new to these students in school, society values, and practices, as well as the academic and school environment.

The challenge of educating LEP students is even more acute when it is indicated that LEP students are more likely to attend high poverty schools than are native English speakers (National Clearinghouse for Bilingual Education, 1993–94). Almost one-quarter of fourth-graders in high poverty areas are LEP, compared to 2% in low-poverty schools. Forty-five percent of low-achieving fourth graders in high poverty schools come from language minority backgrounds (National Clearinghouse for Bilingual Education, 1993–94). A significant number of LEP students are enrolled in compensatory programs such as Chapter 1 (a federally funded program for low socioeconomic at-risk students). Thirty-five percent of United States' LEP students participate in Chapter 1 programs, and they account for 15% of Chapter 1's 5.5 million participants (National Clearinghouse for Bilingual Education, 1993–94). As a matter of fact, the number of Chapter 1 LEP students in middle and secondary school grew far faster than the total Chapter 1 population in these grades, almost doubling between 1985–86 and 1991–92.

LINGUISTIC ISSUES IN EDUCATING LEP STUDENTS

Language is an integral part of life and an integral part of the social system of societal groups. The diversity of the language systems in United States is a reflection of the richness and diversity of American culture. The ability of American educators to recognize and appreciate the value of different language groups will, to some extent, determine the effectiveness of its educational system. All students bring to school the language systems of their culture, and educators have the responsibility to understand cultural and linguistic differences and to recognize the value of these differences while working toward enhancing the students' linguistic skills in the target language. Educators need to recognize that:

- Most students come to school with a great deal of experience with oral and written language.
- LEP students need to have control of formal English in order to achieve academically.
- Language plays an active role in the social learning context.
- Language develops through authentic language use.
- Students need more than social-language skills to be successful in school; they need academic language skills, which involve using both receptive and productive language, thinking and reasoning in all content areas.

Cummins (1984) has argued that language minority students seem to be English-proficient yet perform poorly in school content areas. Cummins explains this phenomenon by suggesting that two sets of skills define language proficiency. The first involves what Cummins refers as 'basic interpersonal communication skills' (BICS) and the second involves 'cognitive academic language proficiency' (CALP). The primary distinction between the two concepts rests in the extent to which the communicative act is context-reduced or context-embedded. BICS refers to *context-embedded* speech (cues that assist comprehension such as facial expression, experiential activities, and body language visual elements); whereas CALP are acts that take place in a *context-reduced* environment (ability to manipulate concepts and solve problems). A context-reduced environment is one in which situation cues, such as those provided by verbal or other feedback, have been reduced. Context-embedded communication is more like what takes place in everyday communication between individuals. The former thus relies on external interpersonal cues whereas the latter relies on internal knowledge of appropriate responses. The reader needs to understand three implications in conceptualizing the English language development of LEP students: (a) language proficiency includes proficiency in *academic tasks* as well as in *basic conversation*, (b) cognitive academic language proficiency may take *five to seven years* to achieve, and (c) skills learned in the first language automatically *transfer* to the second language. Collier's research (1987) supports Cummins' theory that LEP students may need five to seven years to reach native-like control of the English language to perform well on academic tasks. Cummins argues that most language proficiency testing is actually more than an assessment of interpersonal communication skills, and that tests fail to include sufficient assessment of more cognitive academic content. If language minority students do not manifest these two components of language development (interpersonal and academic), they are labeled as 'limited English proficient'. A crucial step in meeting the needs of language minority students is the identification of those students who need language assistance for the development of the English academic language.

What are the characteristics of LEP students? Who are they? Although García (1993) admonishes that describing the 'typical' is highly problematic, he says that a LEP student is one:

- who is characterized by substantive participation in a non-English-speaking social environment;
- who has acquired the normal communicative abilities of that social environment;
- who is exposed to a substantive English-environment, more than likely for the first time, during the formal schooling process.

How can schools screen these students in order to assess further and identify their linguistic strengths and weaknesses? The United States federal government recommends that schools, at the beginning of each school year, begin the identification process by initially surveying and making a list of all students who meet one of the following conditions:

- The student was born outside of the United States or whose native language is not English.
- The student comes from an environment where a language other than English is dominant.
- The student is American Indian, Alaskan Native and comes from an environ-

ment where a language other than English has had a significant impact on his/her level of English language proficiency.

- The student has sufficient difficulty speaking, reading, writing or understanding the English language to deny him or her the opportunity to learn successfully in English-only classrooms

(United States Public Law, The Bilingual Education Act, 1988).

One of the most crucial indicators of a probable need for English language support among English language-minority children is a high frequency of native language use in the home. Initial screening procedures for students of non-English background need to include a home-language survey and a personal interview. The home-language survey usually requires 'yes/no' responses to questions such as 'Is a language other than English spoken at home by the student?' The survey is usually completed by the parent or guardian, but may be completed by school personnel. The interview may occur as a result of the information obtained from the home-language survey or on the recommendation of the school professional who is in charge of registration at the school. Those students who are identified as LEP students will be recommended for further assessment, and this final assessment information will be given to the mainstream teacher to guide her/him in providing the best classroom environment and instructional services under these abnormal learning conditions. Services for LEP students in the mainstream classroom should represent a continuum of appropriate programs, providing language development support such as tutoring beyond the normal classroom. The example shown in Figure 2.2 suggests the content to include in preparing an ongoing profile of LEP students.

Identifying LEP students' language strengths and weaknesses is an important factor in their academic development and is a necessary condition for success in the mainstream, especially as it relates to the acquisition of content area knowledge (Cummins, 1981, 1994). However, in addition to the linguistic skills, there are cognitive skills that need to be considered in providing LEP students with the appropriate learning and linguistic environment for academic success.

Figure 2.2 Using language academic data in the instructional program

Language Development		Academic Achievement
Basic Interpersonal Communication Skills	*Cognitive Academic Language Proficiency*	*Example of Content Areas*
Listening		Factual Knowledge
Speaking		Conceptual Understanding
Reading		Reasoning
Writing		Summarizing and Integrating Ideas

FACTORS TO CONSIDER IN THE COGNITIVE AND ACADEMIC DEVELOPMENT OF LEP STUDENTS

The literature tends to identify cognitive abilities, age, and personality as important factors in the academic and linguistic development of second language learners (Chamot & O'Malley, 1986; Cochran, 1989; Enright & McCloskey, 1988). The cognitive development of LEP students must be launched from within a given sociolinguistic context. The academic success that culturally and linguistically diverse students will experience in school hinges more on how these learners are able to manipulate language in a variety of contexts and purposes than on the specific language they use. According to cognitive development theory, learning is a process of constructing knowledge through the interaction of mind and experience (Dewey, 1938; Piaget, 1952; Vygotsky, 1962). Knowledge always has a concrete basis, and learners need concrete experiences in order to develop knowledge. Learners develop knowledge by interacting mentally and, to some extent, physically with people and objects around them. This interaction requires active involvement. Vygotsky (1962) points out the importance of culture and language to facilitate learning. He stated that language is a social and cultural phenomenon that is central to the development of thinking, and that cognitive development is greatly influenced by one's cultural and social environment. The knowledge that learners remember is that which relates to their interests and social and cultural milieu, and it is in a language that they understand; it is constructed by the learners and includes their active involvement. Given this assertion, it follows that the school's responsibility is to provide a wide range of experiences that will facilitate language development for social interaction as well as language for academic purposes.

Age clearly contributes to the cognitive power of the learner, at least up to adolescence, in that older learners are more cognitively mature than younger learners. Adults and older children in general, initially acquire the second language faster than younger children. A considerable number of studies have shown that older learners are more efficient in second language learning, although their ultimate attainment in the language learning may not surpass that of younger learners who have more time to develop proficiency. Children will achieve more overall communicative fluency because they are likely to receive more years of exposure to the second language and because of interaction with peer groups who speak the target language. Krashen, Long & Scarcella (1979) summarized those differences and similarities. These are:

- Adults proceed through the early stages of syntactic and morphological development faster than children (where time and exposure are held constant).
- Older children acquire faster than younger children (again in the early stages of morphological and syntactic development where time and exposure are held constant).
- Acquirers who begin with natural exposure to second language during childhood generally achieve higher second language proficiency than those beginning as adults (p. 573).

One additional important contributor to the learners' cognitive power is the degree of literacy developed in the first language. Given the fact that language mastery and cognitive development in the primary language will transfer to the second language, language minority learners should first be exposed to conceptual and language development in the language in which they feel more comfortable. The better developed the conceptual foundation of second language learners' first language, the more likely learners are to develop similarly high levels of conceptual abilities in their second language. In the United States there is a strong resistance to home language instruction, despite the evidence indicating that LEP students who develop a strong sociocultural, linguistic, and cognitive base in the primary language tend to transfer those attitudes and skills to the other language and culture (Cummins, 1981; Ramirez, 1992; Wong-Fillmore, 1991a, 1991b).

Clearly, there are variations in cognitive as well as linguistic characteristics in language minority students. This variation affects the communicative and academic interaction in which learners can participate. Cummins (1994) outlined five implications that these cognitive and linguistic characteristics have in the teaching-learning process.

(1) The educational and personal experiences that ESL students bring to schools constitute the foundation for all their future learning; schools should, therefore, attempt to amplify, rather than replace these experiences.

(2) Although English conversational skills may be acquired quite rapidly by ESL students, upward of five years may be required for ESL students to reach a level of academic proficiency in English comparable to their native-English-speaking peers. Schools must, therefore, be prepared for a long-term commitment in supporting the academic development of ESL students.

(3) Access to interaction with English speakers is a major causal variable underlying both the acquisition of English and ESL students' sense of belonging to the English-speaking society; the entire school is, therefore, responsible for supporting the learning and need for interaction of ESL students. ESL provision should integrate students into the social and academic mainstream in whatever way possible.

(4) If ESL students are to catch up academically with their native-English speaking peers, their cognitive growth and mastery of academic content must continue while English is being learned. Thus, teaching of English as a second language should be integrated with the teaching of other academic content areas that is appropriate to students' cognitive level. By the same token, all content teachers must recognize themselves also as teachers of language.

(5) The academic and linguistic growth of ESL students is significantly increased when their parents see themselves, and are seen by school staff, as educators of their children. Schools should, therefore, actively seek to establish a collaborative relationship with parents of ESL students that encourages them to participate in furthering their children's academic progress.

The cognitive development of LEP students is largely influenced by several factors: their literacy in their first language, their educational and personal experiences, involvement of their parents, and the richness of the academic content of the school. All these factors, added to the proficiency in the English language, influence students' involvement in academic areas. Schools need to challenge language minority students, to motivate them, to exhaust their cognitive abilities to the extent that they become successful learners. Schools' active involvement starts with assessment of the students and culminates with the appropriate placement for instruction.

ASSESSMENT ISSUES AND RECOMMENDED PRACTICES

There are several reasons to assess students learning in the classroom: to place students in classes, to measure students' progress and achievement, to guide and improve instruction, and to diagnose students' knowledge on a topic before it is taught. Such assessment must be carried out carefully. In order to assess students' learning, educators need to assure that students have enough language proficiency to be able to understand the content being used for the assessment. Students and teachers realize that most assessment instruments actually test both content concepts and language ability, particularly reading comprehension and writing. Because language and content are intricately intertwined, it is difficult to isolate one feature from the other in the assessment process. Thus, educators may not be sure whether a student is simply unable to demonstrate knowledge because of a language barrier or whether, indeed, the student does not know the content material assessed.

According to the United States Department of Education (1993a) the most common methods used by school districts to determine students' language proficiency are tests of oral language proficiency in English (83%) and home language surveys (77%) However, an examination of mainstream instructional demands yields a listing of content area topics, thinking skills, and linguistic domains necessary for learning, not necessarily assessed through the above instruments. Assessment of English language proficiency as a predictor of school achievement in monolingual English speaking settings provides no information about the probability of success in particular programs. Most assessment of LEP students is based on measuring English language proficiency. Many of the tests are of a multiple choice format.

There has been a growing interest among mainstream educators in multiple choice tests. Usually the only option available from test publishers fails to assess higher order skills and other skills essential for functioning in school or work settings. Also, tests in existence today do not measure academic language proficiency, or they confound content knowledge with language proficiency (Chamot & O'Malley, 1986; DeGeorge, 1988). Language proficiency measures generally sample students' knowledge of a particular language area. In many instances, a standardized English proficiency test is the only instrument used to determine the learner's language dominance or proficiency or to determine when second language learners are ready to perform academically in all-English classrooms. These tests tend to measure language skills that the test developer considers essential to language fluency. Usually, these tests include phonology (the pronunciation and identification of sounds), morphology (knowledge of the functions of words), syntax (grammatical structure of sentences), and lexicon (vocabulary). The extent to which language proficiency tests scores measure the language competence of individual students depends on the degree to which the composite skills on the test reflect students' actual language knowledge and language experiences. It is possible for these students to get high scores on the tests based on their grammatical competence in the language without knowing how to use the language in real life situations. Educators should not over-rely on language proficiency scores only, to determine whether students know enough English to perform in an all-English classroom because tests emphasize aspects of second language speaking and listening development, but provide little information about reading and writing development.

Multiple Criteria Approaches

School districts are turning to a multiple-criteria approach for making instructional decisions about LEP students. Virtually everyone in the field agrees that it is not a good idea to make language and academic decisions about LEP students on the basis of a single test score. Schools should rely on multiple sources of information obtained through different types of data collection, and, thereby increase the accuracy of diagnostic and evaluative functions. The multiple-instrument approach has two main types: *structured* (standardized tests, checklists, observations), and *unstructured* (students' work, samples, and journals). Structured methods are reliable and valid as long as they are properly scored and interpreted. The unstructured methods are somewhat more difficult to score and evaluate but they can provide a great deal of valuable information about the skills of students in the areas of language proficiency, language development, and the acquisition of content knowledge and skills. Since language learning takes place in different contexts for a variety of purposes, observations should involve as many different types of literacy events (reading, writing, speaking, and listening) as possible. For example, in determining reading growth in English, observation of students in different reading activities can provide information of students' growth. These observations may include: shared book experiences, free reading time, formal reading instruction, and reading in the content areas.

We recommend that all culturally and linguistically diverse students enrolled in a given school district be screened and assessed using multi-dimensional procedures that include: (a) information from teachers, or teachers' referrals, (b) information from parents, (c) evaluation of records, (d) appraisal of the student's academic level, and (e) appraisal of the student's language skills. This approach combines multiple instruments in order to assess all aspects of language proficiency and content knowledge from different perspectives. A comprehensive assessment system should include all of the following components:

- Teacher made tests

- Teachers' observations
- Students' works (lab reports, home work)
- Collective group work
- Questionnaires (Home surveys)
- Standardized tests
- Portfolios of students' work

The example in Figure 2.3 outlines recommended domains and types of assessment instruments included in the assessment.

Figure 2.3 A multiple instrument approach

Language Domain	Assessment Instruments					
	Tests	*Interviews*	*Protocols*	*Checklists*	*Rating Scales Inventories Anecdotal Records*	*Language Samples Homework Logs Journals Essays*
Oral language proficiency						
Reading comprehension						
Content-area mastery						
Written language ability						
Overall ability						

The information shown here includes informal indices of behavior and performance in addition to the traditional norm-referenced testing. Teachers' judgments regarding students' ability to process and to use content specific language functions, as well as judgments concerning their general performance in class, can yield valuable information. A list of recommended instruments follows with brief descriptive information.

Language Samples

Any written work students do alone, in class, or at home can be gathered and used to assess students' progress. When students write on specific topics, their products can be scored to assess language and content development. Assessment includes summaries, reflections, scripts for a play, and language experience stories. Logs and journals can be reviewed on a daily, weekly, or quarterly basis to determine how students are perceiving their learning processes as well as shaping their ideas and strengths.

Protocols

This includes asking students to perform a specific academic activity for the purpose of observing specific language skills or content. For example, asking students to read aloud from an appropriate text can provide teachers with information on how students handle cueing systems of language in terms of the semantic, syntactic, graphic, and phonemic aspects. Recording students' oral miscues can provide information to the teacher about students' oral reading level and progress.

Rating Scales/Inventories

This method can be used by teachers to record behaviors and students' progress. These comments can include behavioral, emotional, and academic information; for example, 'Manuel did not write anything in his journal during the first week in school, however in his second week he wrote five times.' These observations should be written carefully avoiding judgmental words. Anecdotal records may take the form of notes written at the end of the school day by the teacher or other school staff close to the student. They may record what occurred in the lunchroom, in the classroom, among students, or by the student alone.

Checklists

It is an observational technique in which observers check only the presence or absence of the behavior or product. Used over time, checklists can document students' rate and degree of accomplishments within the curriculum, since it specifies student behavior or products expected during progression through the curriculum.

Interviews

Interviews can be used to obtain information of interest to a teacher. The interviews can be conducted with a student or a group of students. It is important to keep interviews as simple and to the point as possible.

Tests

There are a variety of tests used in schools to assess students' needs and strengths but the most used fall under three classifications: *standardized* (language proficiency/academic), *cloze*, and *criterion-referenced* which provide information on students' academic status. Cloze tests, for example, provide a measure of reading comprehension. Criterion-referenced tests measure progress through the curriculum and can be used for specific instructional planning. Standardized tests are generally those that measure language proficiency (usually oral) or specific academic areas. Tests of language proficiency should be accompanied by teachers' own judgments and observation data (Canales, 1990).

Great care is needed to develop truly equitable and useful mechanisms for identifying language minority students and providing them with appropriate services. In evaluating the students' overall English ability, it is suggested that as many types of instruments as possible be used to assess the same skill or area. For example, many content areas and cognitive skills from the various subject areas are amenable to assessment by formal tests, yet observation data and information from existing records should also be used in assessing progress in the content areas. English proficiency should not only be measured by a standardized exam. Portfolio information, as well as other evidence collected, should also be used in measuring the language proficiency of a particular student.

This assessment should begin as soon as the culturally and linguistically diverse student arrives in the school; written records should begin to be created in the form of cumulative files, observation notes, anecdotal information, tests scores, and grades. It is also recommended that a portfolio of the student's work be immediately organized, which is kept in school and which provides information on the student's development toward mastery of important content knowledge, thinking skills, and language proficiency. If the student moves to another school, the portfolio should be sent to the new school.

Matching Assessment to Instruction

The assessment should look at: (a) both *interpersonal* and *academic language* proficiencies, (b) evidence from appropriate language and modalities, (c) students' profile progress over time (year to year, semester to semester), (d) students' reflection on their own progress both in language proficiency and academic achievement, and (e) clearer communication with parents about students' accomplishments and needs. The comprehensive assessment approach yields information relative to student mastery or non-mastery of specific content areas, cognitive skills, and language proficiency. Identifying these areas in individual students' profiles can provide sound basis for making instructional decisions about LEP students. Once all assessment information has been compiled, the next necessary step is to use that information for instructional purposes. The example in Figure 2.4 illustrates recommended steps in using assessment data in the instructional program.

Services for LEP students in the mainstream classroom should represent a continuum of appropriate programs, providing language development support beyond the normal classrooms, such as tutoring. The following example suggests the content to be included in preparing an ongoing profile of LEP students. With regard to academic content, and as for all students, instruction should focus on: (a) higher order thinking, (b) depth of knowledge, (c) relevance beyond the classroom, and (d) social support for student achievement. Teachers must insist that tests used in the school take into account the full range of curricular objectives and interactive/experiential models of teaching. If commercial tests that assess communication and higher level thinking skills are not available, teachers should apply pressure in their districts to develop their own criterion-referenced tests. Mainstream teachers should be encouraged to use those methods that have been found very successful in teaching LEP students instead of insisting that these students fit into the mold of a reductionism curriculum, where they are prone to fail.

Figure 2.4 From assessment to instruction

Language and Cognitive Development	Assessment	What are the linguistic and academic characteristics of the student?	
		Assessment from support personnel	Assessment from instructional staff
	Assessment data is analyzed	What instructional program would be most appropriate?	
		Local program options	Local curriculum
	Instruction	Where in the program should the student begin working?	
		Established goals	Instructional adaptations

CONCLUSION

Demographic changes in the United States have brought educational and social issues related to language and academic learning to the forefront of discussion. Language minority students bring cultural, cognitive, and linguistic strengths. Their cultural identity, as well as their knowledge of the first language, are part of the academic foundation of their learning of English and learning through English. Limited English proficient students meet many challenges. They are expected to cope with the acquisition of English in both oral and written form in an instructional program that has been designed for native English speakers. Language minority students do not have knowledge and skills in English, nor do they have an understanding of the school culture. They need time to adjust to the school environment and to acquire the skills necessary to learn through English. Because LEP students represent many diverse ethnic groups and bring to school the richness of many languages, educators need to assess their strengths and weaknesses in a variety of ways. Since research demonstrates that no single practice can work in isolation, schools should set in motion multiple testing mechanisms. Also, because teachers have the most direct knowledge of their students' abilities, they should be involved in the initial and on-going assessment. These practices provide the necessary background to allow the best possible instruction to occur for all learners in the difficult context of the diverse mainstream classroom.

CHAPTER 3

Cultural and Linguistic Diversity in the Classroom

CHAPTER 3

Cultural and Linguistic Diversity in the Classroom

INTRODUCTION

Recent trends and projections indicate that the present influx and growth of diverse ethnic and linguistic groups in the United States will continue. Parents of language minority students come from Europe, Asia, Africa, Central and South America, and the Caribbean, and they settle in the United States seeking a new life filled with opportunities unavailable in their homeland. But these immigrants did not abandon their ethnic traditions when they reached the shores of the United States. Each ethnic group has its own customs and traditions, and each group brought different experiences, accomplishments, skills, values, styles of dress, and tastes in food that linger long after their arrival. Making use of their traditions and language provides them with the moral and social support to survive in the United Sates.

This chapter presents an overview of those cultural and language attributes of the largest ethnic groups in the United States. By understanding language minority students' culture and language styles, educators can organize classrooms to promote multicultural environments and curriculum.

ETHNIC DIVERSITY IN THE CLASSROOM

In United States' school classrooms, most language minority students are likely to come from the following ethnic/racial groups: Hispanic, Asian, African Caribbean (Haitian-Creole), American Indian, Eastern European, and the Middle Eastern (Arabs). Students from these diverse ethnic groups are placing unprecedented demands on teachers, administrators and the entire educational system of the United States. This diversity poses the need for educators to accept the cultures from which language minority students come, and to embrace the imperative to work through that understanding to help these students ease their way into a new language and culture, while still retaining their own culture. Through an understanding of cultural

38

diversity, schools can contribute to the elimination of stereotyping, which influences the way students are perceived and ultimately instructed.

The United states is and has been the destination of about half the World's immigrants, who seek permanent resettlement. A significant percentage of LEP students are children of immigrant parents, usually children of first generation individuals. Immigrants are confronted with the demands of a new society and its assimilation process with accompanying circumstances and hardships which often negatively affect LEP poor students: low wages, unemployment, under-employment, little property ownership, no savings, lack of food reserves, and daily struggles to meet the most basic needs. These hardships easily lead to feelings of helplessness, dependency, and inferiority (Baruth & Manning, 1992). Immigrants and refugees usually find themselves under-employed because degrees earned in their native land are not highly valued by United States employers. Furthermore, as newcomer immigrants, parents often feel a lack of economic and job security and are more threatened by economic depression than those persons born in the United States. This sense of insecurity is transmitted to their children, who easily detect the pressures generated at home. The drive for better economic conditions often affects children's academic achievement and emotional development. Peer pressure on immigrant students is even greater than on American-born students. To be in conformity to their peers, immigrant students must adjust in many areas at the expense of their own cultural heritage. This adjustment takes time, and immigrant students often encounter resistance and objections from their parents, who want to preserve some of their traditional heritage.

Language minority students are racially, ethnically, and linguistically diverse. It is a fallacy to consider all LEP students as one single group. Describing 'typical' culturally diverse students is highly problematic; and educators must be careful to not stereotype all students from the same ethnic group, as many differences exist within the same group (Carrasquillo, 1991; Garcia, 1993). However, there is still room to make generalizations as to the ethnic and linguistic characteristics of these students for the purpose of recognizing, accepting, valuing, and appreciating differences in schools and classrooms. The following section briefly describes the ethnic groups heavily represented in the LEP school population in United States classrooms.

Hispanic Students

Hispanic students are those students who are Mexican, Puerto Rican, Cuban, Central, South American, or other Spanish culture or origin. It should be noted that the use of the term, 'Hispanic', when referring to persons from Spanish speaking countries in the Americas, is not accepted with universal favor (Carrasquillo, 1991). Objection centers mainly on the term's reference to ancestral roots that are solely from Spain. This reference disregards the African American and Native American Indian heritage of many individuals who have Spanish surnames. For many people, the use of the term, 'Latino', is preferred when referring to this population. However, although this view is acknowledged, the word, 'Hispanics' was chosen for use throughout this book because it is the term most often found in the extant literature, especially in statistical data and government reports. It is also the term best known by non-Hispanic groups.

The Hispanic population is a young, diverse, and dynamic group that is experiencing rapid growth in the United States. The Hispanic population in the United States is a community of first, second, and third-generation immigrants who have uprooted their families and left homes, friends, and relatives for economic, political, professional, ideological, and educational reasons. The Hispanic population is the fastest-growing ethnic/racial group in the United States. They numbered 22.7 million persons in 1992 (not counting the 3.5 million persons residing in Puerto Rico), which represents an increase of 53% over the 1980 figure of 14 million (United States Bureau of the Census, 1993). In 1990, six of every ten Hispanics said that they were of Mexican origin, making them the largest Hispanic group in the United States. Persons of Puerto Rican origin constitute 2.4 million persons, representing 11% of all United States Hispanics. In 1993, there were 1.0 million Cubans, representing 4.7% of the Hispanic population. The slow growth of the Cuban population in the 1990s reflects a slow level of immigration (although this rate began to change in 1994 due to the almost 30,000 Cubans who left Cuba by boat). The group of Central and South Americans increased to 3 million, representing 13.4% of the Hispanic population, reflecting the high levels of immigration engendered by political and economic turmoil in their countries of origin. This growth in the Hispanic community is expected to be greater than for any other racial or ethnic group. Although in 1992, Hispanics composed 9% of the United States population, the projections indicate that by the year 2000, Hispanics are likely to represent 11% of the population, increasing thereafter to 15% by 2020 and possibly 21% by the year 2050 (United States Bureau of the Census, 1992).

Hispanic students have a broad range of language and cultural characteristics and needs which impact upon their academic and cognitive development. The cultural patterns of Hispanic students are reflective of those created by their parental heritage, by the length of time their families have been in the United States, and by the socioeconomic level they have achieved in the United States. There are general experiences shared by many Hispanic families in the United States, such as the Spanish language, family structure and characteristics, and Hispanic culture. Spanish language, religious beliefs, family structures, and general customs are enhanced among Hispanics. But, at the same time, Hispanic students represent a diverse group within a group in a country that does not value diversity, but rather values uniformity through a common language, culture and race (Carrasquillo, 1991).

Hispanic students and their families face many challenges to their survival and development in the United States (Carrasquillo, 1991; Carrasquillo & London, 1993). For example, a significant percentage of Hispanic students are poor. The 1993 Census report the poverty rate of Hispanics at 29.3% compared to 18.0% for the whole United States population. The low-status occupations and high unemployment rates among Hispanics translate into low incomes and high levels of poverty. The characteristics of Hispanic students in the United States are listed by Carrasquillo (1991) (see Figure 3.1).

Figure 3.1 Hispanic children and youth in the United States

- Represent a growing population estimated by the year 2000 to become the largest group of minority children in the United States.
- Are not a homogeneous socioeconomic and educational group.
- Suffer economic deprivation.
- Are affected negatively by socioeconomic conditions of the family.
- Share (many of them) the Spanish language and culture.
- May have parents that are marginally employed, under-employed or unemployed.
- Are below the majority population in any array of standard educational measurement.
- Represent a significant percentage of the inmate offender population.
- Suffer from poor health and limited prevention and health related services.
- Are not well represented in institutions of higher education.

In spite of these challenges, Hispanic students show the desire to learn; and their parents show the desire to provide them with the best moral, spiritual, educational and material means. These goals are achieved in a greater or lesser degree due to Hispanics' precarious socioeconomic experience in the United States.

Asian and Pacific Islander Students

These are students whose origins are found among any of the original peoples of the Far East, Southeast Asia, the Indian subcontinent, or the Pacific Islands. Asian students comprise children and youth from more than two dozen different countries of Asia and the Pacific Islands which include countries such as Cambodia, China, Korea, India, Japan, Laos, Philippines, Samoa/Tonga/Guam, Thailand, and Vietnam, just to mention a few. They do not share a common language, a common religion or a common cultural background. When the new Immigration Act of 1965 became fully effective in July, 1968, the number of Asian immigrants to the United States rose immediately and steadily. As required by the immigration rules, these Asian immigrants were better educated and were of higher economic status than their predecessors.

The Asian population grew more rapidly than any other minority group in the 1980s, and there is every reason to believe that it will continue to grow at high rates during the 1990s (O'Hare & Felt, 1991). In addition, the end of the war in Southeast Asia brought more than 1.5 million refugees to the United States. They represent diverse cultural, racial, educational, and occupational backgrounds, and like their children, they encountered a different assimilation process and different problems.

Recent immigration has brought two very distinct groups of Asians to the United

States. One group is educated and ready to move into the mainstream quickly. The other group lacks educational background and skills to move out of poverty (Carrasquillo & London, 1993; O'Hare & Felt, 1991). The average family income of Asian Americans is comparatively high, although their poverty rate has increased during the last decade. Poverty within the Asian American community tends to be overshadowed by the high income of some Asian Americans. Yet, a significant percentage of the Asian community lives in poverty (O'Hare & Felt, 1991; Peterson, 1983; Yao, 1985). One of the most accepted reasons for this discrepancy is that the flood of new Asian immigrants may increase the poverty rate, but many of the second and third generation of Asian immigrants may be moving up in socioeconomic status.

Education has always been highly regarded by Asian cultures. Asian parents passed on their value to their children. Asian American parents have high hopes for their children in the public schools of America as a way to prepare their children for better jobs than the ones they themselves had to take when they arrived in the United States. Today, Chinese, Japanese and Koreans have the highest average of years of education as compared to any other immigrant group in the United States. Because of their high level of education, Asians have entered into many highly skilled professional and technical jobs. But, because of continued prejudice and discrimination, there are still areas of the job market where Asians are not adequately represented. Also, for the Asian group as a whole, the level of employment and income still does not measure up to their level of skill, education, and training.

In general, immigrant Asian students are very sensitive to, and are challenged by, all types of cultural shock during their assimilation process. Yao (1985) indicated that extrinsic cultural traits are changed more quickly than are intrinsic traits. Both verbal and non-verbal expressions must be modified to avoid misunderstanding and embarrassment. The extrinsic culture traits, such as the American style of eating and dressing, are easily mastered in a short period of time. Intrinsic culture traits, such as value systems, social norms, and religious beliefs are more difficult to adjust to in a new country. Yao (1985) indicates that, during their assimilation, the social skills of immigrant Asian students are not as developed as those of American-born students. This results from the quiet, docile way that children from this cultural background are taught to respond once they begin their formal education. Consequently, immigrant Asian students are less verbal and expressive at social occasions and are often completely left out of the festivities. A lack of developed social skills not only hinders their social interaction with others, but also impedes their achievement in the classroom. They need reinforcement from teachers and they work efficiently in a well-structured, quiet learning environment in which definite goals have been established for them. They seldom reveal their opinions or their abilities voluntarily or dare to challenge their teachers. Even when they know the answer to the teacher's question, they may not respond by raising their hand, choosing instead to sit quietly as if they are lost (Yao, 1985). Older students, who are accustomed to structured and passive learning conditions rather than to the American educational approach, which requires critical and divergent thinking, may perform well in rote memorization and mathematics operations but may do poorly in creative writing and analytical commentary (Peterson, 1983; Yao, 1985). This style of learning sometimes conflicts with the teacher's style of teaching, or the learning style of the other students.

Asian students and their parents have perceptions and expectations of teachers that differ from those of American-born parents and children. School authorities, especially the teacher, are highly respected and their advice and orders are strictly followed. The teacher has great authority. In many Asian schools, students must stand up and bow to the teacher and show respect and reverence when the teacher enters or leaves the classroom. The teacher's instructions are to be obeyed and never challenged. Carrasquillo & London (1993) state that it is paradoxical that, in spite of the great authority of the teacher, Asian American students are less dependent on teachers than their American counterparts. Teachers and school counselors must understand the educational values of Asian people and develop a strategic plan that deals with their cultural and educational diversity in the most beneficial way.

American Indian, Esquimo and Aleut Students

These are students whose origins are found in any of the original peoples of North America, and who maintain cultural identification through tribal affiliation or community recognition. In Alaska, a special distinction is made between American Indians and two other groups, the Inuit (often called Eskimos) and the Aleuts. The Inuit and the Aleuts inhabited Alaska long before Europeans arrived, but these two groups did not settle in North America until 10,000 years ago, while the American Indians arrived long before that, probably between 30,000 and 40,000 years ago. Research suggests that most American Indians are descended from only a few original immigrants from Asia to North America. By the 16th century, however, the original peoples of North America had diversified greatly and had formed hundreds of identifiable tribes. Some of these tribes had closely related languages and cultures (Baruth & Manning, 1992; Wax, 1971).

The term 'Indians' came from Christopher Columbus' mistaken belief that his ships had reached the East Indies. The term remains as the most common group name for the people whose ancestors populated the Americas before the Europeans arrived. Most American Indians, while they may like to point out exactly which tribe they belong to, do not mind being called Indians. Another term, 'Native Americans', is also widely used and is generally acceptable as another name for American Indians.

American Indians have not had an easy life in the United States. Settlement by Europeans meant the elimination of the Indian land. Revenge against the Indians came when the Indians confronted the European settlers. By the end of the nineteenth century Indians were confined to reservations, managed and controlled by the Bureau of Indian Affairs. Poor living conditions and diseases in the reservations caused many deaths among American Indians. Reservations brought other problems, such as unemployment, alcoholism, lack of housing, and lack of educational opportunities, which depended in many instances upon the federal government subsidies.

Approximately one-half of American Indians in the United States reside on Native-American lands, while the other half live outside the reservations in urban or other predominantly Anglo-American geographical areas. States with the greatest population of American Indians include California, Oklahoma, Arizona, New Mexico, and Washington. Of the federal reservations, the Navajo Nation is the largest and has a population of more than 165,000 residents (Baruth & Manning, 1992). Although Indians do not want to remain dependent on the federal government, the government's influence in their lives is still strong.

Nearly all literature on Native American education alludes to the vital importance of addressing Native American cultural differences in education. Although each of the many Indian cultures developed its own religious system; no single, undivided 'Indian religion' exists. Nevertheless, certain features are common to many other religions, traditionally practiced by the American Indians. One of these is the belief in a supreme spiritual force, sometimes called the 'Great Spirit'. Another common belief is in the need to search for one's own guiding spirit, a spiritual being who will help seek greater contact with the spiritual world through fasting, meditating, dancing, or using certain natural drugs. Many American Indians also believe that their religious beliefs about how to treat the dead are violated when museums display skeletons and other items from Indian graves.

American Indians speak about 2,200 different languages (Baruth & Manning, 1992; Wax, 1971). Wide-scale differences exist in the American Indian ability to speak English. Some speak English well, but a significant number of American Indians lack proficiency in English. The example described in the following case study taken from Baruth & Manning (1992) is illustrative of the home–school mismatch encountered by many American Indian LEP students:

> 'Harry, a fifteen-year-old boy, has several problems that result, at least in part, from his lack of proficiency in English. He is faced with functioning in a bilingual world. While his family continues to rely on the language it has spoken for centuries, he must speak English at school. Meanwhile, his grades are failing, he does not always understand the teacher (and vice versa) and he experiences difficulty as he ventures outside the social confines of his culture' (p. 49).

Harry, to some extent, is representative of many American Indians with a language and culture different from the Anglo culture represented in the school and the curriculum.

Haitian Students

Haitian immigrants began coming to the United States in the 1920s; but it was not until Haiti's late president-for-life, François Duvalier, took power in 1957 that Haitians began to settle in the United States in significant numbers. The first wave of Haitian immigrants was mostly composed of political dissidents who were members of the intelligentsia, upper class and middle class. In the 1970s, after Jean Claude Duvalier succeeded his father as president-for-life, a second wave of Haitians arrived in New York from the shore of Florida. They were labeled the 'boat people' after landing in the state of Florida in small boats from Haiti. This group, uneducated for the most part, came from the poverty-stricken rural areas of Haiti. The same situation was repeated in 1991 when a military coup expelled an elected democratic president, and the military government punished any individual who was part of the defeated democratic government.

Although in the early 1990s there was an increase in the number of Haitians reaching the United States in small boats, this flow stopped at the end of 1994 when the democratic government was restored in Haiti as a result of pressure and assistance from the United Nations, especially the United States. However, there is still a significant group of Haitians living in the United States with the greatest number of Haitian immigrants residing in New York State. It is estimated that there are about 600,000 Haitians, although this figure is conservative due to the large influx of illegal Haitian immigration.

The most crucial barrier to Haitian adjustment to life in the United States relates to the uncertainty regarding their legal status . They are considered 'economic immigrants' and not 'political refugees', complicating their status and adjustment in the United States. Having come from an authoritarian society, the Haitian immigrant needs extensive orientation to life in the United States. This is due to economic and political differences between the two countries and the vast gap between the two cultures. As with most immigrant groups, language difficulties present numerous problems. These problems are compounded for those Haitians who are non literate and do not have school experience. Haitian Creole is the language spoken by the majority of the people of Haiti, and only a small group of Haitians, usually the middle and upper class, speak and read French. For most Haitian students entering American schools, the language that they speak and can understand is Haitian Creole, not French.

Education, a privilege of a small minority in Haiti, is highly valued by Haitians of all groups as a means toward upward mobility. Haitian parents will make the utmost effort in order to see their children through school. Even if they can barely afford it, they would rather send their children to private or parochial schools, which in Haiti bear more prestige and, in some cases, offer both a higher quality and a religious education (New York State Education Department, 1987). Recent Haitian immigrants to the United States have the tendency to follow the same educational values as those of Haiti. Education in Haiti is delegated to the school. Students are expected to study, do homework, and exhibit prescribed behavior. Parental or community participation is minimal. School officials are trusted to do their job and to be responsible toward their children. The only role parents play in Haitian education, besides that of supervising homework, is a disciplinary one (The New York State Education Department, 1987).

Russian Students

American classrooms are populated by people from diverse European backgrounds, but especially from the eastern and northern parts of Europe. These are students coming from eastern and northern Europe and the states of the former Soviet Union. Most of these families emigrated to the United States because of the uncertainty of their countries, due to rapid political and economic changes. Russian immigrants are, for the most part, those persons who arrived in America from lands currently within Russia. The other half belong to other national and ethnic groups (Ukrainians, Byelorussians, Estonians, Latvians, Lithuanians, Armenians, Georgians, Kazakhs and Uzbeks). These groups speak more than 100 different languages, and have different religious practices as well as lifestyles. Estimating the population of Russians in the United States is problematic because the term 'Russian' was applied to all those groups mentioned before who came from the multinational Russian empire and the Soviet Union. These groups represent, among others, Jews, Poles, Byelorussians, Ukrainians and Germans. Many of these immigrants have settled in metropolitan New York, and California (Los Angeles, and San Francisco). Others fanned out across the American and Canadian landscapes.

Most Russian immigrants left their homeland because of unfavorable conditions, including economic hardships, religious persecution, civil war, the establishment of the Soviet government, a foreign invasion, involuntary displacement, and limited prospects for the future (Magocsi, 1989). Most immigrants saw the United States as their salvation, and made the determination to find ways to leave their countries and settle in 'the land of opportunities'.

The story of Russians in the United States is one of adjustment; they must learn a new language, new life styles, new cultural values and attitudes, and learn to live with other Russians who may have different life styles, religious practices, and political points of view. Referring to the difficulty of many Russians to accept other Russians in the United States, Magocsi (1989) states that: 'A further difficulty awaits the newest immigrants, most of whom are Jews, but neither religiously committed nor are accepted by the older non-Jewish Russian immigrants and their descendants. And for those Russian Jews who are observant, the religious practices they have kept alive in a hostile Soviet society are not always fully in line with the Western religious practice' (p. 103).

Delgado-Gaitan (1994) presents data from an ethnographic study conducted with refugee Russian families in Yolo City, California. The Delgado-Gaitan study indicates that Russians preferred the United States over their homeland, and this preference reflects the strong commitment on the part of these individuals to adopt a new culture and to conform to the new society's expectations. She found that, for refugee Russian families, the church plays an important role: it supports them emotionally, economically, and socially. It ameliorates their tribulations as they learn a new system in a different language, and as they learn to deal with the resultant changing situations in their family structure. Socialization into the new system is accomplished through intense family-education programs. Although immigrant families are unfamiliar with the new system of education, they are, nevertheless, eager to do whatever it takes for their children to succeed in school. Russian families expect their children (and themselves) to learn in English, and they push their children to learn the English language as quickly as possible. In some instances, this strong parental push causes initial distress in students. However, it has been found that young Russian children in elementary school adapt more easily than adolescents and adults (Delgado-Gaitan, 1994). Russian families learn English themselves so that they can help their children excel in school.

Arab Students

The Arabs are made up of several different peoples who live in North Africa and Western Asia (the Middle East) and share a common culture. They descend from 18 countries which share the Arabic language and heritage, but which may differ drastically in political, and religious beliefs, economics and traditions. Most of them speak Arabic, a Semitic language that originated on the Arabian Peninsula. A significant number of Arabs practice Islam, the religion founded by Mohammed, which was spread throughout the Middle East during the seventh century, and which united the people of the region into one of the world's great civilizations. The modern Arab world consists of Algeria, Bahrain, Egypt, Iraq, Jordan, Kuwait, Lebanon, Libya, Morocco, Oman, the People's Democratic Republic of Yemen, Qatar, Saudi Arabia, Sudan, Syria, Tunisia, the United Arab Emirates, and the Yemen Arab Republic. Palestinians live within the borders of several of these countries, their situation began to change in 1994 when Israel ceded the Gaza Strip to them.

Although Arabs have migrated to the United States since the second half of the eighteenth century, a high influx came after 1948. After World War II, due to the political changes in the Arab countries, many displaced Palestinians and other discontented Arabs came to the United States. Since 1948, Arabs have arrived in the United States in search of opportunity from every part of the Arab world. Their descendants have a heritage rich in the traditions of their ancestral homelands and in their long history as Americans.

The United States counts approximately two million Arab Americans among its residents, but any estimation of the size of the current Arab American population is at best imprecise. Many Arabs who came to the United States intended to stay only for a short period of time. Some sought refuge from political and military turmoil that they thought would end soon; some came to study or to reap the benefits of a college education. Many were professionals, lawyers, doctors, engineers, with limited career opportunities in their underdeveloped homelands. They planned to make enough money in the United States to be able to return and live comfortably in the Middle East.

Since a growing number of Arabs are Muslims, it is important to respect their religion in the classroom and to make the other students understand it as well. Most recent immigrants to the United States practice Islam and most come from nationalistic Arab states. Most Arab immigrants retain strong feelings of solidarity with their troubled homelands, especially after their humiliating defeat by Israel in the 1967 Arab–Israeli War. Figure 3.2 presents a list of recommended strategies in dealing with Muslim students in the classroom. This list is commonly mentioned in local school districts' curricula although its original author or publisher is unknown by the authors of this book.

If Arab students are represented in the school, it is recommended that school personnel, and especially teachers, become familiar with their religious and lifestyle practices. A one hour presenɩation to the whole school community by a repre-

Figure 3.2 Strategies in teaching Muslim students

Prayer:	Since Muslim students pray five times a day, give Muslim students time and space to do so.
Fasting:	Muslims fast from dawn to sunset during the month of Ramadan (based on the Muslim lunar calendar). Do not force students to eat if they decide not to.
Dress:	Allow students to wear sweat pants and long sleeve shirts for gym. Allow girls to wear head covers since Muslims are required to dress modestly.
Diet:	When planning parties in the classroom or in the school, remember that Muslims may not eat pork, or foods containing marshmallows, lard, gelatin or animal shortening.
Holidays:	Students may need to be absent to celebrate special Islamic holidays, therefore, prepare assignments and readings beforehand for these students.
Birthdays:	Some Muslims discourage birthday celebrations because Islam teaches them not to be self-centered. Parties would bring too much attention to them.
Christmas and Easter:	Although Muslims recognize and respect Jesus Christ, they do not commemorate his birth and death. Therefore, Muslim parents may be reluctant to let their children join in Christmas and Easter activities.
Valentine's Day:	Some Muslims prefer to refrain from this holiday because 'love' is a private matter and should not be trivialized.
Halloween:	Muslims generally do not take part in trick-or-treating because it emphasizes dark spirits.
Mother's Day/ Father's Day:	The family is valued in Islam as well as respect for parents. Some Muslims do not believe in showing excess appreciation to parents on one particular day, it should be constant.

sentative of the Arab/Muslim community on what it means to be an Arab or Muslim student may be a recommended strategy at the beginning of the school year.

Summary

The purpose of providing the reader with a brief overview of different ethnic and linguistic groups represented in the mainstream classroom was to alert educators to understand that language minority students bring a variety of cultural backgrounds, life styles, religious preferences, educational values, and attitudes to the school/classroom setting. Educators need to be careful in understanding and respecting students' cultural and religious differences, so that they do not clash with school practices. This clarity will avoid future misunderstandings due to unfamiliarity with students' cultural values and attitudes.

LANGUAGE DIVERSITY IN THE UNITED STATES

Language is a critical key to understanding the culture and experience of others. It enables people to develop a sense of belonging and acceptance in a particular group. It is through language that complex cultural concepts and ideas are transmitted and understood. The chart shown in Figure 3.3 illustrates the interrelationship of language and culture.

As can be easily recognized, the complexity of the language issues presented earlier extend beyond verbal communication between teachers and students into other dimensions, such as nonverbal communication and word meanings. Educators should carefully consider language differences and developmental levels in all decisions concerning organizing for instruction, the effect of language differences on working alone or working cooperatively toward achieving educational goals. But gaining fluency in English does not alone ensure success, since many language minority students come from cultures very different from mainstream American

Figure 3.3 Language and cultural domains

Domain	Description
Discourse	Manner in which language is organized in speech and writing beyond the level of the sentence.
Appropriateness	Language used in social context, from informal to formal contexts.
Paralinguistic/Kinesics	Aspects of non-verbal communication (gestures, facial expressions, interpersonal distance, intonation, volume, pitch).
Pragmatics	Norms and expectations as to when it is appropriate to speak, with whom, and how (including taking turns and appropriate topics for conversation).
Cognitive/Academic	Mastery of the language facilitating learning of abstract language concepts.

culture. According to the National Center for Effective Schools (1994) this statement poses the need for educators to achieve a powerful cognitive shift: to accept the cultures from which language minority children come, and to embrace the imperative to work through the understanding to help language minority children ease their way into a new language and culture, while retaining their heritage. The National Center for Effective Schools (1994) goes further and asks: 'How is language linked with culture? Isn't it enough to learn English and merge into mainstream, middle class American society? Is it the school's role to facilitate this, or is the school's role something different? Why is it important for educators to accept and understand the cultures of children from different countries? In short, we are asking why we, as educators, must join the change process to meet the newcomers to our schools' (p. 1).

The multilingual nature of American society reflects the rich cultural heritage of its people. Although the United States is primarily an English-speaking country, there are many other languages spoken. Such language diversity is an asset to the nation, especially in its interaction with other nations in the areas of commerce, defense, education, science and technology. Language diversity in the United States has been maintained primarily because of continuing immigration from non-English speaking countries. The maintenance of native languages other than English depends on the efforts of members of the language group through churches and other community activities. There are over 30 languages in everyday use in the United States. In the largest cities, they represent as many as 100 different countries. This number includes over 200 native American languages (the languages of the colonizers). After English, the most commonly used languages in the United States are Spanish, Chinese, Italian, and Sign language.

The report of the United States Department of Education, *Descriptive Study of Services to Limited English Proficient Students* (1993a), listed the twenty language groups with the most LEP students in United States. These are:

Spanish	Vietnamese	Hmong	Cantonese
Cambodian	Korean	Laotian	Navajo
Tagalog	Russian	Haitian Creole	Arabic
Portuguese	Japanese	Armenian	Chinese
Mandarin	Farsi	Hindi	Polish

Among the English-speaking immigrant students, there are numerous dialects from the Hawaiian pidgin to the southern English to the Caribbean English. Each is distinctive, and each is an effective means for communication for those who share its linguistic style. Language differences ultimately reflect basic behavioral differences between groups of people. Physical and social separation inevitably lead to language differences. For example, while among the nation's Mon-Khmer (Cambodian) and Miao (Hmong) speakers, more than four in ten speak English either not fluently or not at all. Among Chinese, Korean, Vietnamese, Russian and Thai language populations, the proportion is roughly three in ten (United States Bureau of the Census, 1992; National Council of la Raza, 1993). Social variables also contribute to language differences, with both class and ethnicity reflecting those differences. The greater the social distance between groups, the greater the tendency toward language differences.

Language minority students in United States' schools reflect a variety of language backgrounds and proficiencies. While some students are bilingual in English and their native language, others either do not speak English at all, or have limited English-speaking skills. Among those students who are bilingual in English and their native language, there are degrees of bilingualism. Some speak both languages well, others speak limited English, some speak a non-standard dialect, and some use sign language. This diversity is indicative of the multilingual nature of the United States, a result of its multilingual heritage. In 1993, the United States Bureau of the Census reported major demographic trends in racial, and ethnic groups, as well as changes in the overall population. Census data indicated that more than 31.8 million people said that they spoke a language other than English at home in 1990, compared with 23.1 million a decade earlier (United States Bureau of the Census, 1993). This is an increase of three percentage points, from 11% of the nation's population aged five and over in 1980, to 14% in 1990. Spanish was the second most common language spoken in the United States after English. The National Council of la Raza (1993) presented their interpretation of the census data by saying: 'Over half (17.3 million) of those who said they spoke a language other than English reported that they spoke Spanish; by comparison, in 1980, about 11.1 million people spoke Spanish' (p. 7).

ORGANIZATION OF A MULTICULTURAL-SENSITIVE CLASSROOM

Sensitive schools and classrooms promote multicultural environments and curricula, permeating throughout all aspects of the school. The school environment includes all experiences with which learners come in contact: the content, instructional methods, the actual teaching/learning process, the professional staff and other staff members, as well as the actions and attitudes of other students. The classroom environment plays a significant role in ' ow students perceive themselves, both linguistically and academically. It is important that the school/classroom environment demonstrate a genuine respect and concern for all students, regardless of their racial, cultural, ethnic, or linguistic background. The school environment should support school learning and socialization for all students. Teachers are a critical link in students' successful adjustment to school, to the classroom, and to their new classmates. Teachers must be sensitive to students by providing instruction and a classroom environment that capitalizes on and build upon the students' cultural and linguistic diversity. Educators must place a positive value on students' cultural differences in order to encourage development of self-esteem. Gollnick & Chinn (1994) indicated that educators working with a culturally and linguistically diverse population need to believe and practice the following fundamental beliefs and assumptions:

- There is strength and value in promoting cultural diversity.

- Schools should be models for the expression of human rights and respect for cultural differences.
- Social justice and equality for all people should be of paramount importance in the design and delivery of curricula.
- Attitudes and values necessary for the continuation of a democratic society can be promoted in schools.
- Schooling can provide the knowledge, dispositions, and skills for the redistribution of power and income among cultural groups.
- Educators working with families and communities can create an environment that is supportive of multiculturalism.

Cultural differences in language and learning styles are not deficiencies and can be built upon to facilitate learning. A certain degree of cultural compatibility is needed as teachers and students become increasingly aware of each other's cultural differences. Students should not be condemned for their language or culture, and should be encouraged to build upon those differences whenever possible (Sleeter & Grant, 1994). Educators should facilitate learning rather than making learning difficult for students. Informal conversations with LEP students have led to the identification of a list of suggestions for mainstream teachers to employ in order to facilitate language understanding and learning of content in the classroom. The suggestions for teachers are as follows:

- Major concepts should be written on the chalkboard.
- Concepts should not be erased until all students have copied down the information.
- Writing on the board should be simple and legible.
- Handouts and guide sheets should always be distributed to students to help them follow what is being presented during the lecture and which can be used when studying at home.
- Audiovisual materials such as videos, films, and other aids are recommended to reinforce information visually and aurally from lectures or from reading materials.
- LEP students should be allowed to use tape recorders during lectures.
- Speaking needs to be clear and slow.
- Major assignments should provide written instructions.
- In teaching concepts, it is effective to use several examples to illustrate the main ideas or main concept.
- Concepts need to be explained step-by-step.
- When LEP students ask questions, before responding, questions should be repeated, paraphrasing them.
- Jokes and slang in class should be avoided.

These strategies may seem simple and unnecessary to teachers, however LEP students have identified them as crucial in facilitating understanding and comprehension in the classroom.

Another strategy in organizing a multicultural-sensitive classroom is that of a rich and interesting curriculum. Baruth & Manning (1992) recommend the incorporation of literature from the students' ethnic backgrounds in all subject areas in the classroom. This approach not only helps students to see their own literature reflected in the school curriculum but also helps other students grow in understanding classmates and cultures different from their own. Multicultural literature is essential to all areas of the curriculum because these materials meet the needs of all students and help them grow in understanding of themselves and others. Students identify with the people who created the stories, whether in the past or present. They can discover folktales, myths, and legends that clarify the values and beliefs of people for discovering the great stories which form the foundation of various cultures, students can discover the threads that weave the past with the present, and the themes and values that interconnect the people of all cultures. The following children's books are recommended as incorporating literature from the students' backgrounds:

> *How the Garcia Girls Lost Their Accents* (Alvarez, J., 1981).
> *Women Hollering Creek and other Stories* (Cisneros, S., 1992).
> *I'm Nobody. Who Are You?* (Dickinson, E., 1978).
> *Morning Girl* (Dorris, M., 1992).
> *Like Water for Chocolate* (Esquivel, L., 1992).
> *When I was Puerto Rican* (Santiago, E., 1993).
> *The Woman Who Outshone the Sun* (Zubizarreta, R. & Rohmer, H. & Schecter, D., 1993).

There is also the need to make students aware of the ethnic background of their classmates, so that they begin to realize that the classroom is composed of many cultures and many different language backgrounds. The exercise shown in Figure 3.4 is recommended to familiarize students with other classmates' ethnic backgrounds and feelings. *Getting to Know You* fosters knowledge and understanding among students in the classroom. The exercise shown in Figure 3.5 presents another format of the same theme.

Educators should also make an effort to reach out and involve families as much as possible. Research on parental involvement indicates that the alterable curriculum

Figure 3.4 Getting to know you

Directions: Interview a classmate who came to the United States from another country. Use the following questions as a guide: 1. What is your complete name?.. 2. Where were you born?.. 3. Why did your family come to the United States?................................. 4. What were you first impressions of the United States?............................... 5. What are your hopes and dreams for the future?... Summary: What did you learn about your classmate?....................................

Figure 3.5 Character webs

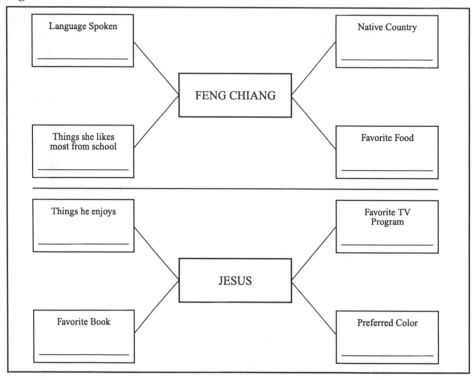

of the home, as well as the teaching home, is twice as predictive of academic learning as is family socioeconomic status (Burke, 1990). Among the benefits of a strong relationship between schools and students' parents are: lowering of barriers to family participation in the schools, increased student attendance, decreased drop-out rate, positive parent–child communication, improvement of student attitudes and behavior, and more parent community support of the school (Carrasquillo & London, 1993). Schools and parents need to understand the necessity of increased participation on their part, so that efforts will be reflected in tangible forms, such as improved attendance at school, and progress in academic performance.

CONCLUSION

The interaction of language and culture is complex, but central to the socialization and academic development of all students. The complex nature of this interaction makes it difficult for students whose first language is not English to master fully the English language for communication and learning purposes. Teaching and interacting with culturally diverse learners requires an awareness of learners' cultural background, knowledge of how culture affects motivation and learning, and the skills necessary to work in close interpersonal situations with students of cultures different from one's own. Being aware that all learners are not Anglo and middle-class represents a significant step toward appropriately providing for the educational needs, knowledge, and skills to work effectively in an American educational system and society. The educator with awareness, but without the necessary knowledge and skills, will be ineffective in providing appropriate and meaningful instructional experiences. At the same time, teachers must enable students to acquire the attitudes, values, and skills, that they will need to participate fully in the dominant American culture.

Educators must reach out to students' families and involve them in the educational process. The families of language minority students are usually not involved in the school, due to educators' perceptions that these parents do not care about their children or would not know how to help them even if contacted. These parents care deeply about their children and would like to help if they are invited, made to feel welcome, and are specifically told what to do to improve their children's educational performance.

CHAPTER 4

Alternatives to Mainstreaming

CHAPTER 4

Alternatives to Mainstreaming

INTRODUCTION

There has been much debate lately in the United States concerning the best way to educate 'limited English proficient' (LEP) students. Much of the debate is centered on which is the best approach to promote cognitive, academic, linguistic, and literacy development of LEP students. There is still a debate as to whether the language of instruction should be English, the child's native language, or both (Ramirez, 1992). Research data suggest bilingual education and English-as-a-second-language as the appropriate instructional approaches for learners for whom English is not their native/primary language. These instructional approaches provide an effective learning environment and instruction, as well as curriculum which addresses second language learners' linguistic, cultural, academic, and cognitive skill development. We recommend that these two instructional approaches receive serious consideration before immersing LEP students in mainstream classrooms. Unfortunately, there is a large group of English language learners who do not receive a specialized language instructional program. These students, whatever their school experience and communicative and academic abilities in their native language may be, are called upon simultaneously to go through the stages of developing interpersonal communication skills, mastering subject area   ntent and skills, and acquiring academic language proficiency for each subject area, all in their second language. These are the students receiving all their instruction in mainstream classrooms.

The content of this chapter is intended for educators of the mainstream classroom to familiarize them with general principles of bilingualism and second language learning and teaching. Understanding bilingualism, successful bilingual educational instructional practices, and second language learning theory and methodology will contribute to help mainstream classroom educators to understand better LEP students' performance and to work with them more successfully.

SECOND LANGUAGE LEARNING

As the school-aged population changes, educators are challenged with instructing more children with limited English skills. Thus, all educators need to know how learners, especially second language learners learn a second language. Average children enter school with a working knowledge of their native language. They have learned to speak and understand this language with little or no formal teaching, and they have learned it at a very early age. Children learn their spoken language by making hypotheses based on the language of other people, especially adults, in their environments. In this process they test a series of language strategies and learn through feedback whether their speech is making sense to the people. Once they go to school they use these same cognitive skills in learning to read and write. It appears that children acquiring a second language follow the same developmental sequence of linguistic patterns as children acquiring a native one, although differences do exist between first language and second language acquisition (Carrasquillo, 1994; Ellis, 1990; Krashen, 1981a; Rivers, 1988).

The acquisition of a second language is an activity undertaken mostly when children, youths, or adults have already nearly or fully acquired the basic structure and vocabulary of their first language. Acquisition of a second language is a gradual process involving the mapping of meaning and use. Children tend to acquire simpler forms first and progress to the more complex grammatical forms, even when they differ in age at the time of second language acquisition. Second language acquisition requires meaning by interaction in which speakers are concerned, not with the form of their utterances, but with the understanding of the messages they are conveying.

Research evidences some differences between first and second language acquisition (Carrasquillo, 1994; Ervin-Tripp, 1974; McLaughlin, 1992; Rivers, 1988). Second language learners are more cognitively developed and have already experienced learning a language, demonstrating a great amount of linguistic knowledge. Second language learners build on the cognitive and linguistic knowledge and proficiency of their native language to learn the second language more effectively.

The following language principles are examples of manifestations of language in the process of development. These language principles have been mentioned in the literature as important variables in the second language acquisition process:

(1) **Language learners go through a silent period before they begin to produce the language orally**. Since children acquire language in meaningful situations, speech emerges in natural stages. Children usually show a 'pre-production period' in which they can begin to comprehend but say very little (Krashen, 1981b; Terrell, 1981). This silent stage helps children to concentrate on the message that is being conveyed to them. In this initial stage, children may concentrate on listening for comprehension, or perhaps in reading comprehension.

(2) **Motivation influences the speed and ease of acquiring a second language.** Positive attitudes toward the target language encourage comprehensible input for language acquisition (Gardner, 1980, 1985; Gardner & Lambert, 1972). It allows the acquirer to be open to input which can be utilized for acquisition.

For example, the desire to be like valued members of the community who speak the second language and the desire to achieve proficiency in the target language for utilitarian or practical reasons are aspects that have been positively related to second-language acquisition.

(3) **Language learning represents a collaborative meaning making process** (Chaudron, 1988; Short, 1991; Stern, 1983; Wells, 1986). Successful second language learners effectively use interpretation, expression, and negotiation of meaning. Language is learned interactively and in context. Listening, reading, speaking, and writing are all active language components, interrelated skills in the process of oral and written communication. Meaning is the key to second language linguistic development, children remember and use the language that is meaningful. Children use language to understand and to communicate meaning. They learn through a creative process of putting together the pieces of the language they know.

(4) **Errors are a natural part of language learning**. Language acquisition is not based on grammatical structures but on meaning. When speakers have something interesting or meaningful to communicate, the listener will make every effort to understand. This very effort will advance the second language acquisition process. Language learners do not have to have a conscious awareness of the 'rules' they do or do not possess. Acquirers may self-correct only on the basis of a 'feel' for grammatically correct forms (Brown, 1991; Carrasquillo, 1994; Krashen, 1981a; Rivers, 1988). With the exception of pronunciation, most second language errors are similar to first language errors. Educators in mainstream classrooms need to expect LEP language errors and need to see them as indicators of progress through stages of language acquisition.

Unlike first language acquisition, learning a second language is often full of difficulties. Beginning learners constantly make errors in producing and comprehending the second language, and initially they have difficulty processing information presented in that language. Even under the best of circumstances, this stage of apparent 'incompetence' can last as long as eight years. Collier's (1987, 1992) findings indicate that it may take from four to seven years for LEP students to reach the national grade level norms of native speakers in language and academic subject areas. Many educators do not realize just how long it takes for students to become proficient enough in English to survive in a classroom where English is the only language of instruction and learning. Educators who are not aware of the length of time it takes LEP students to become proficient in English may have unrealistic expectations and put undue pressure on those students to perform in English. As Hamayan (1990) says: 'This is not only likely to raise the student's anxiety, but it also turns the context from one in which students' achievements are emphasized to one in which students' failures are highlighted' (p.12).

(5) **Language learners' goals and empowerment skills are essential in the process of second language acquisition**. Successful learners share a sense of confidence-building, ego-enhancing, and a quest for competence in some

domain of knowledge or skill (Brown, 1991; Cummins, 1989). Learners need to be empowered to learn language for their own personal reasons of achieving competence and autonomy. Brown (1991) indicates that English language classes and content area classes must provide such empowerment by shifting towards: (a) a focus on process; (b) egalitarian structures; (c) flexible, open-ended curricula; (d) gauging competence and potential; (e) encouraging calculated guessing; and (f) valuing synthesis and intuition.

(6) **Language helps to perpetuate culture and as a tool for that purpose, is vitally connected to a person's cognitive and affective development**. Thus, in helping students to acquire the English language, it is deemed beneficial to validate and preserve the first culture by accepting it and using it in the classroom so that optimal transference can take place (Baruth & Manning, 1992; Carrasquillo & London, 1993; Sleeter & Grant, 1993). All students need to have instructional experiences that include the study of the cultures and the contributions of their own histories, so that LEP students may feel proud of their historical and cultural backgrounds by seeing these aspects reflected in the school's curriculum.

Summary

The second language principles mentioned above help educators to: (a) expect errors and consider them as indicators of learners' language development; (b) provide content and action oriented activities to clarify meanings and functions of the new language; (c) provide opportunities for listening activities and wait for learners to speak when they are ready; (d) plan activities to lessen anxiety among second language learners; (e) introduce language that is meaningful, natural, useful, and relevant to learners; and, (f) recognize the importance of validating first language culture and language skills.

UNDERSTANDING SECOND LANGUAGE PROFICIENCY

LEP students are required to learn subject matter while they are also acquiring English language skills, making it difficult for them to keep up with both academic and cognitive tasks. LEP students may require some time to develop their communicative abilities and basic literacy skills in English before they can start using English as a tool for learning subject matter, or before they can begin transferring what they know from their native language into English. This may result in LEP students being placed in instructional situations that are more complex for them than for students who are already proficient in English (Cummins, 1980, 1994; Tikunoff, 1985). Educators need to understand clearly the process involved in acquiring a second language.

Although language proficiency is a complex phenomenon which is difficult to define due to the various elements involved, it may be described as an indication of learners' current language level (Baker, 1993; Collier, 1987; Ellis, 1990; Chamot & O'Malley, 1986). When we speak of language proficiency in the school context we must distinguish between the level for informal oral and social communication and the need for academic language. In other words, there are two types of language proficiency: the basic interpersonal communication skills and a more abstract cognitive academic language proficiency (Cummins, 1984; Hamayan, 1990; Hamayan & Perlman, 1990). These two concepts were explained in Chapter 2. What emerges is an important distinction between oral proficiency and the academic language proficiency necessary in the content areas of the curriculum, the former being simply the ability to communicate in speech and the latter being the more complex ability to comprehend and produce academic language. Second language communicative competence in social situations does not guarantee success in academic language tasks. Important as the ability to communicate in a social interaction is, it does not provide all the second language proficiency needed for academic success. Oral English language skills alone may be necessary but not sufficient for students to acquire content-area knowledge. Research has also indicated that oral language proficiency measures alone may not be sufficient data for decision-making with regard to the schooling needs of LEP students (Canales, 1990; Chamot & O'Malley, 1986). Educators may need to look at the academic language development of students by assessing it through a comprehensive language and academic assessment battery. Many students in mainstream classrooms may have attained the social skills in English and may, on the surface, appear to be proficient; however, if their proficiency in the more cognitively demanding skills, crucial for their academic success, is inadequate, they are likely to encounter difficulties in content area classes.

The research literature on second language learners emphasizes the need for instruction for limited English proficient students to move beyond effective communication as a primary goal toward a focus on 'academic competence', which implies a stronger focus on literacy development, vocabulary enrichment, critical thinking skills, social skills, and learning strategies (Cummins, 1980; DeGeorge, 1988; Hamayan, 1990; Hamayan & Perlman, 1990; Wells, 1986). Limited English proficient students may require some time to develop their communicative abilities and basic literacy skills in English before they can start using English as a tool for learning subject matter, or before they can begin transferring what they know from their native language to English.

THE ROLE OF THE NATIVE/FIRST LANGUAGE

Second language acquisition is strongly influenced by learners' first language. The native language is a resource second language learners use consciously or subconsciously to help them shift the second language data and the input and to perform as best as they can in the second language. How students use the primary/native language as a resource depends on a series of factors related to the formal and pragmatic features of the first language and the second language and learners' stage of development. Vygotsky (1962) maintained that there are two types of knowledge: spontaneous knowledge which refers to familiar, everyday concepts, and scientific knowledge which encompasses formal, school-learned concepts. Once a number of scientific concepts are mastered, the awareness of learners' development spreads to everyday concepts.

Transferability of skills from one language to another appears to play a critical role in second language acquisition. This is so because there exist a transfer of universal linguistic characteristics and specific knowledge acquired from one language to another (Cummins, 1981; Ramirez, 1992; Vygotsky, 1962). The influence of the first language is likely to be more evident in second language phonology, especially in the accent. This is not to say that it has a negative influence. On the contrary, it helps second language learners by providing a linguistic and cognitive framework, especially at the beginning stage. Researchers also caution against withdrawing home language support too soon and suggest that, although oral communication skills in a second language may be acquired within two or three years, it may take five to seven years to acquire the level of proficiency needed for understanding the language in its academic uses (Collier, 1987, 1992; Cummins, 1981, 1984).

Educators in mainstream classrooms should not discourage the use of the native language at home or in the classroom. On the contrary, its use should be encouraged so that parents and children have the opportunity to communicate using language for effective communication. Giving language minority students support in the home language is beneficial. In the long run, this parent/child, student/peer communication will positively influence the acquisition of the second language. Also, awareness of variables from home life, community life, school life in the native country, and school life in the United States helps educators to create instructional programs to empower English language learners.

INDIVIDUAL DIFFERENCES

Variety in second language acquisition is influenced by individual differences in the way learners learn a second language and the way they use their language knowledge. Learning is affected by many conditions both internal and external to learners. There is in any group a wide range of individual differences in styles, strategies, and pace of learning. These factors influence the rate and success of second language acquisition and have social, cognitive, and affective implications. Social aspects are external to the learner and concern the relationship between learners and native speakers of the second language and also between the learners and other speakers of their own language. Cognitive and affective aspects are internal to learners. Cognitive factors concern the nature of the conceptual strategies used by learners while affective factors concern the emotional responses related to the attempts to learn the second language. Learners are not always conscious of these components, yet their influence or involvement can determine one's success. Aptitude, personality, attitude and motivation, and cognitive/learning style are factors, among others, impacting on a learner's second language acquisition.

Aptitude refers to the special ability involved in language learning. Carroll & Sapor (1959) identified three major components of aptitude: (a) phonetic coding ability (ability to perceive and memorize new sounds), (b) grammatical sensitivity (the individual's ability to demonstrate awareness of the syntactical patterning of sentences of a language), and (c) inductive ability (ability to notice and identify similarities and differences in both grammatical form and meaning). Pinleurs (1966) also has defined language aptitude; his definition includes: (a) verbal intelligence (familiarity with words and ability to reason analytically about verbal materials), (b) motivation to learn the language, and (c) auditory ability. Although the influence of aptitude on second language acquisition cannot be traced accurately, Gardner (1980) indicated that aptitude is a major factor determining the level of success of classroom language learning. Limited English proficient individuals come with different oral bases, different literacy traditions, different writing systems, different concepts of sound–symbol relations, and different modes of normal discourse along with strong patterns, different levels of development in their primary languages. What role does the 'special ability' involved in language learning play? Aptitude may be an important factor in the rate of development, particularly in formal classroom instruction (Ellis, 1990; Gardner, 1980; Krashen, 1981a). Those ESL students with a 'talent' for formal instruction are likely to learn more rapidly.

Personality refers to a number of personal traits in the individual. Although the available research does not show a clearly defined effect of personality on second language learning in general, it has been indicated to play a major role in the acquisition of communicative competence. It has been found that extroverted learners learn to speak the language more rapidly and are more successful than introverted learners because extroverted learners will find it easier to make contact with other speakers of the target language (Ellis, 1990; Krashen, 1981a). Another element mentioned that emphasizes personal dispositions of individuals is social skills involved in second language acquisition. Strong (1983) stated that what contributed to the acquisition of English were those personality traits that controlled the quality of interaction in the second language. One of those factors is the active use of the English second language learners are exposed to. This active use, reflected by traits of talkativeness and responsiveness, might involve not only better concentration but a greater tendency to process what they hear, as well as facility for keeping conversation going.

Attitude has been defined as the set of beliefs that learners hold toward members of the target language group and toward their own culture (Brown, 1991) or as the persistence shown by language learners in striving for a goal. Stern (1983) classified attitudes in three types: (a) attitudes toward the community and people who speak the second language, (b) attitudes toward learning the target language, and (c) attitudes toward languages and language learning in general. Factors that encourage intake and motivational variables have been found to be related to second language acquisition (Krashen, 1981a). These factors encourage learners to communicate with speakers of the second language and obtain the necessary input or intake for language acquisition (orientation of the learner toward the speakers of the target language).

Motivation is one of the more complex issues of second language acquisition. Gardner & Lambert (1972) defined motivation in terms of the second language learners' overall goal or orientation. Research on motivation has focused on Gardner's (1980, 1985) distinction between *integrative* (desire to learn a language stemming from a positive attitude toward a community of its speakers) and *instrumental* (desire to learn a language in order to attain certain career, educational, or financial goals) orientations of second language learners. When the practical value of second language proficiency is high, and frequent use of the language necessary, instrumental motivation is a powerful predictor of second language acquisition. Gardner & Lambert (1972) found that a student's high level of drive to acquire the language of a valued second language community combined with inquisitiveness and interest in the group should underlie the motivation needed to master a second language.

Learning Style refers to an individual's consistent and rather enduring preferences, *vis à vis*, general characteristics of intellectual functioning and personality (Ellis, 1990). Examples of learning styles may include: tolerance of ambiguity; more or less reflective or impulsive; less field dependent/independent; more or less oriented toward imagery; more or less holistic, analytical, or logical. There are a number of hypotheses about the role of each of these terms in second language acquisition. One of the most interesting assumptions is the suggestion that field dependence will prove most facilitative in naturalistic second language acquisition, but that field independence will lead to greater success in classroom learning. Characteristics of 'field dependent individuals', include among others: (a) reliance on external frame of reference in processing information, (b) perception of a field as a whole, (c) self-view derived from others, and (d) greater skill in interpersonal/ social relationships. Field independent individuals are characterized as: (a) reliance on internal frame of reference in processing information, (b) perception of field in terms of its component parts, (c) sensitivity to separate identity, and (d) less skilled in interpersonal/social relationships. The reasoning is that the more social skills learners have, the greater their contact with the target language native speakers, and the more input they receive. On the other hand, in classroom learning, the ability to analyze formal rules is very important. This distinction does not mean that one learning style is better than the other in facilitating second language acquisition. It is assumed that 'field independent learners' will perform some tasks more effectively than 'field dependent learners', and vice versa (Hawkey, 1982).

All of the above factors may have an impact on the ability of students to manipulate one or two languages. If two languages are being used or learned at the same time, learners are usually called 'bilingual'. The next section discusses the bilingualism of language minority students.

THE BILINGUALISM OF LANGUAGE MINORITY STUDENTS

Mainstream classroom educators need to develop awareness of the role of the two languages (L1 and L2) used by LEP students and the instructional strategies that foster the students' bilingualism. The 'bilingualism' of LEP students is related to the different levels of proficiency in the two languages. The speaker's language proficiency in each language is the defining factor in describing LEPs' bilingualism. Although different types of bilingualism are possible, there are two broad types: *balanced bilingual learners* and *dominant bilingual learners*.

> **Balanced Bilinguals**: The term refers to those individuals whose competencies in both languages are well-developed (Baker, 1993; Fishman, 1971) and who have attained an approximately equal level of proficiency in the two languages.

> **Dominant Bilinguals**: The term refers to those individuals who have one dominant language, and show a higher level of proficiency in one language or in some aspects of one language (Fishman, 1971).

Baker (1993) gives a good example of a balanced bilingual: 'A child who can understand the delivery of the curriculum in school in either language, and operate in classroom activity in either language' (p. 8). Unfortunately, most of the students participating in bilingual instruction in the United States are dominant bilinguals, most of them dominant in a language other than English. The literature also mentions the *semilingual learner*, who is an individual who shows deficits or is at an early stage of development in both languages, especially in vocabulary, language usage and functions, and in the processing and using of both languages creatively (Hamayan, 1990). To avoid semiligualism, schools should promote additive bilingualism. The educational program that best promotes additive bilingualism is bilingual education.

As it was mentioned before, most LEP students in the United States are dominant bilinguals. The attainment of proficiency in two languages (bilingualism) may be manifested in two different ways or situations: *additive* and or *subtractive*.

> **Additive Bilingualism**: It is a linguistic instructional context in which learners who have attained the expected level of proficiency in their first language add a second language to their existing repertoire in the first language. The second language and culture are unlikely to replace the first language and culture.

> **Subtractive Bilingualism**: It is a linguistic instructional context in which learners replace the first language and culture with a second language and culture. In most instances the development of proficiency in the second language has inhibiting and sometimes detrimental effects on the first language. It may even result in skills that are below expected levels of proficiency in both languages especially in academic areas.

Goals toward bilingualism in individuals, as well as in community groups, differ depending on the amount of proficiency desired in the two languages by the society in which the use of the two languages takes place. Thus, the language teaching approach chosen by the school usually reflects those long terms goals previously identified by the society. In the United States, as well as in other societies, bilingual education is perceived as an instructional program which fosters bilingualism.

FOSTERING BILINGUALISM THROUGH BILINGUAL EDUCATION

The value that is placed on being bilingual and having access to two languages helps set the tone for promoting achievement of all students in the entire school. Bilingual education refers to instructional programs in which students are able to study subject matter in their first language (L1) while their weaker language (L2) skills are developed. There is a belief sustained by a body of research (Cummins, 1981, 1984, 1994; Garcia, 1993; McLaughlin, 1992; Wong-Fillmore, 1991a) that cognitive development is facilitated by instruction in the students' first language, that students develop more positive attitudes toward school as the result of the use of the native language, and that instruction in the native language actually increases acquisition in the second language. Instruction through the second language cognitive areas begins when students can function in that language and experience no academic handicap due to insufficient knowledge of the language. Although there is variety in terms of the structure and organization of the instructional programs in school, all bilingual programs include the teaching of school subjects in two languages: the students' native language and culture, and the second language and culture.

In the United States, bilingual education is an instructional tool to help students whose first language is not English to overcome their linguistic and academic difficulties and, it is hoped, to perform as well as their English speaking peers in school. Most bilingual education programs are for LEP learners, and it is intended to permit students to develop enough proficiency in English to be able to learn through English. A broad goal of bilingual education is to facilitate the education of students and youth by fostering a positive self-concept facilitating students' cognitive, academic, and language expression. A major aspect of it is the inclusion in the curriculum of the students' historical, literacy, and cultural traditions for purposes of strengthening identity and sense of belonging and for making the instructional program easier to grasp (Baker, 1993; Ovando & Collier, 1989; Ramirez, 1992).

The following elements have been mentioned in the literature (Baker, 1993; Cummins, 1989, 1994; Ovando & Collier, 1989; Ramirez, 1992) as essential for effective bilingual instruction.

- Emphasis on the development of *native language skills*.
- Emphasis on the development of the *second language* including reading and writing development.
- *High standards* for students' achievement.

- Active *teaching involvement* (involving students, high expectations for students, and monitoring students progress).
- *Fluency of teachers* in the language used for instruction.
- *Integration of program* into basic structures of the school curriculum (such as curriculum, administration, supportive environment).
- *Quality of materials* used for instruction (comparable to those used in English).
- *Support* from the community and parents.

The duration of bilingual instruction will vary among different communities depending on the number of years LEP students need to develop proficiency in English and be able to learn through English, along with the community's desire to continue the program so that students will maintain skills in the native language. Also, there are varieties of bilingual education programs. The following four elements have been listed in the literature as key factors in the variation of bilingual programs in the United States.

Manner in which the Students' Native/Primary Language is Used

All bilingual programs use the primary language for instructional purposes. However, there is variety in which subjects are taught in the primary language and which subjects are taught in the second language. In most transitional bilingual programs examined, reading and language arts were initially taught in the native language with the assumption that native language arts and reading skills are later transferred into the second language. These programs were not unified in terms of which language (L1 or L2) to use to teach content areas such as mathematics, science or social studies. Programs examined showed a variety in the type of language emphasis initially as well as the time spent in teaching these subjects. Romero (1991) addressed this issue by stating:

> 'Beyond the amount of time spent in each language across the grades, a critical question in program planning is what the languages are used for, i.e., their assigned functions within the curriculum. More specifically, what is L1 used for at the beginning and end of programs and why? What is L2 used for and why? The broader question is what functions should each language serve as students move from one year to another so that they are adequately prepared for delivery of content exclusively in their second language' (p. 55).

Amount of Time Devoted to Each of the Languages

Classroom-based research in the area of second language acquisition and academic development explores the conditions under which language acquisition and literacy can take place within classrooms (Chaudron, 1988; Clark & Peterson, 1986). One key lesson derived from many of these studies is the critical importance of creating classroom structures within which negotiation of meaning in a weaker language can take place. The amount of time devoted to each language is a primary factor in creating a successful classroom structure.

Not all programs provide exactly the same amount of exposure in each of the languages used for instruction. The proportion of instructional time spent in each language may vary from program to program. Some programs begin with a 90/10 ratio where English is used for about 10% of instruction, but other programs may begin with 75/25, while others begin with instruction equally divided between English and the native language.

Type of ESL Program

Comprehensive English development is provided through both English as a second language classes and the use of English instruction in academic content areas. There are several types of English as a second language programs (holistic, pull-out, intensive). Programs' differences are related to approaches used and skills to be emphasized. Although bilingual education programs are moving toward a holistic language approach of language teaching, there are still several programs in which the specialized ESL teacher emphasizes oral and speaking skills.

Linguistic Goals of the Bilingual Program

Bilingual programs vary with respect as to whether they are intended to maintain the students' native language indefinitely (maintenance/developmental bilingual) or are only to help them ultimately adjust to an all-English program (transitional). Both transitional and maintenance programs always include acquisition of the second language and subject matter instruction in the native language. Differences in goals of bilingual education programs have brought different types of bilingual programs. For example, programs that intend to maintain the primary language and culture (additive) of the non-English speakers are called *maintenance* or *developmental* while those programs that are geared to mainstream students to an only-English classroom (subtractive) are the *transitional* bilingual programs. Thus, bilingual education covers a wide range of types of programs which may vary from school to school and from school district to school district. The most popular bilingual programs in the United States are: *transitional, maintenance/developmental* and *two-way/dual language*. Figure 4.1 presents the most salient features of these three programs.

All bilingual program models use the students' home language in addition to English instruction. The programs are most easily implemented in districts with a large number of students from the same language background. The choice of transitional bilingual over developmental or two-way programs may reflect community, parental, but most importantly, school district preference, or it may be the only bilingual program option in districts with a limited number of bilingual teachers. Most programs in the United States are transitional since the federal government through the Bilingual Education Act (Title VII) favors transitional bilingual programs. Transitional bilingual programs receive most of the federal funding allocations, and few school districts are able or willing to promote additive bilingual education through developmental or enrichment programs.

Figure 4.1 Types of bilingual education programs

Type	Characteristics
Transitional (Early-exit)	• Bilingual education is of transitional nature; it involves homogeneous native language classes in which LEP students begin their studies in their native language until they have learned enough English to be transferred to a mainstream classroom. • Social and cultural assimilation into the dominant culture. • Emphasis on the development of English language skills in order to shift learners to an all-English program of instruction. • Students who demonstrate a certain level of proficiency in English are moved into mainstream classes.
Maintenance/ Developmental (Late-exit)	• Instruction is designed to provide improved language skills in English as well as in the students' native and second language. • Goal of proficiency and literacy in the native and second languages. • Development of students' native language to full proficiency. • Leads to cultural pluralism.
Two-Way/ Dual	• Classes include native English-speaking students as well as native speakers of another language. • The English speakers learn a second language at the same time that the non-English speakers are learning English. • Both groups of students act as linguistic models for each one. • Emphasis on mastery of the regular school curriculum.

RECOMMENDED ENGLISH AS A SECOND LANGUAGE METHODOLOGY

English as a second language (ESL), also referred to as English for speakers of other languages, is the combination of instructional approaches to language instruction designed for those who have a primary language other than English and who are limited in English proficiency. The major objective of ESL programs is to prepare students to function successfully in classrooms where English is the medium of instruction for all subject areas. ESL instruction provides opportunities for students to learn English systematically and cumulatively moving from concrete to abstract levels of language. English as a second language includes instruction in all English communication skills, emphasizing the four basic aspects of the English language in order to communicate in an English environment. English as a second language students need to develop the ability to understand native speakers of English in any situation as well as the ability to read and write materials in English with comprehension and enjoyment.

The term 'specialized' connotes the use of several distinct and varying methods and strategies based on a wide range of innovative learning theories that have been developed over several decades, and which deal specifically with learning and teaching strategies of English to non-native or limited English speakers. The ESL program needs to be sensitive to second language learners' needs, experiences, native languages, and cultural backgrounds. Appropriate second language instruction: (a) emphasizes communication and meaning; (b) integrates the four areas for functional contexts of learning and communication development: understanding, speaking, reading and writing; (c) recognizes students' prior linguistic, conceptual, and cultural experiences to build proficiency in English; (d) respects the values and traditions of students' cultural heritage, and (e) provides for continuation of conceptual development for functional contexts of learning and communication. The program provides adequate opportunity for the child to make adjustments to a new linguistic environment. It allows ESL learners to maintain self-esteem, while continuing to develop academic areas. Before entering the mainstream curriculum, limited English proficient (LEP) students need to use English as a tool for learning subject matter. The general objective of an ESL program is the systematic development of the following areas:

- A *vocabulary* for expressing oneself in different social and academic environments.
- *Automatic control and fluency* in the use of natural and accurate English language, linguistic, and grammatical patterns.
- *Natural communication situations* for meaningful interaction.
- *Creative grammatical and syntactical construction* abilities.
- *Development of strategies* to confront the *process* and varied skills of *reading*.
- Development of *conceptual, grammatical*, and *syntactical* forms of writing.

(Carrasquillo, 1994)

ESL is not a remedial program but a program designed to enhance and develop individuals' linguistic skills, cognitive skills, and content area knowledge. The stigma of seeing ESL as remedial may have been caused by ESL 'pull out' programs in which students receive from one hour to a half hour of instruction in segregated ESL centers or classes. An effective alternative is the 'integrated approach', which relates language learning to content areas and directly provides comprehensible input to the LEP student and can bridge the gap that otherwise can divide language and the content classroom. An integrated approach helps to assure that LEP students use English as a tool for learning subject matter and helps them to progress to full academic proficiency (Short, 1991).

The literature on ESL programs is confusing when it comes to naming and defining the variations in ESL program designs which have been implemented. Although the main objective of an ESL program is the teaching and learning of English, there are different types of ESL programs. Differences in programs depend on the educational goals of the school and the community, availability of ESL personnel, and the number of non-English speakers or limited English proficient students in a given school or grade, as well as the perception of school instructional leaders of the organization, scope, and sequence needed to learn English. This last aspect has not been quite understood by school personnel in charge of providing students with a complete ESL program, who many times have opted for providing LEP students with minimum ESL instructional services. Figures 4.2–4.5 describe key elements of various ESL programs.

Figure 4.2 Free standing ESL program

> - Recommended program when there are many languages or ethnic groups represented in the school and not too many students from one particular language.
> - An ESL program that stands in itself to meet the immediate communication and academic needs of learners whose proficiency in English is limited or non-existent.
> - Instruction is based on a special curriculum that typically involves very little or no use of the native language and is usually taught throughout the day.
> - Provides ESL students with intensive instruction in an ESL format by providing students with the language skills they need to communicate with teachers and peers.
> - Subject areas such as science, mathematics, and social studies are taught in English using an ESL approach.

The free standing ESL program approach may be chosen by the school district when there are a significant number of LEP students in the district and the school staff and parents may want to provide these students with a curriculum specially tailored to their linguistic limitations and cognitive strengths.

Figure 4.3 Intensive ESL program

> - It is mostly used for high school students or adults who arrive in the United States, helping them initially to become familiar with the English language and the school environment.
> - It provides students with a short and intensive English program including survival skills in the four areas of listening, speaking, reading, and writing.
> - Development of English language skills is usually reinforced through vocabulary emphasis, idiomatic expressions, reading comprehension skills, and basic writing skills.

The intensive ESL program is seen as a remedial/compensatory program to be provided on an emergency basis to students who enrolled in the school with no English basic skills.

Figure 4.4 Pull-out ESL program

- English is taught from a second language point of view in language arts classes provided at the students' level of English proficiency.
- Students usually receive forty-five minutes to one hour of instruction in segregated ESL classes.
- The teacher usually goes from classroom to classroom to get the ESL students from different grade levels and programs.
- Content area instruction, if any, takes a broader perspective due to the heterogeneous composition of students in terms of grades and programs.

In the pull-out ESL program, students spend part of the school day in a mainstream classroom, but are pulled-out for a portion of each day to receive English as a second language. Although schools with a large number of ESL students may have a full-time ESL teacher, some school districts employ an ESL teacher who travels to several schools to work with small groups of students scattered throughout the district. This is the least recommended ESL program. However, it is the most popular in the United States, perhaps because it is financially the least costly.

Figure 4.5 ESL in bilingual education

- An essential and integral part of bilingual education instruction.
- Emphasis is on English taught from a second language point of view in language arts and content area instruction.
- As LEP students increase their mastery of English, they are gradually taught content areas in English.
- ESL classes include content of L1 and L2 cultures.
- The ESL instruction may be taught by a certified bilingual or ESL teacher.

In the case of the ESL program, again the focus may vary from district to district depending on school and community goals for LEP students.

As indicated before, the type of instructional program depends on community school goals and preferences. But in all of these programs there is a genuine interest in providing LEP students with appropriate instructional strategies to learn content subject matter through the second language. Sheltered subject matter teaching is one of these strategies. This strategy is discussed in the next section.

SHELTERED SUBJECT MATTER TEACHING

The literature on second language instructional methodologies is abundant. There are several instructional approaches that have been found to be effective for second language learners. These approaches are fully described throughout this book, especially in those chapters addressing appropriate teaching of language and content. The approach to be described in this section is the one that addresses general issues related to the integration of language and content: sheltered subject matter instruction.

One of the difficulties that LEP students encounter in all English classrooms is the simultaneous processing of a new language, especially its vocabulary, and the quantity and variety of cognitively demanding concepts from the different content areas. Mainstream classroom language demands need to be taught specifically and practiced in the context of subject matter learning. Sheltering instruction in the content areas has been recommended as an instructional strategy that attends to meaning and process by examining the curriculum and instructional objectives of the mainstream situation or grade level into which students will be placed. Sheltered subject matter refers to an adaptive teaching strategy to present content area material through a variety of recommended second language strategies to make the material meaningful and interesting to students. Chamot & O'Malley (1986) call it a 'bridge' curriculum which combines the development of English language skills with a focus on the content areas. They also recommend providing training in the use of learning strategies as aids to comprehension. The bridge curriculum requires an analysis of the kinds of language used in the classroom and the uses to which that language will be put. Research has confirmed that students in sheltered subject matter classes acquire an impressive amount of the second language and learn subject matter as well. The technique of presentation, not the content, differs from that of regular instruction. The language used by teachers is characterized by linguistic modifications, such as simplified syntactical and grammatical structures, controlled vocabulary and short sentences. Recommended instructional strategies (Chamot & O'Malley, 1994; Enright & McCloskey, 1988; Hamayan, 1990) include: (a) using illustrations and manipulatives, (b) drawing students' attention to key words in the text, (c) relating new materials to students' experiences, (d) incorporating hands-on experiences in activities that are relevant to the students, (e) employing cooperative learning techniques, (f) teaching core vocabulary in advance, (g) contextualizing a lesson (for example, by adding an introduction to a lesson), and (h) using effective teacher talk.

For language minority students in mainstream classrooms teachers can provide a sheltered approach by:

- Working with students on developing concepts of the content areas by providing concepts from concrete to abstract, avoiding memorization of facts and dates.
- Expanding concepts through reading and writing through collaborative learning techniques.
- Developing students ability to read texts in the content areas using specific strategies such as summarizing, categorizing, identifying main facts, making inferences and comparing and contrasting.
- Providing opportunities to solve problems in the content areas by using thematic units.

- Providing an environment that promotes self-concept and self-confidence in the students as the result of competence in the content areas.

In addition, teachers help students to learn how to learn by finding various ways to organize their reading, to locate main ideas and key concepts, and to predict and integrate as they read. The teacher models the role of the student and goes through a number of activities to develop skills in learning how to study, how to get main ideas, and so on. Students' involvement in cooperative activities are recommended throughout the teaching–learning process. It is also recommended that lessons end with a 'review' activity designed to integrate the concepts presented during the lesson.

CONCLUSION

The research on effective instructional practices for second language learners draws on a rich tradition of educational research in teaching and learning. Particularly relevant to second language learners' academic and linguistic performance is the documentation of the significant role played by two languages (English and the home language) in mediating learning. The best program organization is one that is tailored to meet the linguistic, academic, and affective needs of students because it provides language minority students with the instruction necessary to allow them to progress through school at a rate commensurate with their English-speaking peers.

This chapter reviewed relevant second language/bilingual instruction and teaching techniques that may be most effective to contribute to the development of the target language as well as of knowledge and skills in the content areas. In order to allow LEP students to overcome the barrier of English language limitations, educators need to use an interactive /experiential instructional model that includes guidance and facilitation rather than total control of students' learning, and encouragement of students' interaction through a collaborative learning context in one, but preferably in the two languages.

CHAPTER 5

The Integrated Development of Oral and Written Language

CHAPTER 5

The Integrated Development of Oral and Written Language

INTRODUCTION

Students with a fairly good understanding of language come to school in order to learn what they need to function in the world surrounding them. However, what they may need to learn might not mesh with what the schools think they should learn, because they may not have the language proficiency of the school language. The relationship between school language and students' language is an important one. Knowledge of the English language will help students to pass messages back and forth between learners and teachers, between students and society, between students and the school, between students and friends, and between parents and children, and students cannot learn if they have not mastered the school language. Schools could not function without language. To succeed in the mainstream classroom, students need to be fluent speakers of the language. So, imagine what limited English proficient students face everyday when they come to schools and have a difficult time understanding, producing, reading, and writing in the English language. What can mainstream classroom teachers do to help? This will be the focus of this chapter.

This chapter presents an overview of the four processes of language: listening, speaking, reading, and writing. Theories, principles, and guidelines concerning each of the language processes are reviewed as they pertain to second language learners in the mainstream classroom. In addition, the theoretical background included in this chapter provides the foundation to describe, in Chapter 6, instructional practices integrating the four language areas of listening, speaking, reading, and writing for second language learners in the mainstream classroom.

The authors want the readers to understand that although the focus of this chapter is on literacy development in English, such development in English does not prelude the literacy development in the students' first language in the mainstream classroom. Developing proficiency in the second language does not necessarily mean replacing the first language. The use of the first language in the mainstream classroom provides a linguistic and cognitive framework for students' understanding, especially at the beginning stage. Programs that enable students to acquire initial literacy in their primary language or to expand on literacy development already begun in the home are often most effective. Also, when programs incorporate students' primary language, parents can assume a greater role in their children's education (Schifini, 1994).

THE ORAL LANGUAGE, READING AND WRITING CONNECTION

Language is a complex human mental and physical process, and yet most individuals use it without any awareness of the myriad of processes that take place in producing and interpreting language. As DeMott (1985) indicates, human beings write and read for the purpose of knowing other's responses, and to connect themselves more fully with the human world. As children and adults speak, they focus on accomplishing things with language. Children, as well as adults, are concerned about the success of their attempts at conveying their message to an identified audience. Individuals who have active lives have more to talk about than other individuals who may not have had rich experiences and meaningful contexts. Children learn from their experiences when they explain those experiences to someone who was not present, and who is an interested person who asks questions related to the past experience and thereby aids children in the process of learning from those past experiences. Usually, successful language learners come to school with a broad repertoire of language skills. When children enter school, they have a grasp of the following language concepts: (a) the grammatical structures of language, (b) the various functions of language, (c) the meaning of what language is, and (d) the reason that language is used. This language preparation provides the foundation for successful school language experiences, especially in written language.

Language is an integration of the four processes of listening, speaking, reading, and writing, which are inseparable (Dunkel, 1993; Cecil & Lauritzen, 1994). As Figure 5.1 indicates, the four linguistic processes although independent, are interrelated and work in conjunction with the cognitive process of learning. The language

Figure 5.1 Relationship of language modes

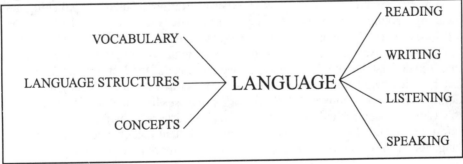

processes share a variety of characteristics, making them interdependent with each other. For example, the abilities used for oral language are the same ones necessary for developing writing abilities. Dickinson (1987) has identified four types of relationships between oral language, reading and writing. These are:

- **A dependence upon language-processing capabilities**. The same abilities that are necessary for acquiring oral language are necessary for literacy development.
- **Interdependence of knowledge structures**. Oral language is interdependent with the control of knowledge structures necessary for reading and writing.
- **Support of acquisition of literacy with speech**. There is a strong relationship between reading and writing development and the ways individuals project themselves orally. Small group work and conversation provide excellent areas for expanding the language/literacy relationship.
- **Interdependence of different modalities**. With proper experiences, students will be able to develop their own spelling and punctuation systems once they have learned some modality-specific information, such as letters of the alphabet.

The connectedness and similarities of these characteristics are evidenced in the struggles and successes of learners in their attempt to embrace a new language and a new culture. Since there is a strong connection between oral language development, reading and writing, teachers develop lessons, activities, and environments that encourage children to increase their vocabularies, extend their manipulation of language structures, and develop new concepts. They make these opportunities meaningful by linking them to the children's past experiences, verbally modeling, labeling the processes and concepts being addressed, and making it necessary for children to create or apply the oral language to the written language. Children learn new words and new concepts through guided experiences that teachers demonstrate and describe. Teachers use new vocabulary words as labels, in context, as they relate the progression of the activity. The children, as part of their experiences, are expected to interact with the teacher, the materials, and their peers in an effort to explore, clarify, practice, extend, and apply new variations of language in familiar or related contexts.

Oral and written language depend and support each other. Whether at school or at home, children need many opportunities to explore language. In other words, language development is a process of experimentation, adaptation, polishing, and meaning-making within the context of the user's life (Flood & Lapp, 1987; Lieven, 1984; Myers, 1987). Language learners begin with the help of others usually through oral language exchanges. Learners' partners structure the exchange in such a way that it is understandable, but slightly above the level of the learner's development. Later, as learners begin to write, they begin to 'converse alone as they have been doing with others' (Dunkel, 1993). The oral processes have laid the foundations for the written processes, and then support what the learners do by feeding knowledge, information, and skills. As learners become proficient readers and writers, written language becomes a tool for making oral language more precise and organized.

Since the four language processes have an inseparable relationship, the teaching of language should be approached from an integrated point of view. Listening, speaking (oral development), reading, and writing in the language classroom should be taught and used together, each fostering and supporting the other. The better students start using language, the more successful they will be at reading and writing the language. In the same manner, ability to read facilitates learning in all content areas. It also contributes to the development of writing proficiency. Research in the areas of language learning have proven that language skills are strengthened as students are encouraged to respond to literature both orally and in writing. School language encompasses the following abilities illustrated in Figure 5.2.

Figure 5.2 School language abilities

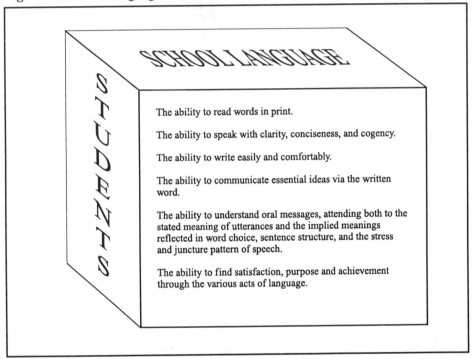

For students who enter school speaking languages other than English, English language acquisition must occur in parallel with efforts in learning to read and write the language. Naturally, this is a challenging task, but needs to be taken seriously by mainstream educators. The development of reading, with its thrust towards understanding and evaluating previously unknown thought, affects the ability to communicate in oral and written forms. Students' English language proficiency needs to be evaluated in the four processes of the language. Language minority students who appear to be proficient in English may only have conversational proficiency rather than the cognitive/academic proficiency required for successful school work (Cummins, 1980). Students with a conversational proficiency may use

English in situations on the playground and in the classroom where there are situational clues (context-embedded) that they may rely on to provide meaning to the situation. However, in situations, whether they be textbook work, teacher lectures, or other classroom activities, requiring high order language skills (context-reduced), the conversationally-only proficient student is at a disadvantage. Cummins (1984) indicates that students may experience difficulties in confronting school activities that require knowledge of academic English language because they may not have experienced the sufficient time required to achieve age-appropriate levels of context-embedded and context-reduced communicative proficiency in English. As it was pointed out in previous chapters in this book, Cummins (1984, 1994) and Collier (1987, 1992) suggest that it takes five to seven years for language minority students to achieve the necessary English language proficiency to function adequately in all-English schools. Cummins summarizes this information in hypothetical curves (see Figure 5.3) which offer a visual explanation of the importance of: (a) providing sufficient time for LEP students for the mastery of the English language, (b) properly emphasizing both less and more cognitively-demanding instructional tasks, and (c) providing a proper context for the integration of the four areas of academic language.

Figure 5.3 Length of time required to achieve age-appropriate levels of context-embedded and context-reduced communicative proficiency (taken from Cummins, 1981: 16)

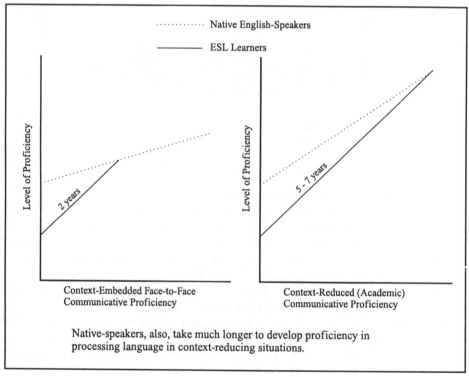

Because the language modes are so inextricably bound up with one another, it is almost impossible to teach one in isolation from the others. Oral and written language develop simultaneously, each facilitating and supporting learners' understanding of the other. Students learn written language by interacting with other learners and users in reading and writing situations, and by exploring print on their communicative processes.

LISTENING COMPREHENSION

Listening is the central process in daily language use. According to (Rubin, 1994), on the average, time spent in communicating school activities divides into approximately 50% listening, 25% speaking, 15% reading, and 10% writing. However, educators often neglect teaching listening skills to students. One reason is that, after all, listening is neither as dramatic nor as noisy as talking. Talking is the center of attention, having speakers' behaviors that are overt and vocal, while listening is often seen as merely being present and not doing any mental activity.

Much of the emphasis of second language instruction has been on oral production, the primary focus on teaching language learners to speak the second language. Most of the time spent in the classroom is on producing the English language instead of comprehending it.

Educators truly believe that, if LEP students learn to speak the English language, listening comprehension will occur simultaneously. However, research on the relationship between listening and speaking tends to suggest that, only if language learners comprehend what they listen to, will speaking develop as a natural process (Krashen, 1981b; Spangenberg-Urbschat & Pritchard, 1994). This notion of listening assumes LEP students to be articulate. Dunkel (1993) indicates that, when students hear, they go through several mental steps and specific cognitive strategies to discover intended mea 'ng. Good listeners, whether native or non-native speakers, use four basic steps plus an array of cognitive strategies to obtain meaning from what they hear. These mental steps are not always carried out in order; listeners may carry them out at the same time, or jump forwards and backwards as they see fit. Dunkel (1986, 1993) identifies these mental steps. They are:

(1) Listeners sort out why they are listening to, and what they want or need to know. Language is to be understood in the same way on similar occasions because listeners or readers must have a pretty good idea about the meaning that was intended in the first place. There must be a reason for listening. (Often in the language classroom, the reason for listening is to pass a quiz on information heard.)

(2) Listeners predict some of the information expected to be included in the utterance and assess how much of the incoming information will be new and how much will be familiar. Good listeners connect experiences and information to the language-related situation. Meaning is brought to language through

prediction, which when said in words is the prior elimination of unlikely alternatives.

(3) Referring back to the initial reason for listening, listeners decide how much of the message is going to be relevant to the purpose of the task, or the initial reason for first listening. This check tells listeners what information in the conversation to ignore and what to select because the first interpretation that comes to listeners is the one that makes the most sense at that particular time.

(4) Listeners then check understanding of the message in a variety of ways. Some examples are: by asking or answering questions, by making appropriate non-verbal gestures, and by acting accordingly. Listeners often receive feedback from the speaker in a real communication situation, or from a teacher in a classroom situation.

Teachers should provide second language learners with listening experiences which include each of these four areas. In addition, teachers should guide listeners through each experience, assisting them to proceed through the four steps and to apply cognitive strategies aimed at uncovering the speaker's message (Dunkel, 1993; Weaver, 1988).

Second-language learners are able to understand more than they can produce, although they may not always show comprehension ahead of production (Clark & Hetch, 1983). Logically, one expects that comprehension will precede production, because when individuals produce an utterance they must make choices among linguistic elements, and to make choices, individuals must understand them. Children understand elements of a construction before they start to produce it appropriately. When successful language learners fail to understand, they devise strategies to get by. When they lack understanding, they demonstrate that the message, information or intention of the speaker is not understood. Thus, we can say that LEP students know and understand more than they actually say or do. Clark & Hetch (1983) and Clark & Barron (1988) suggest that the coordination of production with comprehension is a lengthy process, demanding that language learners match the memory representation they have set up for production with what they already represented for comprehension (Kess, 1992). However, individual LEP students vary very much in the amount of listening they do. For example, they may agree with the quality and manifestation of the speaker through gestures, by painting, and by demonstrating.

THE ORAL PRODUCTION OF SECOND LANGUAGE LEARNERS

The main aspect of speaking is communication. The development of oral language is the foundation for students' literacy development (Goldenberg, 1990). Speaking allows individuals to express themselves concisely, coherently, and in a manner that suits all audiences and occasions. One of the most important observations about language acquisition is that children are not taught how to talk. Children learn to talk by transacting with adults in a language-rich environment. Adults model language for children by speaking to them in natural kinds of language patterns.

Language is used in naturalistic, real-life contexts in which language has a series of functions and purposes. Halliday (1977) suggests that communication takes place when there is sharing of experience, expression of social solidarity, decision making, and planning. This principle is the same for the development of the English language in LEP students, especially oral language in the classroom setting. Spoken language is an important part of the identities of all participants, and second language learners play an active role in speaking the target language to communicate. Thus, context and opportunity play a critical role in how much and how often LEP students use the English language.

The role of oral language development becomes especially critical when students' native languages differ from that of the school language (Carrasquillo, 1994; Goldenberg, 1990). Thus, acquisition of English language skills must be provided in contexts in which students understand what is being said. Students, who have many and varied opportunities to talk about what they have read or written, are better capable of expressing their high-level thinking about texts or any other related cognitive tasks. Talking about what students read and write allows them to interpret the printed word, making their academic and personal world more relevant. Meaningful communication is important and necessary for LEP students' mastery of English, and they need effective language use to help them, not just to survive, but to succeed in an English environment. The elements of meaningful communication are illustrated in Figure 5.4.

Figure 5.4 Prerequisites for LEP students' oral development

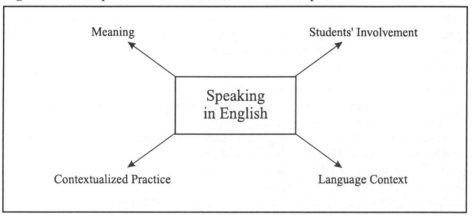

Mainstream classrooms need to provide an environment which emphasizes communication and oral comprehensibility, making it of critical importance to provide instruction that enables students to become communicative and confident users of spoken English for whatever purposes they need. Limited English proficient students' oral language development needs instructional contexts that emphasize the following aspects:

- Content is based on students' communicative needs.

- Instruction makes use of extensive contextual clues.
- Teachers modify their English speech to students' level and confirm students' comprehension.
- The focus is on language functions or content rather than grammatical form.
- Grammatical accuracy is promoted not by correcting errors overtly, but by providing more comprehensible instruction.
- Students are encouraged to respond spontaneously and creatively.

When students are allowed to discuss with others in class what they interpret from readings or their own writing and when they listen to others' interpretations of the same story or piece they evolve in their thinking and are able to structure and restructure their knowledge. Teachers must identify the kinds of situations which require effective communication and the kinds of speaking skills required by those situations.

READING IN A SECOND LANGUAGE

Reading is one of the most important content areas for LEP students to conquer because reading is the window to the knowledge presented in school. Reading is a process of constructing meaning, and the sooner LEP students can read in English, the wider will be their window to their world. Weaver (1988) defines reading as the process of constructing meaning through the dynamic interaction (transaction) among the reader's existing knowledge, the information suggested by the written language, and the context of the reading situation. Constructing meaning includes understanding the information in the text and incorporating the knowledge used to understand the text in the first place. Readers need to be actively involved in the act of reading and interested in the content being read. Whether it is presented through experience charts, basal readers, literature, or trade books, the printed word surrounds every classroom.

Students develop reading comprehension of printed language by having experiences that interpret the print, just as oral experience helps students to interpret spoken language. As students begin to read the print themselves, they use additional systems to assist their efforts in knowing which letter patterns or relationships represent which spoken words. This system of relating sounds to printed symbols in making units of meaning is called *decoding*. As readers look at the words in a text, they engage in an intentional activity; they have a reason for reading. Their purpose for reading will significantly influence the strategies they use and how much they will remember of what they read. Kuccer (1987) has identified four universals which appear to undergird the processes of reading and writing.

> **Universal 1**: Readers and writers construct text-world meanings through utilizing the prior knowledge which they bring to the literacy event.
> **Universal 2**: The written language system operates by feeding into a common data pool from which the language user draws when constructing the text world.

Universal 3: Readers and writers utilize common procedures for transforming prior knowledge into a text world.
Universal 4: Readers and writers display common processing patterns or abilities when constructing text worlds.

These four universal characteristics of learners of reading can be applied to second-language learners. While the process of teaching reading in English to LEP students is, in many ways, similar to teaching reading in the native language, educators need to be aware of students' linguistic knowledge, home and community language, as well as cultural background to provide content that is relevant and interesting. When students with limited English proficiency are mixed with English proficient students, many decisions need to be made about daily classroom practices. But how can mainstream classroom teachers help second-language students learn to read in English? How can all the sounds and meanings of English be presented to LEP students in the mainstream classroom without isolating these students from their classmates and without making these students feel inferior? The following paragraphs give general answers to these questions.

Teachers need to recognize that second-language students begin the process of reading and writing in the second language with very different knowledge from first language students. Although first language learners have already learned somewhere from the order of 5,000 to 7,000 words before they formally begin instruction in schools (Singer, 1981), and have a good intuitive sense of the grammar of the language, second-language learners typically have not already learned a large store of English oral language vocabulary, nor do they have a fairly complete sense of the grammar of the language. Initially, LEP students may need guidance in getting meaning from the printed page. Since comprehension is the purpose of learning to read, language minority students must start with material that has meaning for them.

Differences in reading abilities of ESL students may also be attributed to the social contexts of literacy use in the students' first language. The social context of students' uses of reading in their first language and their access to texts may have a profound effect on their abilities to develop academic reading skills in English. A first issue would be to understand the extent of literacy skills students have in their first language. If students have proficiency in reading in their first language, they do not need to be taught to read again. What they need is the development of the English language foundation to be able to transfer their reading processing strategies to the English reading experience.

Teachers often underestimate the importance that culture plays in reading comprehension. Students must have knowledge and understanding of the world around them as they interact with a text or attempt to write about the topic. Comprehension will take place only when the information in the text triggers a response from readers or writers whose background knowledge has been activated (Carrell, 1989). The classroom teacher must actively deal with the cultural components of a text when teaching reading to LEP students. The student needs to understand the basic assumptions about the world in order to interpret the new information correctly. Students who lack cultural knowledge about the content presented will only be able to make superficial predictions or inferences about what they learn. Teachers should learn as much as they can about the particular community in which they teach. Taking an interest in their students' lives in itself can make a difference in students' academic performance.

Reading in the second language must take LEP students from the isolated view of reading as a decoding process into reading as a holistic act. Reading instruction for LEP students should include the following functions, as indicated by Carrasquillo (1994).

- **Readers must construct purposes for reading**. Why are ESL readers reading a given selection? Only by developing purposes will readers be able to gain the appropriate kind of information and enjoyment from reading.
- **Readers must activate relevant background/prior knowledge**. The knowledge a reader brings to the printed page effects the comprehension of the text.
- **Readers must allocate attention in order to focus on major content and not on less important content**. Given our purposes for reading, some information will be important, and other information will not be important, depending on the purpose of the reader.
- **Readers must critically evaluate the content of the text**. They must determine if the information presented is internally consistent. They must also check to see if the text information is consistent with their own prior knowledge and with general knowledge.
- **Readers must monitor ongoing activities to see if they are actually comprehending the text**. Students' own evaluation of their reading progress and understanding have a tremendous influence in the way they change their learning strategies to become more productive learners.
- **Readers must make and test inferences of many kinds**. Readers are constantly filling in gaps and making assumptions while they read. Interpreting, predicting, and arriving at conclusions are all part of the process of reading for meaning.
- **Readers must select reading strategies that help them to understand what they read**. Strategies are essential in the comprehension of texts. Students need to develop strategies to know when to skip for more points, when to scan for particular information, when to read quickly or slowly, carefully or curiously, silently or aloud.

WRITING IN A SECOND LANGUAGE

Writing is a complex human activity linked with cognitive and social relationships. Writing influences students' oral and reading development (Rhodes & Dudley-Marling, 1988). Routman (1988) indicates that one writes to discover meaning and to figure out what one wants to say. Students write about what they know and have experienced. Such writing may evolve into nonfiction accounts about personal experiences Limited English proficient students develop writing skills through interaction with peers and teachers as well as through the content, purpose, and structure of oral and written tasks. In order to communicate through writing, LEP students need to learn grammar, vocabulary, and the functions of written English.

LEP students can become proficient writers if teachers create writing environments that are interactive and meaningful to *all* the students in the class. In such interactive environments, teachers spend less time telling the students what to do and more time helping them realize options to pursue through writing. Studies support the idea that students, who are given choices in what to write and read, feel a greater sense of ownership and purpose (Graves, 1983, 1991; Hansen, 1987; Hillerich, 1985; Routman, 1988). This assumption can be especially true for LEP students, since it would diminish their anxiety about correctness of grammar, punctuation, and spelling; and increase their focus on the purpose of the task. Independent learners are self-starters, who learn from the consequences of their own choices. Students cannot see themselves as independent learners if they write or read only when the teacher gives an assignment (Hansen, 1987).

One recommended strategy to improve writing in LEP students is the creation of an interactive environment in which shared writing and reading takes place with peers, teachers, and other adults. Group discussion and collaboration are viewed as significant aspects of the development of individuals' writing (Goodman, 1989). In these classrooms, students talk before and after they write. For the LEP students, small collaborative groups are recommended to ensure oral participation. Large group discussions tend to intimidate LEP students, and this lack of confidence or intimidation often translates into silence.

One goal of the teacher should be to make reading and writing functional and purposeful to the student. Current research has shown that literacy learning is not a set of skills but the result of conditions that allow children to be part of a literate community, doing the things that literate people do (Hickman & Cullinan, 1989). Writing letters, dialogue writing, keeping diaries, and reading books to obtain information on a topic that interests them, are learning tasks that have a purpose for students and motivate them to do more and better writing. Rhodes & Dudley-Marling (1988) say that people do not read for the sake of reading nor do they write for the sake of writing. People do these cognitive tasks with some purpose in mind. Teachers should be involved in the process of writing to provide students with the opportunity to see how the process of writing is developed (Newman, 1985). Teachers' modeling can be especially beneficial for LEP students who are trying to learn English and write at the same time. For example, composing on the overhead affords the opportunity to model questions to ask if students become stuck for ideas. Teachers should share writing pieces before and after, thus providing opportunities for questions about reasons for change and further clarifying the process a writer went through (Graves, 1983, 1991; Hillerich, 1985).

Teachers need to encourage students to take risks and to give personal written response when interpreting what they read or heard. Teachers should use questions such as: What did you notice in the story?; How did the story make you feel?; What does the story remind you of in your own life? (Kelly, 1990). Answers to these questions do not demand correct responses. This allows freedom to explore meaning and to express one's own understanding of the text. Short precise answers required in basal readers do not encourage a student to draw upon personal experience, nor do they encourage students to explore their thinking as they write. Open-ended questions about stories and different interpretations about text will be part of the classroom that values students' perceptions. But LEP students need to be guided in writing answers to open-ended questions. They may be intimidated by the lack of vocabulary and language structures to express their thoughts.

Initially, an area of difficulty for LEP students is spelling. Second language students' spelling development progresses along a continuum rather than in neat stages. As students progress in language development, they develop an increasingly sophisticated sequence of rules for presenting words in print. In general, successful LEP students are not taught by teachers how to spell, rather spelling develops naturally through repeated transactions with a language-rich environment as a result of feedback from adults and peers who are focusing on the message they are trying to convey (Weaver, 1988). Proficient spellers move their attention from the whole word to its parts with an increasingly greater focus on the word parts as their rules and the ability to represent words become increasingly more complex.

FROM FUNCTIONAL TO CRITICAL LITERACY

Literacy is the sharing of recreational functional and critical messages though language (Cecil & Lauritzen, 1994; Williams & Capizzi-Snipper, 1990). Literacy has different dimensions and functions. Authorities have identified three broad categories of literacy: functional, cultural, and critical. Functional literacy is often related to basic writing (coding) and reading (decoding) skills that allow people to produce and understand simple texts. For LEP students, functional literacy means providing them opportunities to attain high-level literacy skills. It includes emphasis on native language literacy as well as in the second language.

Cultural literacy emphasizes the need for shared experiences and points of reference to fully comprehend texts. The culture of language minority students influences their reading understanding and their writing performance, it provides a foundation for shared knowledge and traditions.

Critical literacy identifies the political component inherent in reading and writing. To be 'literate' means to be able to recognize the social and ideological nature of the text. Language minority students need to be able to identify the ideological elements used in text and the writer's ideological perspective.

CONCLUSION

Oral language, reading, and writing development should be guided by the notion that language is a social action. The classroom environment, where authentic and motivating reading experiences, as well as meaningful input from peers and teachers are emphasized, promotes LEP students' English language growth. Meaningful contexts for reading and writing development include tasks related to students' experiences.

Mainstream teachers encourage and contribute to LEP students' academic success by providing learning experiences and assignments that enable students to feel productive, challenged, and successful. Emphasis on collaborative learning and activities that combine reading, writing, listening, and speaking, are the most recommended ones. To accomplish this goal, teachers need to utilize techniques like individualization which allows for the adaptation and modification in the mainstream classroom instruction for culturally and linguistically diverse students. The education of LEP students in the mainstream is a challenge for all educators, for students themselves, and their parents.

CHAPTER 6

Instructional Strategies for LEP Students' Oral and Written English Language Development

CHAPTER 6

Instructional Strategies for LEP Students' Oral and Written English Language Development

INTRODUCTION

Research involving second language learners indicates that content-rich, student-centered, integrated language programs are as appropriate for LEP students as they are for native English-speaking students (Carrasquillo, 1994; Chamot & O'Malley, 1986; Enright & McCloskey, 1988; Spangenberg-Urbschat & Pritchard, 1994). Second language learners, the same as first language speakers, learn to read and write by reading and writing about things that have meaning for them and fulfill a purpose in their lives. Under ideal supportive conditions, oral language, reading, and writing may emerge spontaneously as students use them to serve valued functions. In Chapter 5 of this book, the importance, interconnections, and theoretical implications of the four processes of language are explained for second language learners in the mainstream classroom. This chapter expands the theory based notions of the previous chapter into the dimensions of practice by identifying a number of instructional approaches and strategies that promote LEP students' oral and written English language development. These approaches and strategies provide an atmosphere for learning that is positive, meaningful, and sensitive to LEP students' special linguistic and cultural needs, ensuring that each of the processes of language literacy are developed.

INITIAL STRATEGIES TO TEACH READING COMPREHENSION IN ENGLISH TO LEP STUDENTS

Whether LEP students read in their primary language or not, a set of strategies which promote reading comprehension can be organized to guide than to discover reading in English. It is recommended that teachers plan for strategies that involve three categories: *prereading strategies, guided reading strategies*, and *post-reading strategies*. These strategies are briefly described in the following sections.

Prereading Strategies

These are the activities that precede the introduction of the reading text and which provide students with support needed for reading comprehension. Basically, the two elements emphasized during these activities are the provision of *background knowledge* and the development of *key vocabulary* necessary to comprehend the reading. Having sufficient prior knowledge of the topic to be read and the related vocabulary knowledge are essential for successful reading comprehension. Second language learners may experience difficulties in these knowledge areas relative to both the primary and second languages. When language minority students read in the second language, their lack of familiarity with the new language may cause them vocabulary knowledge problems. However, problems can also occur in the primary or first language. The cause of these problems can be attributed to an insufficient background knowledge base on the particular topic to be read. The lack of prior knowledge, which is often academically based, also negatively impacts on the vocabulary background related to the topic. Prereading activities, which make provisions for establishing the necessary background and vocabulary development prior to reading, offer students the support for efficient reading comprehension.

The prior knowledge students have acquired about the world forms the structure through which they assess new information and incorporate it. All students have acquired background knowledge, but there is often a discontinuity between the background knowledge students have acquired and assumptions teachers, authors, and textbook publishers make about that knowledge. This discontinuity is deeper for students who come from a language or culture different from that of students for whom the materials are designed or intended. The activation or development of prior knowledge can often be accomplished through a sharing of the group's knowledge. Knowledge is retrieved from long-term memory, is shared with other students, is discussed in terms of needed vocabulary, and may be recorded in a graphic format which promotes organizing schemata, so that relationships become more clear (Crawford, 1993).

In order for students to get meaning from silent reading, teachers need to familiarize students with the words that provide meaning to the written text, that is, vocabulary. Teachers teach students to infer meaning of new vocabulary from context. Effective vocabulary learning requires both direct and indirect instruction. Instruction should include both specifically focused step-by-step instructional strategies with emphasis on high-priority vocabulary, and more informal immersion-based instruction through which the vocabulary is acquired via wider language contexts. A recommended strategy for doing this is to select some sample text that students are expected to read, or to write. This sample text should include new words with meaning that can be inferred from the surrounding content. Students are then instructed in employing the strategy of utilizing content to determine meaning.

Vocabulary acquisition and development is most effective when it is appropriately contextualized, that is taught in contexts that are natural, functional, and of immediate interest and use. This means that the most effective vocabulary development takes place in lessons in content areas (e.g. Social Studies, Science, Mathematics, or Literature), rather than within a discrete reading period. The linguistic and conceptual contexts of the content areas are more likely to be effective when they contain diverse areas of interest and relevant purposes. In addition, students need to become familiar with the functional use of resources available for vocabulary acquisition, such as encyclopedias, dictionaries, thesauri, card catalogs, maps, and globes.

One useful strategy for providing structure to this process is semantic mapping (Heimlich & Pittelman, 1986). Knowledge is retrieved from long-term memory, is shared with other students, is discussed in terms of needed vocabulary, and is recorded in a graphic format which promotes organizing schemata so that relationships become more clear. Semantic mapping (or webbing) is widely espoused as an effective technique for teaching vocabulary as well as for improving reading comprehension. The semantic map, like a story map, has many attractions. It graphically shows relationships in ways that appeal to and make sense to visual learners. Also, as the map or web grows and interrelates, students can see the conceptual relationships and can develop a fuller understanding of word families (or categories) and how they function as guides to information and meaning. In addition, the process of semantic mapping, provides excellent opportunities for activating students' prior background knowledge, or for building new backgrounds of students during the prereading phase of the lesson. Examples of semantic webbing are shown throughout most of the chapters of this book. Semantic mapping's application should be limited to those important conceptually difficult vocabulary terms which are more in the realm of background knowledge.

The advance organizer is another useful tool for activating prior knowledge. Some stories or literature selections provide a brief summary, often on the back of a soft-cover book. Occasionally, this includes a question or comment designed to entice the reader into reading the selection. Teachers can use these summaries to interest their students in stories, to activate prior knowledge, and to help them make predictions about the story. Even though most vocabulary will be acquired incidentally, some literature selections will contain a few vocabulary words that must be clearly understood for students to comprehend the story. Many of the strategies recommended for the activation or development of background knowledge constitute direct approaches to vocabulary instruction.

Guided Reading Strategies

Guided reading may take the mode of oral or silent reading to provide LEP students with the opportunity to read and get meaning from the printed text. Guided reading provides LEP students with the opportunity to read at their own pace for recreational or learning purposes. Planned, whole group, and silent reading periods are the foundation of guided reading. Teachers direct this process by introducing the students to this reading routine in small time increments and gradually increasing time as students learn to focus their attention on their reading material for longer periods. After selecting a book to read, students are encouraged to attend to the text. An important component of guided reading is the wise and judicious use of questions, primarily through oral language in a discussion format, to orchestrate learning in the classroom environment and to guide individual learning in the most productive direction. For second language learners, especially, teachers need to include *instructional* (to teach some aspects of reading) and *monitoring* (to find out whether students understand what has been read) questions. LEP students need to be asked questions preceding or during the reading to help them get meaning from the reading. Most of the questions should focus on hypothesizing or predicting: '*What do you think this story will be about? What do you think will happen next?*' After asking an inferential question which requires students to project, or predict about coming events, teachers should follow up with specific data acquisition questions to help LEP students to focus on the detailed information in the text. Also, it is important to include appropriate recapitulation or summary questions at the end of the text. When working with longer texts, these questions should be included in the middle of the text to pressure students to mentally review the concepts or ideas of what has been read.

When students begin to read themselves, they may benefit from having their teacher read to them. In fact, the teacher may find that presenting the entire selection as a read-aloud is helpful. The first reading of beginning readers may take the form of group echoic reading with a teacher or lead reader, probably following a read-aloud by the teacher. As the lead reader reads, students try to follow along, reading orally as a group. Also, the teacher's read-aloud lesson provides the teacher with the opportunity to model predicting, thinking about context, and other strategies by talking through some of the metacognitive processes used during the teacher's oral reading. Certainly middle and upper grade students need to be reading silently on an extensive basis, for it is through more rapid silent reading that students can read for the most practice and also be exposed to the most background knowledge and contextualized vocabulary. But it is more difficult for teachers to provide extra support to language minority students because their need for it may be less obvious during the largely independent activity of reading silently. One strategy for providing this support during the silent reading lesson is to guide or structure the reading with questions. Guided silent reading provides an opportunity for students to work at high cognitive levels by identifying cause-and-effect relationships, making inferences and prediction, and applying other critical thinking skills as their comprehension is also supported. Guiding students' reading with questions can provide helpful support through bringing key story concepts to the attention of students as they read, thereby helping them maintain comprehension, and equally important, providing moral support, interest, and motivation.

Post-Reading Strategies

Post-reading strategies are those provided for students to receive extra support for comprehension. Strategies such as students' retelling a story after reading offer a means for reinforcing and supporting comprehension. Retelling also provides a means for integrating writing into the program. Either in groups formed through a cooperative learning process, or through individual, or paired writing, students can record their oral retellings. Building on the knowledge gained through the prereading activities (perhaps involving the activities of prior knowledge and identification of key vocabulary through semantic mapping, and story grammar), students are better prepared to say or write a well-structured retelling. Another post-reading activity not to be overlooked is the most obvious one, more reading. If teachers are successful in promoting comprehension and in providing quality literature that children will choose to read, then teachers can expect increasingly dramatic gains in all areas of the language.

The Language Experience Approach as a Post-Reading Activity

The advantage of the Language Experience Approach for second language learners is the same as for native-English speakers: students read things that are familiar to them and within their range of experiences and capability. Van Allen & Allen (1970) mention different language experiences that can be used to develop students' interests in reading and writing experiences. These are:

- Sharing experiences
- Discussing experiences
- Improving writing style and form
- Dictating words, sentences, and stories
- Telling stories
- Reading whole stories and books
- Using a variety of resources
- Comprehending what is read
- Organizing ideas and information
- Writing independent books
- Expanding vocabulary
- Developing awareness of common vocabulary
- Listening to stories
- Studying words
- Writing independently
- Writing individual books
- Reading a variety of symbols
- Summarizing
- Integrating and assimilating ideas
- Reading critically

The Language Experience Approach uses students' words to create a text that becomes the material for a reading lesson. In the Language Experience Approach, individualized reading and expressive writing reveal the intimate needs, interests, and concerns of the students (Hicks, 1994; Lewis, 1990). Visual materials are essential to this method. Pictures created by the students, or commercially bought, can all be used for teaching. If the class is large, pictures should be big enough to be seen by every student in the classroom.

The first step in introducing the lesson is a teacher-initiated discussion about the reading done. During the discussion, the teacher reviews vocabulary and structures found in the reading. Emphasis will vary according to the level of the group. The teacher asks questions, but does not force anyone to respond. Members of the group can listen to and build upon each other's responses based on the content of the reading and the applications derived from the reading. Next, students summarize the reading or story for the teacher, who acts as a scribe and writes sentences on the board. Students volunteer sentences to add to the story. As sentences are produced, the teacher asks the students whether that idea is already on the board. With students' input, the teacher asks students to consider and reorder until all the story is summarized. Once the story is summarized on the board, students are asked to read it aloud in groups or individually.

DEVELOPING LITERACY THROUGH LITERATURE

Mainstream classroom teachers must work to create a genuine integrated classroom literacy community; a place where the experiences, capacities, interests, and goals of *every classroom member* are simultaneously utilized for students' learning benefit. Literature capitalizes on opportunities to play with language, to experiment with it, and, at the same time, contributes to literacy development. Literature is viewed by many researchers and teachers as the best material for reading (Dunkel, 1986, 1993; Goodman, 1989; Kelly, 1990; Weaver, 1988). Literature not only contributes to the development of students' reading, it promotes oral and written growth. Vocabulary development and syntactic maturity have been found to be influenced positively by reading and listening. Through literature, students are exposed to a diversity of ideas, oral and written, which typically demand high levels of background knowledge; vocabulary, and language structures that are challenging to students. Studies have revealed that children, who did well in writing, tended to do well in reading, and vice versa (Morrow, 1993; Weaver, 1988). Exposure to literature helps students to:

- Develop sophisticated language structures.
- Accumulate background knowledge useful in learning to read.
- Increase interest in learning to read.
- Build a sense of story structure.
- Form a natural setting for the foundation of comprehension skills.

Exposure to literature enhances listening skills, vocabulary, and grammatical and syntactical knowledge of the English language. The learner is introduced to new words; these words are learned within a context of a story, not in isolation. Vocabulary enhancement is especially important for second language learners, since they may speak a different language at home or make use of a limited English vocabulary. Literature, when it is read to students, also promotes listening skills. Students learn pronunciation of new words and develop skills in interpreting or telling of stories. These skills are especially important for language learners, since they can hear language being modeled. This modeling can also be done by the students as they read in groups or by echoing. Thus, literature provides excellent models for students as they learn to read or write. Regardless of age or culture, when individuals relate stories they have read or heard, their retelling follows a set of patterns. For example, narrative retelling of stories develops a sense of setting, climax and ending. Retelling stories also gives the learner a sense of grammar and structure. This sense of syntax enhances the reader's understanding of a story read, even when the reader is a second language learner, who may be unable to decode each word.

One of the primary goals in using a literature approach to improve English skills among LEP students is that these students learn to enjoy reading and voluntarily choose to read in English, both as a recreational and learning activity. Teachers play an important role in achieving this goal, especially when the students being introduced to English reading are students who may not have achieved proficiency in the English language. When introducing LEP students to English literature, the following instructional practices or principles need to be considered:

(1) Initial instructional emphasis is on shared reading which contains traditional, easy stories that many students already know by heart. Usually, there is no attempt to isolate or break down any of the words or sentence elements in this initial reading; rather the focus is on the rhythm and pattern of the story.

(2) The content of the literature should be used to emphasize aspects of the structure of the language that needs to be pointed out such as phonics, and sight-word vocabulary. A recommended strategy is the use of the cloze procedure or pocket charts for identifying words and structures taken from the text. This instructional aspect should follow the reading and discussion of vocabulary.

(3) The content of the literature material serves to engage students in writing activities using the literature as models for the instruction. The students' stories are reviewed by the teacher for improving the mechanics, and these stories are then shared with other classmates.

(4) It is recommended to ask students to keep a journal of their thoughts and ideas as they read literature. The teacher, or other students, may react to this journal writing by responding in writing with their ideas back to the students.

There are good and specific ways to use literature in the mainstream classroom. The following strategies are especially recommended because they are founded on the premise that students' language is enhanced by exposing them to a variety of language models and patterns.

The Shared Book Experience

The Shared Book Experience strategy is an interesting, multisensory way for students to model the reading strategies that good readers internalize naturally (Hicks, 1994). In this strategy, the teachers or other students read aloud a literature book which contains a story that fits the interest and background of students, and has a writing style that is strong, descriptive, and figurative. During the reading, the listener has a copy of the text so that he/she becomes familiar with pagination, illustrations, directionality, and new vocabulary. As the reader continues the reading, intervals of class discussion about comprehension, sentence structure, and vocabulary development are encouraged.

Content Themes

Students read a set of literature pieces that have a common theme. Students and the teacher agree on specific activities to pursue, related to the theme. In order to be able to accomplish the proposed activities, students need to read and analyze the reading materials related to the theme. These literature materials may present either one perspective of a theme or several perspectives. Teachers need to exercise care to ensure that students are provided with literature that presents different points of view of a theme. If students are well-guided by the teacher, it can become a meaningful opportunity to contribute to the development of higher levels of thinking skills, such as inference, application, and evaluation.

Literature Groups

The teacher selects five or six titles she/he feels sure that the students can relate to, make sense of, laugh or cry over, literature that can move students (Weaver, 1988). The teacher briefly introduces the books, the students write the titles of their first and second choices, and then are placed in groups comprising five or six students who have chosen the same book. They read the book individually or in the group, and discuss it or carry out activities related to the reading.

Collaborative Groups

The teacher and students agree to collect, read, discuss, and share literature for a particular purpose. The purpose may be recreational, or for students and the teacher to become knowledgeable about a particular area of interest. Reading material generated by teachers and students should be of cultural relevancy, spark interest in further reading, and keep the promise offered by the power to read. Students can collect specific literature, such as fables, proverbs, and short stories on their own or under the guidance of the teacher. This is also an opportunity to ask students to share materials from their own ethnic background. Several sources for finding these materials include school and community libraries, court houses, historical societies, and materials from the students' homes or from their parents' or grandparents' homes which may reflect the local culture.

Story Maps

Story maps are a good way of introducing LEP students to the reading of a story with a purpose in mind. A specific purpose for reading is determined prior to reading the selection or passage. The literature is then read for the specified purpose, with the intention of identifying the particular story elements that provide the purpose setting information. A story map may be used to sequence the story, and serve as a framework for organizing the elements. A sequenced story map may include the discussion of an outline which includes the elements shown below.

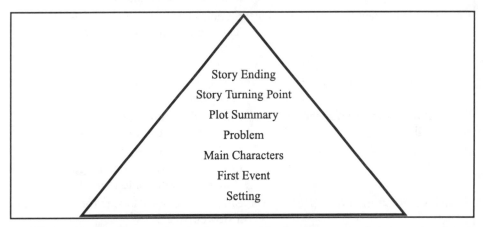

Story Ending

Story Turning Point

Plot Summary

Problem

Main Characters

First Event

Setting

All these strategies need to be integrated in the language classroom to expose students to reading literature for different purposes. In planning instructional programs teachers should incorporate the use of these respective strategies at the appropriate times.

WHOLE LANGUAGE CLASSROOMS

The whole language philosophy embraces the definition that whole language instruction is the simultaneous, integrated teaching of listening, speaking, reading and writing within a meaningful context, based on students' strengths, backgrounds, and the experiences that they bring to the classroom. Many educators support a whole language approach to the teaching of reading which includes the development of word-identification skills. In many ways, this approach is closely related to the language-experience and the literature-based approaches to reading instruction. Oral language, reading, and writing are seen as interrelated as a means for enriching the whole experience of the students' language. The language of the students is the critical base for all reading instruction. For second language learners, initial reading instruction is most effective when it focuses on the students' language rather than a contrived language with controlled vocabulary. Figure 6.1 illustrates the benefits of whole language classrooms for LEP students.

The whole language approach is rich in resources in what students should be using in the classroom to learn listening, speaking, reading and writing skills. Whole language classes, because they necessitate meaning-focused, learner-centered experiences, look different from traditional classes, which provide more skills focused,

Figure 6.1 Benefits of whole language classrooms to second language learners

Characteristics of Whole Language Classrooms	Benefits for Second Language Students
Curriculum is learner-centered.	Second language students can choose topics they can relate to.
Language is learned from whole to part.	Students can enjoy literature while learning meaning, pronunciation, and spelling.
Listening, speaking, reading, and writing are used from the beginning.	Students can improve all four processes of language in the mainstream classroom.
Curriculum is meaningful and functional.	Students' culture, customs, and even language will be valued in the class.
Students' interaction is enhanced.	Collaborative instruction will give opportunities for second language students to contribute to the lesson.
Students learn at their own pace.	Students are not set aside for working at a slower pace.

teacher-centered instruction. For example, in whole language classrooms, there are no isolated spelling, phonics, handwriting, or guided writing classes. Instead, teachers find integrated language, where all of the above mentioned skills are taught interchangeably.

Another advantage of the whole language approach for LEP students is the significant feature of the emphasis on collaborative learning strategies that encourage group work. The collaborative environment of the classroom is central to developing both oral proficiency and academic literacy. Students in groups become more responsible for one another's success or failure. English-proficient students can help LEP students finish the task by collaborating with them in those related areas where second language learners may not have an adequate English language foundation to accomplish the task by themselves. Work groups offer opportunities to make meaningful connections with others who are willing to interact in speech as well as in writing. Students become communities of readers, writers, speakers, and listeners. Teachers interact with these communities and serve as models of language behaviors in how to use the four modes of language appropriately.

In summary, whole language emphasis is on using students' language development and interests to motivate them to get meaning from the classroom language environment and the printed material. Whole language requires arrangement and organization of people (students and teachers), materials, activities, and a complete spectrum of language and life found in the classroom. In whole language classrooms, LEP students are expected to learn to read as they learn to speak the English language, gradually, naturally, with indirect and direct instruction, and with encouragement. Learning is emphasized more than teaching, and students read and write every day. Oral and written language are considered integrative components of the curriculum.

INSTRUCTIONAL STRATEGIES FOR THE DEVELOPMENT OF WRITING PROFICIENCY

Developing English writing proficiency in LEP students is geared to motivating students to write for a variety of audiences and purposes with acceptable writing standards, to respond to others' writing, and to progress through drafts of their own works. Teachers become advisers and critics by helping students clarify their own thinking and by helping writers communicate the intended meaning to others. Carrasquillo (1994) indicates that, in order to be able to produce successful writers, teachers need to emphasize the following areas in the classroom:

- Provide sufficient time for students to write frequently and for varied purposes.
- Provide writing activities for students with opportunities to use a process/product approach as well as a programmatic approach.
- Give students opportunities to select their own topics so that they become personally invested in their writing.
- Encourage students to share their writing with their classmates as well as to respond to each other's work in constructive ways.
- Encourage students to make reading/writing connections so that their favorite authors become their writing teachers.
- Give students opportunities to 'publish' their work so that their writing is treated as literature.
- Model the writing process and share their product with the class.

Three of the instructional strategies that have been identified in the literature for developing writing proficiency are: (a) the integration of process and product, (b) journal writing, and (c) pragmatic writing. In the following sections these strategies are briefly discussed.

Integrating Process and Product

Limited English proficient students need support in understanding that writing is a process that, in most instances, culminates in a product. In the writing process model, writers are taught how to identify and investigate a topic, identify a readership, and develop a piece of writing in a manner that reflects the fact that writing is fundamentally a dynamic process. The instruction focuses on equipping writers with the skills, knowledge, attitudes, and habits of writing clearly to an audience (i.e. the teacher, their parents, themselves) for a specific purpose (the product). Writing as a process is based on the assumption that writing is developed through stages, and students need to be aware that it takes time and requires several revisions within the process of completing writing tasks. The teaching of writing needs to be carefully planned, to initially familiarize students with the steps to be followed in planning, writing and producing a good piece of writing. Writers, especially LEP students, need guidance and practice in utilizing the sequential format shown in Figure 6.2 when engaging in the writing process.

Figure 6.2 The writing process

Planning. Writers choose a topic of interest and engage themselves in thinking about the ideas they want to express. During this stage students begin gathering the materials from external sources.

Drafting. Drafting is the act of putting thoughts down as written words. For second language learners, this stage is very difficult because there are so many elements the writers must consider at the same time, including highly abstract ideas, spelling, punctuation, and the perspective of the audience.

Revising. Revising is the process of making changes in the text and developing new thoughts about it. Revising gives writers the opportunity to reshape and restructure their work.

Editing. Editing is the process of making corrections and adjustments, often rather minor ones, to prepare the work to be read by others.

Publishing. Publishing involves making the work public or accessible to others.

This process is recursive and overlapping rather than linear. Students, especially second language learners, are continually making changes in the text, and they move freely back and forth from and between these stages. For example, the writer may move from drafting to revising and then back to drafting again. This model is viable for second language writers whose limited mastery of written and spoken English can make it frustrating to learn, using only the product method. By integrating process and product, the development of writing proficiency focuses on meaning, the elements of the structure and style, as well as punctuation and grammar.

Journal Writing

Journals are booklets of blank paper that the students use for recording their thoughts and ideas. Used on a daily basis, the students go from learning the skills of writing to the habit of using writing as a tool for organizing and thinking about their experiences. Teachers may select one or more of the following instructional uses of students' journals.

Recording

The student records in the journal what is on his/her mind. This writing is private. Only the selections the student chooses are read by the teacher or by other children. Some students may elect to read their writing to other individuals or to the group. The main teaching role is to motivate the writing and to support it by (a) giving students words, (b) commenting appropriately when asked, and (c) consistently respecting the approximations of the beginning writer.

Interactive Writing

Students and teachers use the journal for communicating with each other. The student writes and the teacher responds to the writing with thoughts, ideas, and related experiences. Teacher comments do not reflect evaluation of the writing skill, the content, or the quality of the students' thinking. It is a written, nonjudgmental discussion. In later grades, this is referred to as 'journal dialoguing', with the teacher carrying on a written dialogue with students via the journal.

Instructive Writing

As an outcome of instruction, the students use the journal as a collection of their guided and independent practice responses. Teachers may assign work to be completed, or may actively use the students' writing as a source for teaching one of the writing processes, such as revision.

LEP students benefit when teachers provide opportunities for journal writing in the classroom. Not only do they write more on a regular basis, but they also begin to experience the varied functions and modes of writing.

Pragmatic Writing

Writing is a social action, carried out with the purpose of accomplishing a particular social function, such as a writing of a letter to the school principal expressing a particular school-related concern. Limited English proficient students need to see writing as a social tool. They should know how to use the writing activity for a social purpose: to write to get information, to express an opinion or desire, and to introduce themselves to a particular audience. Pragmatic writing is reactive rather than structured instruction. Teachers need to motivate students to see the need to write, to help them identify the information, and to use the most appropriate type of writing. For second language learners, the teacher's role is very important because students' writings need to be guided and monitored, especially when students do not have the language mastery (grammar, spelling, syntax, functions) and may not feel motivated to write. The chart in Figure 6.3 illustrates ideas of how pragmatic writing may be addressed in the classroom.

THEMATIC UNITS

To insure an integrated curriculum in the mainstream classroom that is sensitive to LEP students' needs, the most common recommendation for teachers is to develop a theme approach. Mainstream classrooms should organize instruction around thematic projects that are initiated by either teachers or students. The theme approach to learning promotes a mode of teaching and learning that is a meaningful enterprise. These projects are used to facilitate students' learning and usually follow a problem-solving format. For LEP students, themes that integrate the content of the different subject areas are the most recommended. Figure 6.4 illustrates the benefits of this approach for second language learners.

Thematic teaching provides an opportunity for the integration of the curriculum,

Figure 6.3 Pragmatic writing: What to include and for whom

Elementary School

- A letter to a relative or a friend.
- A personal note to the teacher.
- A request to the parent or guardian.
- A request to the principal or teacher.
- An application to do voluntary work.

Middle School

- A letter to a special friend.
- A response to a school/community issue.
- A letter to a relative.
- An explanatory note.
- A letter requesting a change of grade.

High School

- A college application.
- A response to a part-time job advertisement.
- A request to take a test.
- Asking for a letter of recommendation.
- Filling out a medical chart.

Adult Learners

- An application for a job.
- A response to an advertisement.
- A personal letter.
- Filling out a résumé.
- A business/professional letter.

whether integrating it across the curriculum or only within the Language Arts. Figure 6.5 illustrates the interdisciplinary concept model of curriculum.

Students select a project such as building a model shopping center, or investigating all the advantages and disadvantages of living near a park. Teachers act as process monitors, coordinators, and facilitators in the students' progress toward their project's goals. With this process, teachers create and implement ways for students to experience Mathematics, Reading, Writing, Science, and Social Studies in an integrated way related to the projects. Independent reading in this setting, usually relates to the students' project goal. These types of themes must be able to make connections across the content areas, provide depth in learning, provoke experimentation, research, and imagination, and provide effective use of time. Two fundamental principles for selecting themes in the mainstream classroom are: (a) the learning to be integrated must be of worth in itself, and (b) the connections between the subjects in an integrated curriculum must be worthwhile. The success of these efforts

Figure 6.4 Benefits of the thematic approach to second language learners

Characteristics of the Thematic Approach	Advantages for Second Language Students
Easier for students to understand why they are doing a particular task in the classroom.	The teacher introduces same concept using different content areas, mediums and activities. By providing different learning opportunities to accomplish a particular task, it increases understanding in the classroom.
Creates more flexible problem solvers that can transfer information across content areas.	Students are not as afraid to try something new or different, because it is acceptable to make educated guesses.
Promotes metacognitive awareness.	LEP students can practice different types of study skills that will facilitate a more extensive variety of ways to learn one concept.
Everyone is engaged in learning.	Promotes positive attitudes towards reading and writing.

Figure 6.5 Interdisciplinary concept model

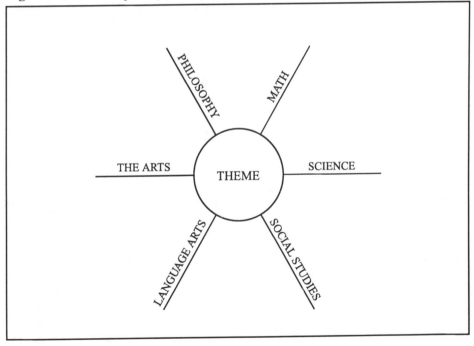

will rely, as always, on a knowledgeable teacher who is willing and able to make discriminating decisions and respond to students.

CONCLUSION

Oral language, reading, and writing go together and must be taught to students using meaningful and enjoyable experiences. Mainstream educators need to recognize the strengths and needs of LEP students in order to work strategically with these students to help them become independent problem solvers. Teaching LEP students to learn how to learn and to find ways to learn more effectively are skills that all teachers should emphasize in the classroom. It is important that schools employ comprehension support strategies to help students succeed in school. These strategies should include such components as guided reading instruction, group instruction, and self-teaching. For LEP students, learning how to use these strategies is very important, since it is possible that they may not have been exposed to such strategy use before.

By providing whole language classrooms and whole language schools, educators immerse students in reading and writing, and provide the leadership needed to help them use their own competencies to develop specific knowledge about how written language works. By doing this, educators can create winners for our multicultural society.

CHAPTER 7

Integrating Language and Social Studies Learning

CHAPTER 7

Integrating Language and Social Studies Learning

INTRODUCTION

Limited English proficient students develop and strengthen English language skills while acquiring knowledge and skills in the content-area subjects. Social studies is one of the most challenging subject areas because it is closely bound to literature, to English literacy and because of the difficulties of the instructional texts. Limited English proficient students may not have the language skills necessary for social studies instruction and learning. There is a significant amount of reading to do in most social studies classrooms, and most of the readings are expository, rather than narrative in style. Long reading passages are filled with abstract concepts and unfamiliar events and names. In addition, social studies books are not well written, often lacking coherence and cohesion between sections (Short, 1994). Therefore, educators need to create social studies classrooms that integrate *language development* with *subject area content development and critical thinking*. The integration of these three areas can help LEP students manipulate, apply, and expand language in order to increase their knowledge of the concepts and facts presented in the social studies class. Social studies content, if well presented and taught, provides opportunities for natural language learning, allowing the learner to focus on the content or meaning rather than on the structure of the language. The social studies class can provide opportunities for students to develop an awareness of how to use what they know in order to understand relationships and solve problems.

This chapter outlines strategies for integrating social studies content and language development. Two main topics emphasized throughout the chapter are (1) how to prepare students for the social studies class, and (2) how to help teachers become facilitators of learning by using effective instructional strategies.

INTEGRATING LANGUAGE AND CONTENT

Social studies instruction develops critical thinking by enabling students to make decisions about issues confronting themselves, the society, and the interdependent world. Social studies represents the content and concepts from several disciplines. These include history, geography, anthropology, sociology, political science, and economics. Students social studies knowledge will increase as a result of studying a body of knowledge that includes history, geography, economics, and political science, while drawing upon relevant interdisciplinary sources. These concepts are based in human interactions and lend not only to the integration of disciplines, but also to the integration of language and content (Abrams, 1993). Authorities such as Ravitch (1988) and Parker (1989) have written about the powerful influence of the social studies content on students learning. They say:

> Properly taught, history encourages the development of intelligence, civility, and a sense of perspective. It endows students with a broad knowledge of other times, other cultures, other places, it presents cultural resources on which students may draw for the rest of their lives. (Ravitch, 1988: 149)

> Social studies lessons built on firmer ground express a distinctive view of teaching and learning: of learning, not as the warehousing of facts, but as the progressive construction of understandings; of teaching not as telling facts, but as leading a construction project. The teacher acts as a contractor — not actually building a house but contracting out the sorts of labor that will culminate in a house. (Parker, 1989: 41)

But the cumulative nature of social studies often creates situations in which LEP students may fail to grasp concepts or ideas because they have missed previous instruction, background knowledge, or because they lack sufficient English academic language skills. The literature on social studies (Crandall, 1987; Ovando & Collier, 1989; Short, 1994) lists elements that may negatively affect LEP students' academic success in the social studies classroom. These are:

- LEP students may not have had social studies instruction in their native countries.
- Social studies concepts may not have been adequately developed in classes LEP students have attended previously.
- The content of American social studies instruction may differ greatly from that of other countries (there may be gaps in students' knowledge).
- LEP students may lack the English language skills needed to participate on grade level instruction in social studies classes.
- Social studies material is often too difficult for beginning and intermediate LEP students (texts assume a specific reading level for each grade).
- Teachers may feel unprepared to integrate ESL and social studies instruction (mainstream teachers need training in ESL methodology, and ESL teachers need content area preparation).
- LEP students may be unfamiliar with the social studies vocabulary and may

have trouble keeping pace with native-English speaking students who have a broad vocabulary base in social studies.

Mainstream educators need to become more language sensitive in conducting classes that include LEP students. For all students, but particularly for LEP students, subject matter content can and should be interwoven into language lessons. Content and language development are complementary and cannot be separated. For this reason, the most logical place for instruction in reading and thinking strategies is in social studies and science rather than in separate reading lessons. Social studies educators argue that communication skills are best taught in social studies (National Council for the Social Studies Position Statement, 1989) because content or context is necessary to develop language. The language system acts as the mixing bowl in which new information is blended with previous knowledge to create new meaning. Authentic language use, which refers to the utilization of language processes from the acquisition of content, can be promoted through the social studies areas. But language development or literacy involves far more than just the students' facility with the written text. Literate people have a particular stance toward the universe; one of constant engagement and learning (Graves, 1990).

Certain cognitive skills are global across the disciplines of the social studies. Abrams (1993) summarized the most recurrent skills: understanding cause–effect relationships, comparing and contrasting; collecting, organizing, and interpreting data; hypothesizing; and making inferences. Other skills are specific to respective disciplines. Geography content is based on understanding spatial relationships and geographic literacy or place awareness. The latter implies the ability to identify and describe a region according to its physical and topographic features, and to understand the effect these elements have on migration patterns and development (National Council for the Social Studies Position Statement, 1989).

Although language teaching and learning should be an integrated systematic process, there is the need to recognize that the language used for academic instruction is different from the language used for social communication. Academic language relies on cognition, conceptual development, and the more formal language used in textbooks and lectures. The cognitive academic language proficiency of LEP mainstreamed students may not have been developed enough to cope with the demands of the social studies curriculum. In preparing the content and scope of the skills to be emphasized, teachers need to assess the level of English language proficiency of their students. Cummins (1984: 138) provides some guidance by outlining the behaviors to be manifested in the surface and deeper levels of language proficiency.

Classroom teachers need to be aware that cognitively demanding social studies content will only make sense to students when it is appropriately understood by students according to their level of language proficiency. For example, efficient text processing requires that readers construct a multilevel text representation having a surface level and a deeper level. The former is literal and restricted in meaning while the latter is a knowledge based on elaboration or interpretive text level. It is not

Figure 7.1 Surface and deeper levels of language proficiency

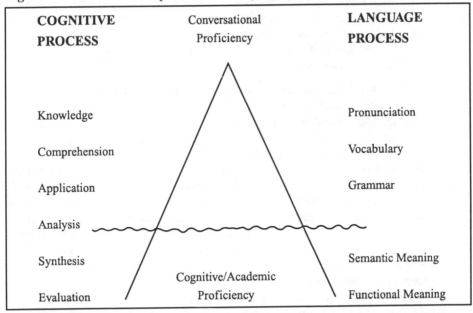

recommended that social studies content be simplified; on the contrary, what is recommended is that the content to be taught be challenging and interesting and that its delivery be done in a way that promotes cognitive development, especially the development of thinking skills (Cummins, 1980, 1984; Schallert, 1987; Short, 1991, 1994). Educators challenge students, not only with social studies academic curricula, but also with activities for creative, cooperative, reflective, and responsible citizenship. But teachers need to prepare LEP students for a social studies lesson by making use of a series of pre-lesson activities.

PREPARING STUDENTS FOR A SOCIAL STUDIES LESSON

An important component in integrating language development and social studies content is the preparation of a series of activities to be used before or during the lesson to make sure students will understand the content and language of the lesson. This preparation will put students at ease with the material under study. The following section identifies specific recommendations for preparing students for a social studies lesson.

Recommendation 1:
Teaching core vocabulary and terminology in advance

The meaning of words is crucial to understanding content of oral and written messages. The more word meanings learners know, the better their comprehension acquisition will be. One of the difficulties that LEP students face is the simultaneous processing of new vocabulary and the understanding of cognitively demanding concepts. Limited English proficient students are in need of becoming familiar with the core vocabulary that will be essential in the lesson. If students are familiar with the core vocabulary of a particular lesson, they are more likely to understand new concepts presented through these words. Recommended ways of familiarizing students with the necessary vocabulary words include:

(1) **Identification of a list of content specific words for each lesson**. These words are written on a sheet of paper, indicating the chapter in the textbook from which they came. These words are then discussed with the students making sure LEP students can identify their meaning as they are used in the text and are able to explain their meaning in their own words.

(2) **If the textbook has the content-specific vocabulary already identified, teachers can scan for other words LEP students may not be familiar with**. Teachers also need to be aware that pointing out a list of vocabulary words in the textbook does not guarantee that students are getting the meaning of those words as they are used in the text. Pictures or other manipulative materials are used to get the meaning of these words for LEP students so that they will have a comprehensive list of words that they can use in understanding the ideas or concepts presented in the lesson.

(3) **Preparation of a written list of words specifically for LEP students**. This list is given to students prior to the lesson, preferably the day before the lesson is presented.

(4) **Preparation of a list of words by the students themselves**. Teachers may ask students to try to find the meaning of these words by using the dictionary, by asking another student, or by guessing their meaning. Students may use the words in sentences.

Although pre-lesson vocabulary development may be initiated in the social studies classroom, the high frequency of unfamiliar words may still present a dimension of difficulty to understanding the main ideas or concepts of the lesson, due to the many unknown words of the lesson. Consequently, teachers need to teach students to begin thinking of ways to figure out the meaning of these words, such as locating unknown words and finding a strategy to get the meaning of the word. Students should be consciously aware of *what they may do* when they encounter an unknown word, so that in future situations they will be able to think through the problem themselves and resolve it independently.

But teaching students vocabulary words is only one aspect of the preparation involved for the social studies lesson. In order to prepare LEP students for success in the lesson, it is necessary that teachers be cognizant of the background, experience, and cultural orientation of each of the students in their classrooms.

Recommendation 2:
Using prior knowledge information

The huge scope of information and knowledge which falls into the category of social studies, combined with the difficulty in understanding textbooks, makes the component of background knowledge an integral element in student comprehension and successful teaching. Beck & McKeown (1991) state that, in order for information to be understood, a learner needs to be able to connect new information with what is already known. Social Studies educational literature (Beck & McKeown 1991; Maria, 1989; Short, 1991, 1994) reveals that many students have only superficial knowledge of central themes in the social studies curriculum. This knowledge is often vague, disjointed, and/or inaccurate (Beck & McKeown, 1991). The language used in the expository texts of social studies books too often presumes unrealistic background knowledge on the part of the students. Beck & McKeown (1991) interviewed fifth graders to determine their prior knowledge regarding the Revolutionary War. In particular, they questioned students on their knowledge regarding the phrase 'no taxation without representation'. Students' knowledge was shallow, and yet the textbook presumed that students would be able to form a coherent comprehension of representative government, elected assemblies, democratic representation, and other ideas central to the Revolutionary era and American history.

Social studies educators must realize that background knowledge clearly influences the understanding of text and content (Beck & McKeown, 1991). Learning is continuous and progressive, and what is learned is based on what is already known. Background knowledge of the student is a crucial ingredient in any successful educational experience. Administrators and teachers need to find ways to create meaningful learning situations that build on previously acquired knowledge, and are realistic for the culturally different and LEP student. Through meaningful learning, new material becomes an integral part of existing cognitive structures. Smith (1993) contends that a learning situation can be meaningful only if the learner can relate the new learning tasks in prior knowledge and if the task is related to an existing knowledge structure. Assessing and developing prior knowledge is crucial for all students, particularly students from culturally and linguistically diverse backgrounds. These students may have had limited experiences related to American culture, and periods of interrupted schooling, which would deprive them of the considerable background knowledge that social studies textbooks assume students have (Maria, 1989). It is the job of the teacher to 'connect' the lesson with the students, not the student with the lesson. Accomplishing this task necessitates teachers' appreciation for the background and experience of each student. Freeman & Freeman (1991) summarize this thought by saying: 'Students improve their comprehension of reading materials when teachers learn about and draw on the students' background knowledge and strengths in order to help them make connections between the reading and their lives' (p. 30).

The role of background knowledge is heightened when we consider that learners are active, constructivists who generate and test hypotheses. Learners learn by the process of cognitive conflict, by testing and questioning hypotheses. Thus, inadequate domain knowledge, lack of participatory testing, and lack of questioning of hypotheses do not lead to learning. Knowledge is actively constructed by individual minds. Each individual has a theory of the world in his/her head. This is a constructive view of learning. This theory posits that a construct or schema is already in place in the mind of the individual. The background knowledge needed for history is different than the background knowledge of chemistry. Higher domain knowledge lead to better performance on domain related skills. Inadequate knowledge leads to poor representation. Overall, the research on background knowledge suggests that social studies educators should focus on fewer topics which are presented in depth using a variety of genres that draw on learners' background knowledge (Maria, 1989; Langer, 1984). For example, if the theme of the third grade social studies curriculum is *Communities around the World*, one of the topics of study is of 'communities around the world that have different ways of governing themselves'. It may be recommended to brainstorm and discuss the concept of 'community government', before discussing the unit. Some LEP students may not have the prior knowledge of what a community government is because it may not exist in their native countries. It is also recommended to analyze only *one community* rather than studying several types of governments or communities.

Individuals learn by assimilation or accommodation. Assimilation is the process in which knowledge is restructured by being integrated into the existing schema. These schemata are influenced by social and cultural interactions. Schemata are systems and have three major components: *concepts or knowledge, membership connections*, and *interrelationships*. These schemata are semantic maps and concepts or meanings. Schemata help learners create expectations and relationships. A text that addresses the schemata and background knowledge of students contributes to students' learning. It has been said that the genre used influences the acquisition of knowledge (Abrams, 1993; Smith, 1993). Texts that account for more background knowledge will be more effective in connecting readers' knowledge with text representation. The greater use of historical novels, biographies, and literature in the teaching of social studies, the greater the opportunities for students to learn the content of the material (Smith, 1993).

How can background knowledge be considered, and integrated in classroom instruction? Teachers should start with the most basic concepts and gradually develop related ideas into broader units of study. Teachers need to draw from the students' personal experience to enable students to see how the topical area is most closely related to them. For example, if the lesson is related to the Civil War, students may be asked to tell about any experiences they may have had with war in their native countries and the reasons/causes or the results of that war. A good activity to activate background knowledge is to divide the class into small groups and ask each group to list everything they know about the topic to be presented, which is the Civil War. In this case, groups are asked to organize the information according to the different categories they have listed. They may complete this activity using graphic organizers such as the web format presented in Figure 7.2.

It is recommended that a display of pictures illustrating time and location of the

Figure 7.2 What do I know about the Civil War?

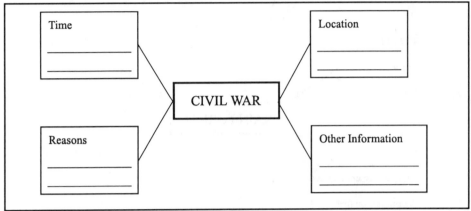

Civil War be given to help students initiate the dialogue. A list or display of key vocabulary words with their meanings may also be helpful to students throughout the discussion.

Recommendation 3:
Providing information about the content

Meaning is constructed by integrating perceptual, linguistic, and conceptual processes from the content with the learners' own knowledge base. Information presented in social studies lessons is often catalytic for further academic language learning. The motivation for language learning arises naturally as students become involved in understanding concepts of history, geography, and anthropology. The social studies class should be concerned with more than historical facts, geography, and terminology. It should promote the development of critical concepts of American history, thereby helping culturally diverse students to understand their new country and its origin.

But, in order for students to understand all the above concepts, they need three types of knowledge: *declarative*, the 'what' of learning; *procedural knowledge*, the 'how', and *conditional knowledge*, the 'when' and 'why' of learning. An introduction to a lesson helps clarify the context in which new concepts are to be presented. The teacher needs to familiarize students with the general area under consideration and to give students an idea or plan with which to make sense of the new information. For example, if the unit under consideration is the 'Rain Forest', introduction to the unit can be presented in a semantic mapping format (see Figure 7.3).

Semantic mapping uses discussion along with brainstorming in constructing a visual map that organizes the background activated in brainstorming (Stahl & Vancil, 1986). The lesson may start with brainstorm of the 'rain forest' concept, a topic that is central to the lesson. Each student provides a piece of information. Although individually their knowledge is sparse; together it may be extensive . Thus,

Figure 7.3 The rain forest

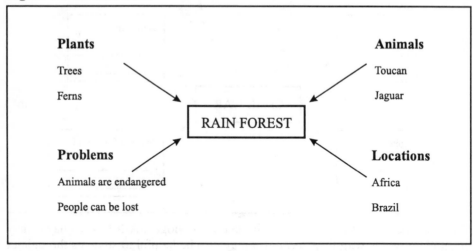

while not every student has the appropriate background for the lesson, the collective knowledge of the group organized through the use of semantic main and group discussion can develop the appropriate prior knowledge base for each student.

RECOMMENDED TEACHING PRACTICES

Classroom teachers striving to strengthen LEP students' academic language competence, develop and implement social studies lessons that are sensitive to the cultural and educational backgrounds of the students; and promote students' multicultural resources in the social studies class. There exist alternative techniques which employ all four linguistic processes and have thus enabled the social studies curriculum to be an effective component of language instruction, one rich in descriptors, varied in type and methodology, and as a result, more meaningful to students. Short (1994) indicates that with respect to social studies pedagogical practices, LEP students benefit from instruction that:

- Offers opportunities to communicate about social studies: oral, written, physical or pictorial form.
- Makes connections between the content being taught and the students' real-life experiences.
- Taps the students as resources of information about their native countries.
- Activates students' background knowledge.
- Provides hands-on and performance-based activities.
- Promotes critical thinking and study skills development.
- Pays attention to language issues and makes accommodations that will help students represent information and identify relationships.
- Uses graphic organizers to help students represent information and identify relationships.

- Incorporates cooperative learning activities and seeks peer tutors among classmates.
- Is process-oriented and provides models to help students make the transition to academic tasks.
- Opens discussion to different perspectives of history.
- Adjusts instruction for the different learning styles of students.

Instructional strategies must involve interactive group discussion which connects the students' knowledge to main ideas or central concepts. Students must be actively involved in making that connection or no learning will occur. Specific teaching practices have proven to be effective in teaching LEP students (National Center for Effective Schools, 1994; Cochran, 1989; Edmonds, 1979). The discussion of the following four teaching practices: historical literature, cooperative grouping, emphasis on paraphrasing and summarizing, and use of manipulatives and multi-media materials illustrate how teachers can use social studies content to engage language development and, conversely, how teachers can use language classes as a means of expanding social studies knowledge.

Historical Literature

History is typically defined as a written or orally communicated record of past human events. The cognition of these events requires the receptive processes of language. Social studies is, in this sense inextricably bound to literature, since much of its content has been communicated through both the oral and recorded medium of storytelling. A topic is discussed from the perspective of combining different genres that were written about a specific topic, or were written for that historical event. The explanation in Figure 7.4 provides information as to how to use different pieces of literature on the topic of the United States' national anthem.

Figure 7.5 is an example of how to use historical literature on the topic of 'Coming-

Figure 7.4 Historical literature in the social studies classroom: *The Star-Spangled Banner*

The Star-Spangled Banner	
Historical Perspective	**Literature on the Topic**
Poem written in 1814.	Biography of F. Scott Key.
United States was at war with Britain.	The national anthem *Star-Spangled Banner*.
United States was losing the war.	America's Historic Places (Readers Digest, 1988).
The poem represents the hope of the American people to succeed as a nation.	The New Emily Post's Etiquette (Post, 1975).
The poem is US national anthem since 1931.	Novels and short stories on the topic of the significance of the national anthem.

Figure 7.5 Historical literature in the social studies classroom: Coming-of-Age

---

Historical Perspective: It is a ceremony which represents the change from childhood to adulthood.

Related Literature: There is a long list of literature written on this topic. The following are recommended books on the topic:

- *Mexican American Youth* (Heller, 1967).
- *Youth of Europe* (Kerr, 1964).
- *Rites of Passage* (Kett, 1977).
- *Adolescence Transition from Childhood to Maturity* (Lambert, Rothschild, Atland & Green, 1972).
- *Tough Change, Growing Up on Your Own in America* (Lefkowitz, 1987).
- *Children of the People* (Leighton & Kluckgohn, 1969).
- *Coming of Age in Samoa* (Mead, 1961).

---

of-Age', a common ceremony in both the American culture and other cultures around the world.

Cooperative Grouping

Cooperative grouping is a classroom technique that promotes learning among heterogeneous groups of students (Johnson, Johnson & Holubec, 1988, 1991; Slavin, 1981, 1990). In cooperative groups, students of different levels are assigned roles which encourage them to work independently on specific tasks. Working cooperatively on assignments and projects with native speakers of English increases the opportunities language minority students have to hear and produce language and to negotiate meaning with others. Cooperative learning activities provide a non-threatening atmosphere in which language minority students feel accepted and more confident about themselves, thus raising their self-esteem. Also, friendships develop among students of different backgrounds.

Heterogeneous cooperative groups (both linguistically and in reading ability level) are the most recommended grouping. Cooperative grouping allows students to get to know each other in ways that do not happen in a whole-class setting. LEP students are mixed with English proficient students, students who are having difficulty reading the textbook work alongside with those who are reading at or above grade level. The roles that are assigned in groups vary, but the following types of roles are common to different models of cooperative grouping:

Material Director: Responsible for getting and putting together the material needed for the accomplishment of the different tasks of the activity under study.

Time Keeper: Responsible for making sure that the group keeps track of the task and time involved.

Coordinator: Responsible for making sure the group is doing what it is supposed to do, leading the group's discussions.

Reporter: Responsible for either writing or informing the rest of the class about the group's accomplishments or productions or solutions.

Monitor: Responsible for making sure that everyone in the group is on task.

The assignments are changed occasionally so that every student has a chance to experience the different roles involved. It is essential, however, that a role be assigned to each student to ensure that no one is excluded in the development of the particular task.

There are other types of cooperative learning structures. Holt, Chips & Wallace (1992: 27–28) have summarized them as shown in Figure 7.6.

Paraphrasing and Summarizing

Paraphrasing and summarizing are essential skills for LEP students. Too often, teachers assume students will develop these skills independently, when, in fact, these skills must be taught and reinforced through repeated practice. There are many different ways of summarizing information. The teacher needs to work cooperatively with the students to demonstrate the various ways of summarizing, while guiding them with necessary briefing and vocabulary. Below is a list of recommended strategies:

- Writing sentences that summarize the main points of the lesson.
- Skimming each section/paragraph of a reading for the main ideas.
- Restating the idea in their own words.
- Using restatements for a chapter/reading summary.

The outline illustrated in Figure 7.7 may help teachers to make sure that students are able to understand the concepts and skills emphasized in the lesson.

Use of Manipulatives and Multimedia Materials

When there are a significant number of LEP students participating in a social studies program, a learning environment rich in multimedia materials and manipulatives must be created. Representing information visually benefits language learners because it highlights important topics or points out and reduces dependence on written text. Many of the concepts presented in social studies lessons are abstract ideas that may be particularly difficult for non-native English students. Pictures are very important in the social studies classroom, they provide students with visual experiences that transcend language barriers. For example, describing a scene from a forest is not the same as showing a photograph or picture of the forest. The visual image makes an immediate impression on the viewer while not relying solely on an oral or written explanation that may not be understood by LEP students.

Real objects or historical artifacts that reinforce social studies concepts provide students with active as well as visual experiences. Concrete objects bring ideas to

Figure 7.6 Cooperative learning structures. Reprinted by permission from Holt *et al.* (1992: 27–28).

Team Building
- *Round Robin.* Each student in turn shares some information with his or her team-mates.

Class Building
- *Corners.* Each student moves to a corner of the room representing a teacher determined alternative.

Communication Building
- *Paraphrase Passport.* Students correctly paraphrase the ideas of the person who has just spoken and then contribute their own.
- *Spend-a-Buck.* Each student is given four quarters (or four votes) and must make a decision about what to 'spend' them or use them for in a particular situation.
- *Group Processing.* Students evaluate their ability to work together as a group and each members' participation, with an aim to improving how the group works together.

Mastery
- *Number Heads Together.* The teacher asks a question; students consult to make sure everyone knows the answer.
- *Send-a-Problem.* Each student writes a review of a flash card and asks team-mates to answer or solve it. Review questions are passed to another group.
- *Cooperative Review.* Students engage in a variety of games to review the weeks material.

Concept Development
- *Three-Step Interview.* Students interview each other in pairs, first one way, then the other. Students share with the group information they learned in the interview.
- *Brainstorming.* Students encourage each other to generate ideas regarding a particular topic or problem and build upon each other's ideas.
- *Group Discussion.* The teacher asks a low-consensus question. Students talk it over in groups and share their ideas.

Multifunctional
- *Roundtable.* Students pass a paper and pencil around the group. The paper may contain several choices for ways of doing something. Each student in turn writes his name by his preferred strategy.
- *Partners.* Students work in pairs to create or master content. They consult with partners from other teams.
- *Co-op Co-op.* Students work in groups to produce a particular group product to share with the whole; each student makes a particular contribution to the group.
- *Group Investigation.* Students identify a topic and organize into research groups to plan learning tasks or sub-topics for investigation. Individual students gather and evaluate data and synthesize findings in a group report.

Figure 7.7 Content summary

Topic: ....

Main Idea: ....

Other Important Facts/Ideas

a. ....

b. ....

c. ....

d. ....

e. ....

life and make learning exciting and fun. By including manipulatives in the class, teachers may reach students who are at the lowest level of English proficiency as well as those who are English proficient. Pictures help students to relate new vocabulary and concepts. What are some of these manipulatives for the social studies class? Here is a limited list:

- maps
- photographs
- calendars
- globes
- video cassettes
- transparencies
- encyclopedias
- filmstrips
- weather charts

Short (1994) indicates that, although pictures are useful instructional tools, teachers must exercise caution with those pictures found in social studies textbooks. Social studies illustrations often represent the scene of an event, a portrait of a famous person, or a land form. These are somewhat helpful because they provide students with definite images, but they do not provide the diversity of concepts presented by the written information in the text. LEP students may also expand their knowledge of concepts and process skills by using sequential illustrations that demonstrate processes and by increasing the use of graphic organizers such as timelines, flow charts, and semantic webs.

AN ECLECTIC MODEL

Coming-of-Age was a topic presented earlier in this chapter as an example of the use of historical literature in the social studies classroom. Austin (1994) has developed an eclectic model on this topic which includes five components.

Component 1: Pre-Lesson Activities

The initial stage in the lesson involves students in becoming familiar with unknown vocabulary words (such as rite, passage, puberty, tradition, and ceremony) and the assessment of background knowledge. This could be accomplished through brainstorming activities, the use of semantic or word-webbing, and teacher-led discussion. Some of the questions that might be used to elicit discussion and connect the lesson with the student are:

(a) Why is the Coming-of-Age Ceremony an important one?
(b) What is a tradition? What purpose does this ceremony or tradition serve?

Several good examples of literature describing coming-of-age ceremonies should be introduced to elicit meaning of unknown words. Stories and story telling offer the familiar narrative context which supports learning.

Component 2: Developing Interest in the Topic

By using the above questions and other questions generated by students and teacher, a motive for students' inquiry would have taken place. Usually, at this stage a general question is asked that sets the purpose for the inquiry and motivates students' involvement in a series of learning activities. The culmination of these activities is the ability to answer the purpose setting question. The question may be:

What is the Coming-of-Age Ceremony? Is that an important ceremony? Why?

Teachers may need multiple and varied resources at this level (picture books, books, personal stories, audiovisual material, games, computer software, community events, and people from the community).

Component 3: Learning Activity 1

Cooperative learning activities and the formation of dyads or triads are suggested for students to explore the identification of coming-of-age traditions within their own cultural experience. The ultimate goal of this component is the group contribution to a working definition of what constitutes a Coming-of-Age ceremony.

Component 4: Learning Activity 2

Students work in groups to study a chosen foreign culture with a well delineated rite to passage ceremony. The teacher has previously prepared all the resources necessary for the students to carry out the activity. Students are assisted by the teacher and the librarian in gathering information from other sources. The group task is to present the information as informatively as possible, using pictures, slides, audiovisual, and written material of the passage-of-age of the cultural group or country they have selected. Students' presentations should involve each member of the group in some way. Students who lack experience in expressing their ideas in writing or orally, should be encouraged to contribute through art, a display, or perhaps the audiovisual part of the presentation.

Component 5: De-Briefing

The class as a whole reflects on the topic. Questions to guide the conversation may include:

- What did we learn from this study? Why was it useful? How can we use this knowledge in our understanding of people from other cultures?
- What do similarities in coming-of-age ceremonies tell us about ourselves, our values, and our ideas about becoming adults?
- Do you have to go through a formal or informal ceremony to become an adult?

The described model presents the lesson in a way that can accommodate the many levels of language development, cultural diversity, and learning disparities that are represented in the social studies classroom.

CONCLUSION

Teachers and curricula must accommodate the needs of language minority students as they learn the content of social studies. An effective social studies curriculum promotes the development of effective social and cognitive skills, enabling students to deal with the complexity of modern times from a point of strength and in the best interest of the whole school community. A good social studies program needs to develop cognitive/language skills in interrelationship with subject content and concepts. Instruction and accompanying materials must provide adequately to assess, correct, and build on existing information and skills, care should be exercised to avoid too many overly complex concepts and vocabulary, provide linguistic supports that allow for competent language use, utilize subject content to develop higher level cognitive skills, and use text that is both coherent and considerate. There are pedagogical implications for LEP mainstreamed students. There are a variety of instructional approaches, readily accessible publications, and curricular materials in the general social studies field that challenge and motivate students and teachers. At the same time, where there is a dearth of social studies resources and teacher training guidelines specifically focused on LEP students, teachers need to search out for and use what is available to provide the best social studies curriculum for their students.

CHAPTER 8

Integrating Language and Science Learning

CHAPTER 8

Integrating Language and Science Learning

INTRODUCTION

Science is fundamentally an attempt to describe and explain the world. It is a way of understanding the world through observable patterns and the application of these patterns to the unknown through observation, the testing of hypotheses, and the design and carrying out of experiments, including the measurement and evaluation of data. It is the role of the school to help students develop *scientific literacy*, which can be defined as an active understanding of scientific methods and of the social and economic roles of science as they are conveyed through various media and is thus built on an ability to acquire, update, and use relevant information about science (Sapp, 1992). Science is an activity, not a passive reception of facts; it is a process that should be part of the thinking of daily living. As a thinking process, science learning involves the use of literacy processes. Literacy processes are the root system for growth in scientific knowledge; they are the means by which science content is not only learned, but conveyed, since content information is rooted in written and oral language. Scientists and science learners must be literate in the basic literacy process in order to be able to communicate effectively their ideas or discoveries. English literacy, which is a prerequisite to learn effectively about science processes, concepts, and skills, presents a problem to language minority students who are not fully proficient in the English language. Students attempt to make sense of the world in which they live in terms of their current knowledge and use of language, and in many instances, LEP students do not have the necessary English language proficiency to be able to understand science content and processes.

On the other hand, the science classroom provides an excellent atmosphere for developing the kinds of social and scientific behaviors LEP students need in order to find solutions to local and global problems (Fathman, Quinn & Kessler, 1992; Sutman, Allen & Shoemaker, 1986). But, in teaching science to LEP students, the

125

main objectives are to make the science material understandable and meaningful, to motivate and involve students, and to enhance the acquisition of the concepts and skills of science as well as the development of the English language. This chapter describes the processes involved in developing *science* concepts, skills, and terminology. Science is a meaning-making process, for this reason a list of curricular and instructional recommendations are enumerated throughout the chapter to facilitate the integration of science and language learning. The communication of ideas through listening, speaking, reading, and writing helps support the development of science knowledge. On the other hand, meaningful science content and methodology can facilitate the acquisition of proficiency in the English language.

SCIENCE PROCESSES AND THE LANGUAGE OF SCIENCE

Science is, in itself, a language and each different science (biology, physics, chemistry) is a separate language. Science involves the acquisition of concepts and processes, specific vocabulary, phrases, and terminology. The ability to manipulate this language and its processes will provide the necessary instruments for the mastery of the science curriculum.

The following theoretical principles of science need to be included in the teaching process. These are:

Science is a way of thinking. Science is a way of thinking; it involves doing, acting, investigating, gathering, organizing, and evaluating. Active teaching promotes learning and it is through science activities and experiences that students do, act, investigate, gather, organize, analyze, and evaluate information. Science processes and skills are the tools which allow learners to gather and think about data for themselves, involving skills such as measuring, communicating, classifying, and inferring. Science offers a unique way of looking at the world; it provides opportunities for asking questions, gathering and interpreting data, and explaining findings. Scientific thinking involves particular attitudes that includes making judgments based on adequate data, striving to be rational and analytical, and maintaining a sense of wonder of the complexity and beauty of the universe. The science curriculum, as well as the teaching of science, needs to be geared to the development of inquiry and thinking skills. Science is not finding one solution to a problem, but rather exploring many possibilities. Engaging students' minds through argument and discussion fosters science learning, because science can only be learned by doing, not by listening (Steen, 1991). When planning lessons, teachers must create opportunities to focus on thinking skills. Thinking skills can be developed through teacher–student questioning or through scheduled activities like problem-solving and decision making. Short (1991) gives examples of how to develop these skills in the different phases of the lesson:

- *Predicting, categorizing and inferring* — warm-up and motivation phases of a lesson.

- *Observing, reporting and classifying* — presentation and application phases of the lesson.
- *Sequencing, summarizing and justifying* — lesson reviews.

Science draws on and constructs the body of facts, principles, laws, and theories that attempt to explain physical, biological, and behavioral phenomena. This body of scientific knowledge forms the framework for understanding the processes of science and the result 'product' of those science processes. Students must use the tools of science, or the process-inquiry skills, which include observing, classifying, measuring, using spatial relationships, communicating, predicting, inferring, defining operationally, and formulating hypotheses to become actively involved in hands-on science. Educators need to understand that the teaching of science involves several phenomena: behavioral (i.e. human behavior), biological (i.e. the human body), physical (i.e. seasonal changes). All these elements of science need to be included in the school science curriculum.

Science includes a technological component. Science information has been a crucial factor in the development of technology. Said in different words, technology uses knowledge from science to accomplish tasks and to solve problems. Science learning is an excellent context for using the vast knowledge that can be provided through technological resources such as the computer and the video-discs. Computers can stimulate ideas to engage in first hand, which would otherwise be very abstract requiring unavailable resources. Video-discs and optical data material are a relatively new technological resource, and are beginning to be popular in science classrooms due to their practicality in presenting complicated science concepts in a visual and concrete way.

The science classroom is the perfect environment for experimentation with technology. For example, video discs and optical data provide teachers with rich material to enhance science instruction, displaying graphics and film clips on monitors. Using optical data, students can explore extreme weather conditions, physical forces, geological forces, time sequences, and biological factors much as if they were gathering laboratory and field data. By observing, classifying, collecting, and analyzing data, students relate to the information presented through the video-disc or the optical data information by generating activities into real world applications.

Science involves a behavioral component. Science can help people to understand certain phenomena, but knowing is not always doing. Part of science education, then, is linking knowing and behaving. Teaching science to students conveys the idea of being able to make behavioral changes in students' attitudes and ways of performing science-related tasks. To promote the development of English through science, it may be helpful to examine science and learning principles that aid in the acquisition of both *language* and *content*. Teaching for understanding science and the language of science means that learning needs to be seen as:

- **Goal oriented**: Skilled learners are actively involved in constructing meaning and becoming independent learners.
- **Developmental**: Science content learning provides opportunities to link new information to prior knowledge.
- **Strategic**: Science knowledge provides opportunities to organize knowledge in the solution of problems and in the understanding and classification of science concepts.
- **Self Guided**: Learners must develop a repertoire of effective learning strategies as well as awareness of and control of their own activities.
- **Sequential**: The acquisition or development of science knowledge occurs in phases; learners must think about what they already know, anticipate what they are to learn, assimilate new knowledge, and consolidate the knowledge in meaningful concepts.
- **Influential**: Science knowledge acquisition is influenced by development, and there are important developmental differences among learners.

Science needs to be taught in a way that is understandable, is active, and includes a meaning-making process that has relevance for multicultural students, as it promotes increased English language proficiency. To be successful teaching science concepts and skills to LEP students, teachers need to give simultaneous attention to the language used and the content presented. Through the use of specific teaching strategies that reflect learning and teaching principles appropriate to limited English speakers, teachers can help students, who are acquiring English to understand basic science content while improving their English skills. Therefore, in order for new knowledge to be acquired by LEP students, it is essential to integrate science and English language development.

SCIENCE: A MEANING-MAKING PROCESS

Research in second language acquisition indicates that a critical element in effective English instruction is access to comprehensible input in English (Krashen & Biber, 1988). One way to provide comprehensible input is by teaching meaningful content in English, using strategies and techniques that facilitate content understanding for second language learners. Emphasizing the way of discovery learning, teaching for understanding, and teaching for concept development and vocabulary development are ways to provide comprehensible input. By making use of such instructional procedures to integrate content and language instruction in the science classroom, it is expected that LEP students will increase both their understanding of key science concepts and their English proficiency levels as well (Short, 1991).

Discovery Learning

Science should be taught as science is practiced, by investigating and evaluating data (Steen, 1991). The purpose of using inquiry/discovery strategies in the science classroom is for students to find out science information through their own efforts, to think about and apply science concepts, and to formulate complete thoughts in

English. In a discovery environment, students have the opportunity to find the answers to the questions they themselves pose about a topic. They articulate the problem, and the possible ways to solve the problem. Students investigate a topic of their own choosing, rather than one recommended by the teacher. They identify the problem, hypothesize causes, design the procedures or experiments, and conduct research to try to solve the problem. LEP students need guidance at the beginning to formulate complete thoughts in English and to express their questions and answers. For example, if LEP students are in Early Childhood classrooms, they will enjoy a science environment that includes live animals and plants. They will learn to respond to stimuli and to improve their language skills as they observe and handle living things, some of which may be an integral part of their native culture. They can also transfer the expanded knowledge of their own language gained through science activities to English. Moreover, experiences with plants or animals lay the groundwork for understanding the more abstract ideas presented in later science instruction. Whether observing a demonstration, participating in a group, or working individually, students should develop an understanding of how to investigate through scientific observation and the collection and interpretation of data.

Teachers should provide a variety of resources to support students' discovery activities: materials for science laboratory investigations, reference books, newspapers, magazines, access to libraries for additional materials, classroom visits from specialists in the community, field trips, films, and computer programs. Science curriculum needs to stress the cognitive processes of *observing, inferring, predicting, hypothesizing* and *experimenting*. These skills provide a rich environment for simultaneous cognitive and linguistic development.

The use of a pre-writing activity such as semantic webbing is also an excellent task for students before they read, discuss, or conduct an experiment. Students may list items first and web later; or they may web as they list, creating new strands as categories occur to them. Figure 8.1 shows the beginning of a web as students think about and discuss general ideas that come to their minds when the concept of *food* is presented to them. This initial conversation can guide and motivate students to investigate how human beings came to an understanding that food is an important part of their lives.

Figure 8.1 Food: An important part of our lives

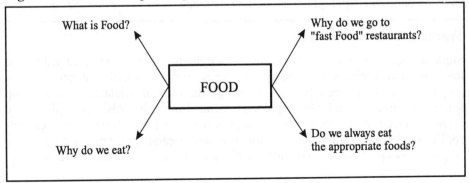

After students have had the opportunity to discuss the areas shown in Figure 8.1, the teacher can use the information gathered to invite and guide students to study the topic of *Food: An Important Part of Human Beings' Lives*. Students can work on collaborative activities to come up with specific facts about the topic. This type of activity is a good means of integrating other curricula areas (mathematics, language arts, reading, and social studies). Discovery items may include the activities shown in Figure 8.2.

Figure 8.2 Discovery activities

Make a list of 'fast food' restaurants in your neighborhood. Why do you consider them 'fast food' restaurants?	**Social Studies**
Write an advertisement for a 'favorite' food.	**Language Arts**
Collect advertisements of foods in newspapers or magazines. Discuss or write about the technique used.	**Language Arts**
Make a chart of 'food stories'. Categorize them by 'real' or 'magic'.	**Literature**
Compare the health benefits of two products: fried chicken and roasted chicken.	**Science**
Make a chart of food samples that are : (a) high in fats, (b) low in fats.	**Science**
What do the following books say about eating? *Little House Cook Book, Swans, Grunts and Snickerdooles, Gregory, the Terrible Eater.*	**Reading**
Make a chart of different types of food and where they come from.	**Social Studies**
Make a diagram of the travels one kind of food takes to get to your table.	**Social Studies**
Classify seeds with their plants.	**Science**
Make a chart of different types of foods and their prices.	**Mathematics**
Make a prediction almanac of future meals and future habits.	**Social Studies**
Read the books *The Bread Factory* and *The Funny Little Woman* and write a paragraph about their message.	**Literature**

Teaching for Understanding

Students need to understand science as a dynamic, cross-connected enterprise involving mathematics, technology and the natural and social sciences. Science prepares students to view the world through the eyes of science and to develop scientific habits of mind. One approach to achieving these goals is to explore each science concept in different ways. This provides students with multiple occasions for listening to and using language structures and vocabulary related to a particular science concept. Science educators (Fathman, Quinn & Kessler, 1992; Sutman,

Allen & Shoemaker, 1986) suggest a model for teaching science to LEP students in which science concepts are examined through three types of activities:

Step 1: A teacher demonstration.
Step 2: A group investigation.
Step 3: An independent investigation.

Students learn primarily through their own cognitive efforts, drawing on their interactions (transactions) with others, and with the external environment to construct their reality. An important dimension of science instruction is recognition of the learners' cognitive characteristics and how they interact with particular strategies to determine the overall effectiveness of instructional programs. We have found that the use of science logs (see Figure 8.3) is very useful in helping LEP students in understanding science concepts and main ideas.

Figure 8.3 A science log

Topic:	
What I did understand	What I did not understand
1.	1. ....
2.	2. ....
3.	3. ....
4.	4. ....
5.	5. ....
What I learned:	
....	
....	
....	

The above exercise can serve a number of important functions such as : introducing a concept, creating interest in a topic, stimulating thinking so that students are ready to continue investigating on their own, showing students how to do something, and raising questions or presenting problems to solve. Before beginning topic development, teachers should find out what students already know about the particular topic. In this way, students' prior knowledge is activated.

Concept Development

Concepts are the essential units of human thought, and are learned best when they are encountered in a variety of contexts and expressed in a variety of ways. Students need to understand conceptual change in which scientific principles are applied to new phenomena, and to integrate those principles into their personal and scientific knowledge. LEP students do not always understand the concepts that are being introduced in the classroom because they are unable to distinguish between important and unimportant data. Many concepts are also abstract, which leads to difficulty in comprehending the information. Scientific concepts need to be explicitly introduced and taught to students. Students must understand that scientific concepts are different from their own previous ideas, but not so strange or difficult that they cannot be understood (Rutherford, 1989). For all students, but especially for LEP learners, key concepts need to be emphasized through such devices as repetition and highlighting (using bold print or italics and putting key concepts in boxes). Fathman, Quinn & Kessler (1992) identify several strategies that may be useful in helping LEP students to understand the main concepts in a given lesson. These are: (a) using visual reviews with lists and charts, (b) paraphrasing the salient points where appropriate, and (c) asking students to provide oral summaries themselves. Fathman, Quinn & Kessler (1992) list a series of steps outlining how teachers can develop activities on a science concept or theme. The steps are as follows:

(1) Select a topic; e.g. *heat, light, animals*.
(2) Choose a science concept, e.g. *light bends, water, water condenses*.
(3) Identify the language functions necessary for science activities, e.g. *requesting, directing, informing*.
(4) Design a teacher *demonstration* related to the concept.
(5) Design one or more student *group investigations* to explore the concept.
(6) Design *individual or paired student investigations* to explore the concept.
(7) Plan *oral exercises* for developing listening and speaking skills.
(8) Plan *written exercises* for developing literacy skills.

Before the delivery of instruction, it is important for teachers to understand the concepts related to a particular topic. For example, if the topic under discussion in an Early Childhood science class is *safety*, concepts may include, components of a *first aid kit*, the *concept of pain, safety habits*, and ways to *deal with emergencies*. When teachers have a clear understanding of these concepts, they can organize and deliver instruction more appropriately to all students. This instructional organization and delivery of instruction previously discussed include components, such as emphasis of language skills, providing background knowledge, or developing the necessary prior concepts for those students in need of language reinforcement.

For students learning English, new science concepts can pose difficult problems. Fathman, Quinn & Kessler (1992) say that abandoning previously acquired knowledge is a challenging process and may be accomplished only superficially, even after formal science teaching. This is particularly relevant for learners who come from diverse cultural backgrounds with world-views that may differ from those reflected in the science classroom. Relevant examples and exercises for LEP students should be used to illustrate content. For example, on the concept of *pollution*, some LEP students, because of their varied environmental experiences in their own countries, may not have heard of the problem caused by pollution. It does not mean that, in their native countries, the problem of pollution does not exist. Rather, it means that due to ignorance or indifference, the idea may not even be discussed in their native country and society at large, much less in the school

Figure 8.4 Solving pollution problems

Directions: The following table presents several environmental problems. Identify the possible causes and consequences of each problem and explain how we can help solve these problems. The first one is done for you.			
Signs Of Pollution			
Problem	**Cause**	**Effect**	**What Can We Do To Solve This Problem?**
Soil Erosion	Wind, water, poor farming practices.	Soil minerals are lost and the remaining soil can no longer support desirable plants.	Farmers should not leave the soil uncovered after harvesting. Humus can be added to the soil to prevent its erosion.
Oil Spills			
Smog			
Tree Cutting			
Global Warming			
Endangered Species			
Thinning of the Ozone Layer			

curriculum. The exercise shown in Figure 8.4 describes a recommended strategy to initiate students in understanding that there is a pollution problem.

Texts written for native speakers of English may assume previous knowledge about concepts or objects that are unfamiliar to students from another culture. If the teacher suspects that a particular topic may not be familiar for LEP students in the science class, she/he has the obligation to provide all students with the background necessary to understand written science materials.

Vocabulary Development

Science content material deals with the learning and application of new vocabulary. Specialized vocabulary is closely tied to the specific content of science. Knowing vocabulary is not just identifying the scientific jargon. It includes the ability to use the vocabulary of science to make informed decisions about science issues which would affect society as well as students personally. Science relies upon the presentation of many key vocabulary words. It is important to incorporate vocabulary development into science lessons, to ensure that students understand the science concepts being introduced, and at the same time, it is a good opportunity to improve English language skills. The introduction of vocabulary should be limited to fewer than twelve words per lesson (Fathman, Quinn & Kessler, 1992; Kessler & Quinn, 1987). Students' knowledge of scientific terms in their native language may be helpful in identifying the meaning in English of the same word. Vocabulary can best be introduced using real objects, pictures, and other visual devices. Teachers facilitate students' understanding of the English terms or names to be used in a lesson by:

- helping students to label with stickers the items to be used in an experiment;
- verbally describing what the students are doing;
- using language appropriate for the students' proficiency level.

Teachers should follow up by asking students to repeat the activity and describe it in their own words. Semantic mapping is a good activity to organize vocabulary into conceptual groupings. For example, if the concept to be developed is the one of *birds*, teachers may use the two exercises shown in Figures 8.5 and 8.6 to review the concept as well as key vocabulary related to the concept of birds.

Teachers need to contextualize the lesson being presented. We have found that an interesting introduction (with visuals and technological devices) to a lesson helps clarify the context in which new concepts are to be presented. Teachers need to

Figure 8.5 Semantic map of subordinate words

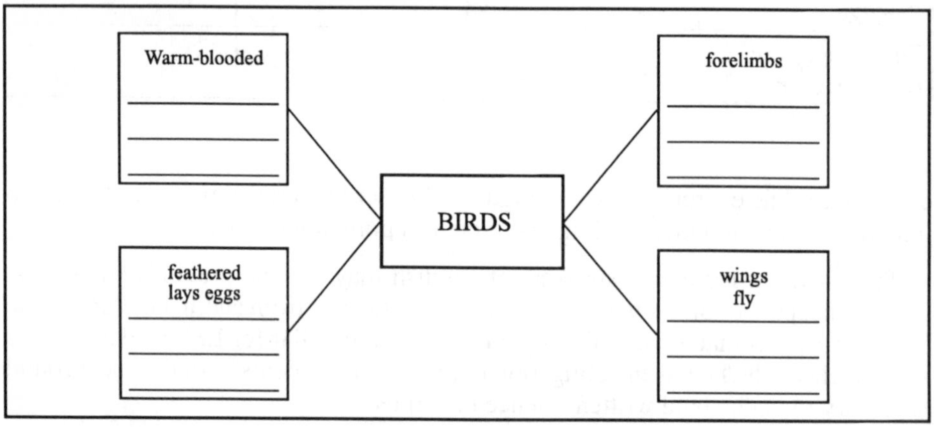

Figure 8.6 Can you identify words that are related to the concept of birds

familiarize students with the new area or topic under consideration (Kessler & Quinn, 1987; Short, 1991; Mohan, 1986) and to give students a set of ideas or plans with which to make sense out of new information. Also, teachers should analyze textbook chapters from the point of view of facilitating the comprehension of those materials for English learners in their classes. It is relatively easy for teachers to identify important facts and vocabulary in written materials. The teacher then can prioritize the vocabulary and facts to review, before presenting the information to the students.

COLLABORATIVE INTERACTIONS IN THE SCIENCE CLASSROOM

Students' experiences and engagement in science activities modify prior beliefs, yielding a scientific knowledge that is uniquely personal. To ensure effective learning, science educators must employ strategies that make students active participants in their own learning, not passive receivers of knowledge. Collaborative strategies are effective instructional tools for improving students' participation and academic performance in all subjects. Collaborative strategies in the science classroom are particularly important and necessary because these strategies contribute to fostering content knowledge and skills, as well as language development through inter-student communication. For LEP students, collaborative work in science provides an ideal environment in which to learn a new language. Language is acquired naturally as students listen to others and express themselves while working in a group. Collaborative strategies promote collaboration among students' peer groups or teams of students who are stronger in English language proficiency and can help others with weaker language skills to perform the necessary learning tasks. Most complex problems demand the talents of many different people. Yet, science is often taught in a competitive manner that encourages isolated student work. Science students, and especially LEP students, must learn how to work with others to achieve a common goal: to plan, discuss, compromise, question, and organize information. Second language learners who work together effectively in heterogeneous language groups take responsibility for each other's learning and develop a positive attitude toward their new language. Teachers of science can help LEP students understand the basic content of science, while improving their English skills, by using specific teaching strategies that reflect learning and teaching principles appropriate to limited English speakers. To teach science concepts and skills successfully to LEP students, teachers need to give simultaneous attention to the language used and the content presented. In doing so, Fathman, Quinn & Kessler (1992) recommend the following strategies:

- promoting collaboration between teachers and among students;
- modifying language;
- increasing relevancy of science lessons to students' everyday lives;
- adapting science materials; and
- using language teaching techniques in presenting science concepts.

Students should also be given ample opportunities to test their own ideas. A major goal of science instruction is to develop students' ability to interpret and apply what they have learned. In order to accomplish this, students need maximum involvement in the lesson. Students should be given ample opportunity to make choices and decisions within the groups and personally about how to organize their own work, to challenge each other's explanations and approaches, and to discuss the information being presented as much as possible.

These strategies provide for diversity and individuality in learning styles and aids students in the socialization process. Collaborative strategies, such as cooperative learning or holistic approaches to instruction, are beneficial in facilitating the following processes and skills:

Science Investigations

Science investigations are personally relevant, socially meaningful, and academically challenging. If done in collaboration with other students who are conducting an investigation, this activity can foster conversation, scientific inquiry, thinking and interaction on meaningful problems. Students share responsibility for analyzing and participating in activities. As Fathman, Quinn & Kessler (1992) say, this is particularly helpful for second language learners who may have the cognitive ability to do the tasks and construct scientific meanings, but may be limited in demonstrating this ability through English. Science investigations allow students to discover new information on their own with guidance from the teacher. Teachers help organize the data and sometimes set out the procedures for students to follow. Students, either individually or preferably in groups, report the results of an investigation. Diagrams can be powerful tools that can help students summarize the information gathered and to communicate ideas more effectively. By creating their own diagrams, students have a far better chance of understanding the relationships of science elements.

Expansion of Concepts

Science classrooms need to provide the opportunity for the expansion of concepts. In this way, students can apply concepts and skills that they have learned on a specific topic. In providing a student with opportunities to expand already known concepts, educators should allow for students to choose the topic, as well as the activity involved. The following activity was observed in a mainstream classroom in which there were several LEP students. The activity is called *My Invention*, and groups of students were invited by the teacher to think about an invention that they would design and describe the process involved in carrying out such an invention. The steps of the activity are shown in Figure 8.7.

The Language Experience Approach (LEA) is another good strategy to summarize a concept already learned and to expand ideas of that concept (Short, 1991). After students have an experience (e.g. going on a field trip, finishing an experiment) they work in small groups to summarize what they have learned through that

Figure 8.7 My invention

Problem: Identify a reason you feel your invention is needed.

Purpose: Tell what task your invention is supposed to accomplish.

Description: Describe what your invention would look like. Include a diagram on the back of this paper.

How it works: Describe how your invention would function.

---

experience. The most proficient student in the group can write the group's ideas while other students contribute by discussing, organizing and dictating the information. Then, the whole group edits and prepares the final copy of the summary.

Problem-Solving Situations

Students often complain that science is 'boring' because instruction stresses problems that are to be solved by one proper method, yielding a single correct answer. Students need to see science from another perspective, from the point that science is exploration, conjecture, dead-ends, what-if-analysis, strategizing, and most important, vigorous arguments which are the norm of scientific practice. Problem-solving situations show this face of the science classroom. In problem-solving, students must select and order varied types of data, using concepts that they already know to guide their search for answers to questions. This process leads to an understanding of new concepts and their relationships. Associated with this process are the efforts LEP students make to convert these experiences to appropriate language.

Problem-solving situations encourage discussion, which is necessary for LEP students language development. Unfortunately, most talk in a science class comes from teachers, not from the students. In typical courses, students serve as scribes, taking notes, and asking questions for clarification. None of these activities engage students' minds as effectively as does vigorous argument and discussion. The role of evidence in science can be learned only by doing, not by listening.

In problem-solving situations, students investigate a topic of their own choosing and teachers act as facilitators. They identify a problem, hypothesize causes, design procedures or experiments, and conduct research to try to solve the problem (Short, 1991). Students work together, sharing information while practicing their language, negotiating meaning and practicing critical thinking skills. Designing questionnaires and interviewing respondents are useful activities for heterogeneous student groups. Interviews may be conducted in the students' stronger language, although the responses must be reported in English. A report and analysis of the interview responses may be conducted orally or in writing. Paired and group activities promote students' interaction and decrease the anxiety many students feel when they perform alone for the teacher or in front of the class. It is important for each student to have a role to play in the completion of the particular problem-solving activity (recorder, illustrator, material collector, reporter). The ideal number for grouping students into problem areas should not exceed five students. This allows each student to have opportunities to socialize and play a significant role in developing and reaching a solution to the problem.

Development of Thinking Skills

When planning each lesson, teachers must create opportunities to focus on thinking skills. Thinking skills can be developed through teacher–student questioning, or through scheduled activities like problem-solving and decision making. All the strategies mentioned throughout this chapter focus on the development of thinking skills.

Development of Study Skills

LEP students frequently need assistance in learning how to study. There are several strategies that have been recommended to facilitate LEP students' ability to process academic content. Among those recommended, graphic organizers, diagrams, and mapping are the most popular ones. Short (1991) recommends the use of graphic organizers as shown below. By graphically organizing information, students may be better able to understand, store, and retrieve information (see Figure 8.8).

Figure 8.8 Graphic organizers

Types	Skills
Outlines	summarizing, making predictions.
Timelines	organizing and sequencing events chronologically, comparing events.
Flowcharts	showing cause and effect.
Mapping	examining movement and spatial relations.
Graphs and charts	organizing and comparing data.
Diagrams	comparing and contrasting

Diagrams are recommended when LEP students have to read information in a text that may not be easily understood, due to language or content complexity. Students have a far better chance of understanding the relationships of science elements if they are given the opportunity to create diagrams themselves.

The use of semantic mapping, a recommended strategy to develop concepts or vocabulary, was described in the previous chapter. It is a visual way to apply schema theory in the science classroom. Teachers and students arrange concepts and connect them to knowledge previously learned about a topic.

WHAT OTHER ELEMENTS FACILITATE THE ACQUISITION OF SCIENCE CONCEPTS AND SKILLS TO LEP STUDENTS?

Mainstream classrooms need to make sure that instruction, curriculum, and the classroom environment carefully attend to students' linguistic and cultural diversity. Focusing on students' language functions, the cultural relevancy of the classroom and the provision of a variety of manipulatives, facilitate the acquisition of science concepts and language skills among LEP students.

Language Functions

Language functions are specific uses of language for accomplishing certain purposes (Fathman, Quinn & Kessler, 1992). An analysis of the kinds of functions needed in science activities is an essential first step in choosing a language focus for science lessons. The grammar focus can be determined by the structures necessary to express each language function. By focusing on functions used in science lessons, teachers provide students with information that has immediate practical value for understanding and communicating both in and out of the classroom. Fathman, Quinn & Kessler (1992) have identified language functions that are frequently used in the science classroom. These are:

directing	refusing	describing	disagreeing	praising
requesting	accepting	expressing opinions	advising	cautioning
questioning	defining	agreeing	suggesting	encouraging

Cultural Relevancy

Students bring varied and often rich experiences from their own cultures. They should be encouraged to share their personal experiences when exploring science topics. Personal experiences increase students' interest in a topic, make a new topic relevant to previous experience, and motivate students to explore and learn about a topic. Fathman, Quinn & Kessler (1992) give as an example of a relevant topic, that of the weather differences in the students' native countries and how weather affects the way people live and dress. An easy way to make science relevant to students is to point out the role it plays in their everyday lives. Using students' own diets to explains food types and nutritional content is another example of personalizing learning.

Hands-on Materials

Teachers should introduce topics whenever possible by using demonstrations, oral previews, real objects, pictures, films, and other visual or physical clues to clarify meaning. For example, in the science class, teachers should make use of real objects such as thermometers, telescopes, computers, and weighing scales.

Teachers should plan for students to manipulate new material through hands-on activities, such as role plays and simulations (see Figure 8.9). Total physical

Figure 8.9 A practical response to the problem of pollution

> **Situation:** You live in a neighborhood in which people do not place garbage in litter baskets. The appearance of the neighborhood is spoiled, in addition to the threat of contagious illness created by the abundance of rats, roaches, and other animals.
>
> **The Roles:** A small meeting (10 people) is scheduled between people from the Sanitation Department, the Police Department and The Neighborhood. Each member will discuss the problem and present one strategy to solve it.
>
> **The Solution:** A list of solutions will be discussed and a written flyer prepared to be distributed among all the members of the community.

response activities, laboratory experiments, drawing pictures, and topic sequences are necessary activities in the science classroom.

An oral preview (oral discussion) on a topic using objects and visuals can facilitate reading comprehension on that topic for second language learners. Oral discussions may include teacher-directed summaries, audio tapes of summaries of readings, language master cards of key words, or oral activities such as role plays.

CONCLUSION

Most students would benefit from a curriculum that reflects the power and richness of the sciences. Science learning thrives in vigorous communities that help students make connections with issues of importance to them. But educators cannot forget that limited English proficient students bring language and cultural differences to the science classroom. Integrating the teaching of science with language learning through collaborative interaction can result in the active negotiation of meaning through which these students come to learn scientific inquiry processes, English vocabulary and structures and social interaction skills. Teachers of mainstreamed LEP students have the opportunity to help their students progress in understanding science concepts while developing English listening, speaking, reading, and writing skills by applying specific teaching strategies that incorporate language functions and structures into science activities.

In the science classroom, students should be involved not just in learning facts and completing practice exercises. Rather they should be actively engage in the activities and practicing the skills of scientific literacy, which include explanation, description, prediction, and control of objects and events in the natural world. Students in such classrooms learn science from sources of authority such as text-books and the teacher, from evidence they acquire by working with natural objects and events and from communication with each other and their teacher.

CHAPTER 9

Integrating Language and Mathematics Learning

CHAPTER 9

Integrating Language and Mathematics Learning

INTRODUCTION

As in the other curriculum areas, as also in mathematics, schools across the United States are challenged to meet the needs of an increasingly diverse population of students, including those with limited English proficiency. Mathematics instruction for LEP students needs to take into consideration the students' *language proficiency* and *content* knowledge in order to provide experiences that bridge gaps in mathematics literacy, expand the students' communicative competence in English, and ultimately, prepare them for success in future mathematics course work and experiences.

Mathematics is a very important, useful component of learning. Mathematics understanding and problem solving help students not just to learn mathematical concepts but provide the process to improve the ability to think, reason, and solve problems (Rowan & Bourne, 1994). Mathematics' concepts such as money, measurement, size, shape, addition, subtraction (which leads to being able to do bookkeeping, balancing checkbooks and bank statements, buying goods and services) come into play in everyday life, and students must be comfortable with their processes and functions. But, in order for mathematical thought to be understood and developed, connections among various mathematics and real-world events need to be emphasized and discussed. Beginning in kindergarten and continuing through every grade, skills such as measuring, computing, estimating, and verifying are all taught together, often in the context of real-world situations. The level of sophistication increases in every grade; but learners investigate geometry, algebra, reasoning, and statistics beginning in the early primary grades.

Although all educators agree with the need of teaching mathematics for understanding and for the solution of every day problems, there is little opportunity in the mathematics classroom for students to interact verbally with other peers about mathematics' real issues. There is little opportunity for students to express, in a familiar manner, mathematical ideas they need to understand for their present and future needs. Students need to learn the language of mathematics and be able to express its concepts and skills so that they may solve ordinary life problems. Students are not only expected to perform mathematical functions, they also have to read, analyze, and interpret information in order to solve mathematical problems. Every student creates a personal understanding of mathematics and the world through a process of *experimentation, conjecture* and *discussion* of the ideas in the context of *real-world situations*. LEP students are often quick to develop the social language skills that enable them to communicate with their peers outside of the classroom. However, within an academic context, this basic proficiency is inadequate because LEP students may be inexperienced with the mathematical world or the terminology and writing styles particular to mathematics. These students may not be prepared to perform the higher order language and cognitive tasks required in rigorous academic content courses, especially in the area of mathematics.

This chapter presents an overview of issues to address in classrooms where LEP students may be grouped with English proficient students to learn concepts and skills in mathematics. The language of mathematics, the content and the process of the mathematics curriculum, as well as recommended instructional strategies are listed and discussed in the next sections.

THE LANGUAGE OF MATHEMATICS

A language is an agreed upon set of symbols and sounds, and it is used to communicate ideas and thoughts. Mathematics is a language that expresses the size, order, shape, and relationships among quantities. It has an established vocabulary, syntax, semantics, and discourse based on representational symbols in its various branches including arithmetic, algebra, geometry, calculus, and number theory. The question raised by mainstream educators is how to ensure that the language of mathematics is effectively taught and communicated to LEP students when they do not have the necessary English language proficiency to understand mathematics content and skills. Lack of language proficiency in the language of instruction has harmful effects on students' ability to deal with content-area texts, word problems, and lectures (Cummins, 1980, 1984; Krashen & Biber, 1988; Wong-Fillmore, 1991a). Language educators (Cazden, 1986; Chaudron, 1988; Goodman, 1989; Weaver, 1988), as well as mathematics educators (Burns, 1992; Dale & Cuevas, 1987; National Council of Teachers of Mathematics, 1989; Rowan & Bourne, 1994; Short, 1993; Short & Spanos, 1989; Stenmark, 1991), have offered arguments suggesting that the nature of math language imposes a heavy burden on all students regardless of the language of instruction. The National Council of Teachers of Mathematics in their *Curriculum and Evaluation Standards for School Mathematics* (1989) referring to non-native speakers of English, stated:

> Students whose primary language is not the language of instruction have unique needs. Specially designed activities and teaching strategies (developed

with the assistance of language specialists) should be incorporated into the school mathematics program in order for all students to have the opportunity to develop their mathematics potential regardless of a lack of proficiency in the language of instruction. (p. 142)

The concepts and the message of the following poem, although relevant and clear to English-proficient students, may be difficult for LEP students to understand due to the complexity of its language. There are *vocabulary words* that may be unfamiliar (swapped, traded, cheeks), *contractions* ('cause, don't), *idiomatic expressions* (down the seed-feed store, shook his head) that may impede LEP students from understanding the main idea and the mathematical message of this poem. This interesting and meaningful poem with its rich language may require the inclusion of pre-language mathematics activities if used with LEP students.

SMART

My dad gave me one dollar bill
'Cause I'm his smartest son,
And I swapped it for two shiny quarters
'Cause two is more than one!

And then I took the quarters
And traded them to Lou
For three-dimes — I guess he don't know
That three is more than two!

Just then, along came old blind Bates
And just 'cause he can't see
He gave me four nickels for my three dimes,
And four is more than three!

And I took the nickels to Hiram Coombs
Down at the seed-feed store,
And the fool gave me five pennies for them,
And five is more than four!

And then I went and showed my dad,
and he got red in the cheeks
And closed his eyes and shook his head —
Too proud of me to speak!
(Taken from Shel Silverstein, *Where the Sidewalk Ends*, 1974: 35)

Back in 1983, the National Commission on Excellence in Education determined that United States' school children were falling short in their mathematical (problem solving, critical thinking, and reasoning) abilities. An interpretation of that statement is that the problem which stems from a deficiency in language development may interfere with students' abilities in solving word problems (Rowan & Bourne, 1994). A close examination of any mathematics exercise indicates that students are not only expected to perform mathematical functions, they also have to analyze and interpret information in order to solve mathematical problems. The connection between language and mathematics has always existed, although educators have only recently discovered this fact. Mathematics has its own language; it is abstract, difficult, and precise. The language register for mathematics is composed of meanings appropriate for the communication of mathematical ideas, together with the vocabulary terms used, the specific syntax and semantics, and the appropriate discourse needed to understand and express ideas and structures. The different components of the language of mathematics are discussed in the following sections.

Vocabulary

The subject of mathematics has vocabulary words and language structures that may interfere with LEP students' understanding and processing of mathematics concepts and skills. The following examples illustrate the complexity of the terminology of mathematics.

(1)   A significant number of mathematics terms and terminology are new to most students, but these words are especially foreign to those students for whom English is a second language. LEP students may not have the concepts nor the English labels for words such as:

theorem, mode, angles, profit, variables, integers
tenths, mixed numbers, whole numbers, three-quarters.

(2)   There are many different words in the English language that can be used to express the same mathematical operation. Examples are as follows:
- LEP students may be familiar with the word *add*, but may not know similar words such as *plus, sum,* and *increase.*
- LEP students may be familiar with the word *multiply*, but may not be familiar with the words *by* and *product.*
- LEP students may be familiar with the word *subtraction*, but may not know similar words such as *less than.*

(3)   The language of mathematics is composed of a complex set of phrases that describes a concept. In these mathematical abstractions, two or more mathematical concepts are combined to form a new concept, compounding the task of comprehending the words as a very important component of the process. For example, concepts such as: *least common denominator, a quarter of a pound* need to be recognized by students if they are going to understand the process being presented and explained.

Syntax

The 'syntax' of mathematics is seen as the relationship and comparative structures of mathematics as part of the language of mathematics. The following three examples illustrate the syntactical complexity of the language of mathematics.

(1)   The identification of a concept is difficult for LEP students to process when the

concept is made up of the relationship between two words. The following list shows examples of word relationships:

greater than	as much as	taller than	more than
less than	as many as	shorter than	the same as

(2)   Mathematics sentences present complex structures in which LEP students may not be able to do the mathematical operations because they cannot understand what is asked in the sentence. Munro (in Dale & Cuevas, 1987) listed some of these complex structures which include:

Nouns :	Twenty is five times a certain number. What is the number? How much is one half of twenty?
Prepositions:	Eight divided by four. Twenty multiplied by five.
Passive voice:	Ten is divided by two. Twenty is represented by one half of forty.

(3)   Logical connectors (words or phrases which carry out the function of making a logical relationship between two or more basic linguistic structures) create confusion for all students, but especially LEP speakers. Words such as *then, that is, but, consequently, either* can be very difficult for LEP students to understand. The following examples illustrate how difficult it may be for LEP students to interpret what process is being asked for in the following sentences:
 • If four is equal to two plus two, then eight is equal to _____ plus _____.
 • The summation of two plus two is equal to four, that is, assuming that _____.
 • Two plus two is four, but two by two is _____.
 • If two plus two is four, consequently three plus three is _____.

Semantics

Language development and communication require that students reach a consensus about meanings of words and recognize the crucial importance of shared definitions. In order to understand the language of mathematics, students need to have the ability to infer the correct mathematical meaning from the language. The following examples illustrate the semantic complexity of the language of mathematics:

(1)   Some symbols play different roles in different countries. For example, in many Spanish-speaking countries, the concept of a *decimal* may be presented as 1,5 instead of the common American way of 1.5. We have found that the way that Dominican and South American students visualize their division operation is different from the American division representation. Twenty divided by two is represented as 2/20 instead of 20/2. LEP students in American schools may have difficulty with the way in which the process is executed because the order of operation in the United States is different from that in their native countries.

(2)   Students need a strong language background in order to make inferences in mathematical process. For example, in a particular problem *a number* and *the*

number may mean the same but language minority students may interpret them as two different concepts.

(3) Mathematical syntactical structures in English may not follow the students' native language syntactical structures. For example, in the English language there is the practice of naming the ones value before the tens value only with the teen numbers, which may cause difficulty in understanding the concept for native Spanish speakers (Rowan & Bourne, 1994) since Spanish speakers name the ten value first.

ENGLISH	SPANISH
sixteen	dieciseis
seventeen	diecisiete
eighteen	dieciocho
nineteen	diecinueve

Teen numbers may need to be explained to LEP students in the context of meaning and linguistic structures. When students have the opportunity to explain their thinking based on their backgrounds, connections such as in this example, can be made and misunderstandings can be corrected (Rowan & Bourne, 1994).

(4) There is also everyday language included in mathematics that takes on new meaning when used in specific mathematical contexts such as common, equal, irrational, column, table. Observe the following sentences.

Common
> Find the least common denominator.
> Two is a common number.

Equal
> Two plus three is equal to five.
> Shang Lee and Peter worked equal hours.

Irrational
> — is an irrational number.
> This situation is becoming irrational and hard to understand.

Column
> Add the two columns.
> The columns of the building are wide.

Table
> Explain the information provided by the table.
> That table has four chairs.

Discourse

Verbalizing a thought is an important element in making mathematics useful to LEP students. It helps them to focus on main ideas and organize their thinking. It solidifies concepts and processes and serves for future reference. Dale & Cuevas (1987) define the term *discourse* as: 'chunks of language — sentences or groups of sentences or paragraphs — that function together as textual units, each with specific meaning and purpose in mathematics' (p. 20). It includes the communicative aspect of the language, including the language expressed in textbooks, as well as the language expressed in word problems. Dale & Cuevas (1987) mentioned that mathematics texts lack redundancy or paraphrase, this causes difficulties for LEP students by inhibiting their ability to understand what is said or asked as impeding their understanding of the process to be followed. When LEP students explain their thinking, they have the opportunity to decide for themselves whether or not they are correct. The process of explanation enables them to revisit their thinking and confirm their thoughts. It also serves to clarify wrong assumptions that lead them to incorrect responses.

Word Problems

The solution of word problems is a difficult task for all learners of mathematics. The problem is even greater for LEP students. It is not because they are lacking in computational ability that LEP students are unable to choose the correct operation to solve the problem, rather it is due to a lack of English proficiency in such areas as vocabulary, syntax and semantics, LEP students are unable to choose the correct operation to apply to the problem. Students not only have to figure out the mathematical operation to solve the problem, but they also have to deal with the interpretation of the context of the language. In order to solve word problems, students have to connect the appropriate mathematical processes to the meaning of the particular problem. To do this, students need to understand the mathematical processes in ways that enable them to make those connections to the word problems. The difficulty for LEP students is knowing the correct way to connect the mathematical operations to the situation in order to arrive at a solution. They may be unable to answer questions needed for problem analysis. 'What does the problem ask? Do I have to add, subtract, multiply, or divide?' The following examples illustrate the complexity of word problems.

Example 1:

A grocery store owner buys a carton of 18 boxes of corn flakes for $10.50. He sells each box for $.85. Find his profit for selling all 18 boxes.

Example 2:

A car which was selling for $13,500 was sold at 20% discount. The sale taxes added 8%. (a) Find the dollar amount of the discount for the car. (b) Find the amount of the taxes to be paid. (c) Find the final cost of the car including the taxes.

MATHEMATICS: CONTENT AND PROCESS

It is essential that the mathematics classroom environment is structured and organized to facilitate understanding and process development. Teachers need to prepare the classroom in such a way that the appropriate language and communication are used to communicate concepts, processes, and applications of mathematics. The following areas need to be emphasized in the development of content and process of mathematics: constructing meanings, solving problems in meaningful situations, using thinking strategies to learn basic facts, and the integration of mathematics with the other content areas. The National Council of Teachers of Mathematics (1989) in its publication *Curriculum and Evaluation Standards for School Mathematics* recommends instruction to fulfill the following basic student goals:

- Learning to value mathematics.
- Becoming confident in their ability to do mathematics.
- Becoming mathematical problem solvers.
- Learning to communicate mathematically.
- Learning to reason mathematically. (pp. 5–6)

The Standards emphasized the need for teaching students to learn to solve mathematical problems and understand conceptual mathematics. To achieve in mathematics means that all students should learn to value mathematics, communicate mathematically, reason mathematically, and become confident in their ability to do mathematics, as well as to become mathematical problem solvers. These goals redirect the school curriculum to integrate language and mathematical skills within the same framework. Instruction can no longer aim toward an answer-oriented curriculum, but one that values process and calls for evaluation of student needs, the continual interaction of students with their environment, and the construction, modification, and integration of ideas. Placing students in carefully planned situations provides opportunities that extend natural modes of learning to benefit mathematical ends. The content of the curriculum may be the same, but the processes and end goals are broader in the sense that students have been asked to reflect about mathematics. The content of school mathematics includes the areas shown in Figure 9.1.

These areas are included at all grade levels with greater or lesser degrees of emphasis in content as well as processes.

Construction of Mathematical Understanding

Teachers engage students in the construction of mathematical understanding through the use of group work, open discussions, presentations, and explanations of mathematical ideas. Instead of students passively memorizing and using only rote memory, students must be actively engaged through various modes of communication. Limited English proficient students should be encouraged to discuss with one another how to analyze and solve mathematical problems. This approach enables students to share mathematical problem solving methods and learning strategy usage.

The exercises in Figure 9.2 provide examples of how teachers can teach mathematics to LEP students so that the mathematics lesson may have meaning for them.

As LEP students reflect upon their experiences, they gradually construct their own understanding of the relationships between concepts. Students must construct

Figure 9.1 The content of school mathematics

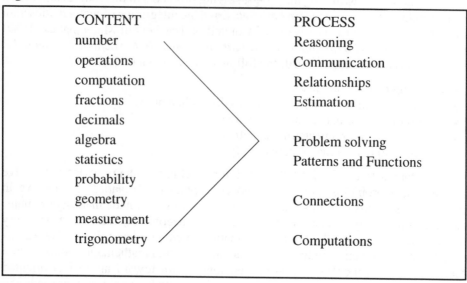

CONTENT	PROCESS
number	Reasoning
operations	Communication
computation	Relationships
fractions	Estimation
decimals	
algebra	Problem solving
statistics	Patterns and Functions
probability	
geometry	Connections
measurement	
trigonometry	Computations

Figure 9.2 Using mathematics

1. List all the situations outside the school for which you have used mathematics during the past month.

....
....
....

2. List three ways or methods you used when using mathematics during the past month.
   ( ) calculator
   ( ) paper and pencil
   ( ) mental arithmetic
   ( ) Others ....
3. Which method did you use with the most frequency? Why? ....
4. Which method did you use with the least frequency? Why? ....

for themselves personal understandings of mathematics concepts and processes. Each LEP student is seen as an individual, who given a meaningful situation in the proper setting, is able to wrestle with a problem and devise a workable solution. The focus of the process is on building an understanding so that it can be transferred to their situations. How can mathematics understanding be developed? Burns (1992) recommends the following strategies:

- Introduce mathematics concepts to students in real-world contexts.
- Develop number sense and understanding of relationships between the operations.

- Integrate arithmetic with the other strands of the mathematics curriculum.
- Build on children's own ways of thinking and language for describing their thinking.
- Rely heavily on estimating mathematical computation.
- Encourage students to develop their own ways to do mathematics calculation.

Solving Problems in Meaningful Situations

LEP students initially need to be guided to build understanding of mathematics so that they can construct their own knowledge with the focus on valuing the mathematics process. In the problem-solving process, students need to develop their own procedures in which they can discuss, explain, modify, and write about their understanding. LEP students need to be placed in problem-solving situations with meaningful and culturally relevant problems, especially those that connect mathematics to other disciplines which will lead them to develop their own ideas and understandings. The following strategies have been recommended in the literature to promote students' mathematics concepts and process:

1. A step by step problem-solving process which allows students to understand, compute and revise (if necessary) in order to solve a mathematical problem (Rowan & Bourne, 1994). The suggested plan requires four steps:

Step 1: Understand the problem.
Step 2: Develop a plan that they feel will solve the problem.
Step 3: Try the plan to see if it works.
Step 4: Look at the results to see if they make sense for that problem. If the results do not make sense, they go back to the first step of the process and begin again with the guidance of the teacher.

Although the above plan focuses on students' own process, teachers can present situations for students, either individually or in groups, in which the above four steps are followed. Teachers will provide instruction to implement, evaluate, and revise the plan with all the students involved in the lesson. By providing relevant problem-solving situations through planned classroom instruction, educators are showing students that they respect their cultural and linguistic backgrounds, can apply sound educational principles, and are able to accommodate to the needs of all students in the classroom.

2. Cooperative groups can provide an optimum learning setting for LEP students to share their understanding of problems while receiving the necessary linguistic and conceptual background which enables them to participate in the problem-solving task. Vygotsky (1962) emphasized the strong influence peer interaction has on learning. Learners construct knowledge through coordinated, mutual interpretations of each other's intentions as are realized through action and speech. He also promoted the idea that what students can do cooperatively today, they will be able to do individually in the future. Partners/peers can provide support for LEP students and enable them to use the available resources to develop those skills over which

they do not have explicit and conscious control. This practice enhances and enriches the basic language skills of LEP students by utilizing the expressive and receptive components of communication.

3. Literature provides a good source for making the connections between mathematical processes and the applicable contexts. For example, the poem *Smart* presented in a previous section, if understood by LEP students, is a good vehicle for students to listen, read, interpret and reflect on the content and the message of the poem. Stories such as *Count by Twos* (J. Nelson, 1990), *Anno's Math Games* (Philomel Books, 1987), and *The Magic Money Machine* (Modern Curriculum Press, 1990) help students explore new concepts through active participation, integrating new ideas, and predicting new outcomes. Students must first see and understand the need and context for computational skills. Literature can serve as that link between using concrete material and abstract activities (Nevin, 1992).

4. Story problems are often used to motivate specific areas of mathematics content and require the development of specific problem-solving strategies. The following example presents an activity in which students need to understand the problem to perform the required task.

Activity: Draw a picture to depict the events of the story.

Alice had some toy dinosaurs. She gave one eighth of the toys to Jimmy. Now Alice has 15 dinosaurs. How many did she have to start with?

5. Thinking strategies are helpful in learning basic mathematical facts and how to apply them to problem-solving, mental arithmetic, and estimation situations. To develop this knowledge, students must continually be placed in situations in which they need to know and have the means to determine simple facts. Over time, the facts will naturally become committed to students' rote memory.

Example: If you don't know the sum of 12 + 8, how could you figure out the answer?

Using Thinking Strategies to Learn Basic Facts

Authorities in the field of mathematics education (Burns, 1992; Rowan & Bourne, 1994; Steen, 1991) have called for a curriculum which includes development of language and enrichment of mathematics by:

- **Actively engaging students to participate in mathematics hands-on activities**. Calculators and hands-on materials can facilitate the investigation and culmination of mathematical problems.
- **Encouraging team work so that students can share verbal and/or written alternative strategies to problem solving**. When students are encouraged to work in teams and are given hands-on materials, they create solutions to mathematical problems and internalize through their involvement in productive mathematics communication.
- **Encouraging discussion to expose students to explaining and defending**

their responses. The more students can verbalize their understanding of the processes of mathematical operations, the easier it is for them to be able to solve mathematical problems.

- **Including varied writing activities to clarify their own understanding and conclusions**. Writing helps students reflect on and clarify their thinking.
- **Developing the concepts of each lesson**. In each lesson there are strategies to be followed for investigating or solving mathematical problems or operations.

How, should a class be carried out for students who are limited in the English language? In a class of LEP students, teachers need to employ a variety of instructional activities that include the elements previously discussed (i.e. vocabulary development, simplification of syntactical and discourse structures, and expansion of semantic structures). Cuevas (1981) provides a model, *Second Language and Mathematics Skills* (SLAMS), that includes language and mathematics development for second language learners. SLAMS is based on the assumption that, in order for students to master mathematical concepts, the language of the concepts must be first mastered. This model outlines two curriculum strands: *the language strand* and *the curriculum strand*. The scope and sequence of the SLAMS model is presented in Figure 9.3.

Figure 9.3 SLAMS model (Cuevas, 1981)

Mathematics Curriculum Scope and Sequence	
Language Skills	*Mathematics Content*
Analysis of the Language Used	Analysis of Mathematics Skill
Diagnosis of Content Language Skills	Diagnosis of Mathematics Skills
Strategies of Content Language	Strategies for Mathematics

The following steps are included in the presentation of this model.

- The teacher introduces the aim, builds background from prior knowledge, develops vocabulary, and reviews concepts and skills.
- The teacher breaks the class into small groups or teams and assigns a task related to the aim.
- The children come together as a group.
- Does the student recognize the symbols and terms that pertain to the skill?
- Can the student pronounce them?
- Can students write them?
- Can students define the terms used?
- Are students mathematically knowledgeable of the structures used, so that ideas and relationships are understood?

RECOMMENDED INSTRUCTIONAL PRACTICES

As was said earlier, in teaching mathematics, educators must build an understanding of mathematics concepts and language. There are a series of instructional ideas that, although not unique to the teaching of mathematics, have been found to be very successful in teaching second language students.

Pre-Mathematics Language Activities

When teaching mathematics in a mainstream classroom that includes LEP students, teachers need to focus on factors that may affect the involvement of these students in mathematical problem solving or mathematical operations. The most prevalent language difficulties for non native English speaking students include the understanding of lexical items, and the use of comparative terms or structures. Prior to the mathematics lesson, the teacher should make sure that students have enough understanding of the key words of the lesson (not necessarily mathematics vocabulary) to be able to follow the mathematical concepts and processes that will be introduced in the lesson. Activities such as semantic mapping, reviewing prior knowledge and experiences, brainstorming, and defining words in context are suggested activities for assuring that the vocabulary to be used in the math lesson is understood by everyone including LEP students. The teacher can use this approach with everyone in the class but emphasizes them with LEP students by questioning them and asking them to respond by rephrasing the information in their own words. Specific question may include:

(1) Do you understand the problem or operation asked for?
- Restate the problem in your own words.
- Explain what are you trying to find out?
- How do you think you might solve the problem?
(2) If you don't understand the problem:
- What are some of the difficulties you encounter in solving the problem?
- What are the language difficulties of this problem?
- What are other areas that cause you difficulty in solving the problem?

Conducting Productive Class Discussions

Educators are encouraged to provide opportunities for LEP students to verbalize and discuss specific ideas that will later be included in the mathematics lesson. Teachers need to encourage students to talk to one another as they work in pairs on these activities. Mathematical language must be used in order for it to develop and be mastered. Encourage the use of English, but do not discourage students from using their first language.

Use of Manipulatives

Manipulatives are any objects that can be treated with or operated by the use of hands in a skillful manner. These objects serve as concrete representations of mathematical concepts. Teachers can utilize everything from color tiles, beans, rods, and number blocks to fingers and toes to serve as manipulatives. The materials need to be accessible to students for use in counting, classifying, patterning, constructing, and exploring. Their value lies in the ways in which they are incorporated into the class lessons. Manipulatives, when used effectively, aid in contributing to conceptualization and understanding. Progression in concept development starts from the concrete and then moves to the abstract. Centers and games can be made with various manipulatives that reinforce and build upon concepts under current study. Incorporating the use of concrete materials enables teachers to make better assessment and meet the needs of individual students as they construct their mathematics knowledge (Ross & Kurtz, 1993).

Manipulatives need to be seen as the bridge to make the connections between the concrete objects, pictures or technological devices, and the mathematics concepts. Manipulatives, in themselves, are not the answer to all the difficulties LEP students encounter in the mainstream classroom. Manipulatives provide the initial concrete step procedures to understand the words or the symbols of the mathematics language.

Integration of Mathematics and Other Content Areas

Students should encounter mathematics throughout their curriculum in language, reading, social studies, science, art, and physical education. Mathematics integration is beneficial to all content areas; it fosters the development of interpreting information, visualization of concepts, and the implementation of solutions. Interdisciplinary units concentrate on organizing themes or concepts and enable students to integrate scientific processes, communication skills, problem solving, critical thinking, and creativity. But activities used in the mathematical classroom need to be tailored to the needs and interests of a specific group of students. Rowan & Bourne (1994) list some sample prompts (see Figure 9.4) taken from a variety of classes. We recommend that the list be given to LEP students to choose one or two activities. These prompts integrate reading, writing, art, science, and social studies. By giving students the list to choose from, not only are they asked to choose a preferred activity, but they need to read all of them, which becomes a meaningful reading exercise. In addition, they need to evaluate mathematically which exercises they can carry out.

Writing about mathematics is another way of integrating content areas in the mathematics classroom. The following list illustrates types of meaningful writing activities recommended for all students, especially LEP students.

(1) Restate the problem in your own words. What are you trying to find out?
(2) How do you think you might solve the problem?
(3) Explain how you solved the problem. Include all the steps so that someone else can use your method.
(4) How do you know your answer is right? Is there more than one possible answer to this problem? Why? Why not?

CONCLUSION

Mathematics has a language that is diverse and broad, yet it is an integral and necessary part of everyday living. In teaching mathematics, educators need to place emphasis on content as well as in the process, and in making connections between disciplines. This ensures that students engage in mathematics for understanding and

Figure 9.4 Sample prompts (from Rowan & Bourne, 1994: 102)

- Show three different drawings for the number five (5).
- Write three story problems that have five (5) as an answer.
- Write about your favorite number. Tell why it is your favorite.
- Make up a pattern and tell about it.
- Find out how many windows are in your home. Tell how you did this.
- Write three story problems for the picture on page 45 of your book. Tell how to solve your problems.
- Find out the favorite ice cream flavor of ten people you know. Invent a way to show this information to our class.
- Spin the roulette ten times. Tell what happened. Tell why you think it happened.
- What was easiest for you in today's math lesson? Why?
- What was hardest for you in today's math lesson? Why?
- What did you like most in math this week? Why?
- Write ten problems that use the number 10.
- Try to solve the problems mentally (no paper, pencil or calculator). Write how you solved them.
- Write about how you would tell a younger child to do the work we learned in math today.
- Make up ten math problems that you think are easy to do without paper, pencil, or calculator. Tell why you think they are easy.

to solve problems using various information sources and strategies. Only when students learn how to incorporate and communicate their mathematical knowledge effectively, do they become literate in mathematics. Mathematical literacy is a skill that all students must achieve to succeed in the technological world that requires students to face a myriad of yet-undetermined needs.

All students are unique. They enter the school and the classroom situation with different backgrounds and different language proficiencies, and they exhibit distinctive learning styles. Students' language development and their ability to understand and communicate mathematically are critical in helping them construct links between their informal, intuitive notions and the abstract language and symbolism of mathematics.

Although LEP students interpret and connect ideas differently, if given the proper linguistic supports they can construct the connections and relationships among concepts that are essential for understanding mathematics.

CHAPTER 10

The Role of Teachers in the Development of Linguistic, Cognitive and Academic Skills of LEP Students

CHAPTER 10

The Role of Teachers in the Development of Linguistic, Cognitive and Academic Skills of LEP Students

INTRODUCTION

There is an extraordinary interest in the United States to identify 'effective' 'successful', 'exemplary' characteristics for teachers in general. Two decades of research on effective teaching have provided a base of information about the skills and knowledge teachers need to demonstrate to instruct students from the nation's mainstream culture successfully (Brophy, 1979; Clark & Peterson, 1986; Edmonds, 1979; Goodlad, 1990; Tikunoff & Ward, 1991; Wittrock, 1986). This research has extended to teachers who are working with a student population which is culturally and linguistically diverse (Garcia, 1993; Ramirez, 1992; Tikunoff, 1985; Trueba, 1989; Wong-Fillmore, 1991a). As schools become more diverse, all teachers must ultimately assume greater responsibility for the development of LEP students both in the English language and in the academic content of all subject areas. A report conducted by the United States Department of Education indicated that a significant number of mainstream teachers provide instruction to LEP students. For example, about 15% of the Nation's teachers had at least one LEP student in their classes, and two thirds of teachers serving LEP students serve those students in mainstream classrooms. But, only 55% of all teachers of LEP students had taken relevant college courses or had received recent in-service training related to teaching second language learners. Only about one-third of teachers of LEP students had ever taken college courses concerning cultural differences and implications for instruction, language acquisition theory, and teaching English to LEP students (United States

Department of Education, 1993a). These findings suggest that although it is becoming increasingly common for mainstream teachers to find themselves teaching LEP students, most of these teachers have not been trained to address the particular learning needs of LEP students (Hamayan, 1990; Milk, Mercado & Sapiens, 1992; Rigg & Allen, 1989; Wong-Fillmore, 1991a, 1991b). Because mainstream educators are the most important influence in students' school academic performance, this chapter's content revolves around the teacher's role and responsibilities in promoting language minority students' cognitive, academic, and linguistic development.

This chapter discusses the role of mainstream teachers in promoting language acquisition and learning in the classroom. Competencies of mainstream teachers as they relate to the integration of English language development, content area acquisition in the different school subject areas, and the creation of an appropriate classroom environment are addressed in this chapter. The chapter concludes with a section discussing the value of teachers using a reflective practitioner approach to create an optimal instructional environment for the delivery of effective instruction.

COMPETENCIES OF SUCCESSFUL MAINSTREAM TEACHERS

Teachers are the most powerful influence on students' behavior and learning. Teachers' attitudes, expectations, behaviors, and actions affect students. Teachers unconsciously and consciously project and carry out the school's and their own desires for their students. Mainstream teachers, who have LEP students in their classrooms, must integrate *English language development* with *content knowledge acquisition* if instruction is going to contribute effectively to LEP students' linguistic, cognitive, and academic development. Review of the literature on teacher education (Brophy, 1979; Edmonds, 1979; Garcia, 1993; Ramirez, 1992; Tikunoff & Ward, 1991; Wittrock, 1986, 1987) suggests a set of fundamental skills, knowledge, and attitudes that all teachers, but especially those working with linguistic and culturally diverse students (including mainstream teachers), should possess. Competencies of effective teachers include:

- Organization and Effective Delivery of Instruction.
- Knowledge of Second Language Acquisition Processes.
- Knowledge of Students Developmental Language Practices.
- Familiarity with Students' Native Language and Cultural Background.
- Familiarity with Students Learning and Cognitive Styles.
- Effective Classroom Management.
- High Expectations for their Students.
- Facilitators of Parental Involvement.

These characteristics are discussed in the following sections.

Organization and Delivery of Instruction

Excellence in teaching has been defined as consistent instruction, relevant instruction, and efficient instruction. The outcomes of the learning process should be consistent over time between sections of the same class or subject. In other words, good teaching is the delivery of consistent, reliable, and relevant instruction that produces positive results. The relevancy of an instructional program can be defined as the degree to which what is being produced reflects sound teaching practice. Effective instruction should foster efficient instruction; or said differently, the instruction needs to be practical. Effective instruction of culturally and linguistically diverse students begins with teachers' mastery in the use of instructional practices directly related to increasing all students' performance with regard to the achievement of the basic skills and content (Tikunoff, 1985; Tikunoff & Ward, 1991). Two key questions frequently asked in the areas of organization and delivery of instruction are:

(1) How can teachers effectively organize instruction to meet the needs of all the students in the classroom?
(2) How well do teachers deliver instruction?

Tikunoff's (1985) study *Significant Bilingual Instructional Features* reported commonalities in the 'significant' teacher's response to organization and instruction in the classroom. Three instructional features were identified for effective teachers of LEP students that may lead to answers to the two broad questions raised:

- Specification of the task outcomes and identification of the specific activities students must do to accomplish those tasks.
- Use of active teaching behaviors that are found to be related to increased student performance on academic tests of achievement in reading and mathematics.
- Mediation of instruction for LEP students (i.e. by using the students' native language and English for instruction, alternating between the two languages whenever necessary to ensure clarity of instruction).

Although the last area may not be directly related to effective mainstream teachers, it does imply that all teachers need to demonstrate a sensitivity to and understanding of students' linguistic strengths, although those strengths may not necessarily be in English. According to Tikunoff (1985) teachers need to plan their learning activities based on the task outcome specifications as well as provide successful strategies for the on-going assessment of students' learning. Through these teaching practices, effective teachers of language minority students: (a) provide praise and positive motivation, (b) spend more class time on teacher-directed whole class activity, (c) ask more cognitively demanding questions, and (d) monitor students when they work independently or in groups.

By planning and organizing instruction, language development and knowledge of content are enhanced. Tikunoff & Ward (1991) identify five ways in which effective instruction can promote English language development and acquisition of subject matter content and skills:

- Calling students' attention to the language the teacher uses in the lesson.

- Presenting the structure of the language used in the lesson to the students as well as its content and meaning.
- Summarizing newly acquired/applied words and language structures during and at the end of the lesson.
- Providing new vocabulary to be used in the lesson.
- Asking questions that require more than yes/no responses and encouraging students to expand upon and classify their responses.

The above activities serve to clarify the intent and the different modalities to deliver instruction to students. Brophy & Good (1974) and Tikunoff & Ward (1991) indicate that an important component of effective instructional abilities is the clarity of intent of instruction on the part of both teachers and students along with clear specification of tasks to be completed and procedures to follow in their completion.

Additionally, teachers who are competent in organizing and delivering instruction show:

(1) **Ability to make instruction comprehensible**. Able teachers clarify how students are to function appropriately while completing assigned tasks, and establish mechanisms through which students may demonstrate their English learning by providing opportunities for students to seek feedback regarding the accuracy of the task's completion (Tikunoff & Ward, 1991). One important aspect of making instruction comprehensible is the attention teachers give in helping students learn facts which are both easily used and recalled and can provide a context for concept development. Grade level students should finish their schooling with a store of significant, supportable concepts that are usable in daily living. Teachers should intentionally plan concept development by providing quality instruction in which process and product are both empha-sized. Teachers should focus on academic goals, plan to teach an ample amount of content, keep students involved, select and pursue specific objectives, use carefully chosen materials, monitor students' progress, structure learning activities, provide for immediate feedback, and create classroom environments that are task oriented but relaxed. Brophy (1979) mentions additional teachers' obligations as they relate to instruction: To 'have a mind' to instruct thoroughly; to use time as a precious commodity; to teach personally rather than through surrogates; to be unafraid to use resuscitation, drill and practice; to use whole-group, small-group, and individualized teaching judiciously; where necessary to encourage-over learning to the point of mastery where necessary; and to manage the classroom well.

(2) **Knowledge and articulation with regard to the instructional philosophies that guide them**. Competent teachers can explain 'why' they are using specific instructional techniques and usually couch these explanations in terms of a theoretical position that underpins their role with regard to teaching and 'how' students learn (Garcia, 1993). The teacher's philosophy of teaching is one that is comprehensible and includes current theories of teaching that have been put into practice in the classroom and have proven to enhance students' learning

and language development. Effective teachers' philosophies have been developed by university courses, in-service training, as well as by individual readings, practice, and reflection. Effective teachers are individuals who have a broad and firm understanding of the teaching process and of the interrelationship between language and learning. Such teachers not only apply these theories of learning in the classroom, but also have the skill and sensitivity to make the needed theoretical accommodations to provide for the diverse student population of their classrooms.

(3) **Knowledge and mastery of the content areas**. These are teachers who have a solid and confident understanding of the material (i.e. mathematics, social studies, science, reading, language development) being taught. When teachers start teaching they bring to the classroom a university preparation in teaching in a specific content and school level. This preparation is manifested in the adequacy and relevancy of the content of the teaching as well as in the use of varied instructional strategies in the delivery of this content. Effective teachers are aware that knowledge is continuously changing due to new discoveries and new ways to look at old concepts. The same way that doctors are in a continuous process of inquiry to serve their patients better, teachers' knowledge needs to be complete, current and accurate. It is only then that they are able to transmit the most recent and complete knowledge and concepts to their students.

(4) **Strong feelings about classroom practices that reflect the cultural and linguistic background of LEP students**. Competent teachers feel that cultural knowledge is important to enhance students' self-esteem and academic development. Instructional practices evidence teachers' understanding of diversity when all students in the classroom accept peers' linguistic and cultural differences, and they do not see these differences as 'deficits' but as contributing factors for learning about other cultures and other societies. The content of the instruction reveals that teachers value diversity when the curriculum includes the study of other cultures and other peoples on a regular basis and when classroom materials for teaching about culturally diverse groups and concepts are provided. Chapter 3 provided detailed discussion on this topic.

Knowledge of the Second Language Acquisition Process

Teachers can promote English language development while teaching subject matter content and skills. It is beneficial to have an understanding of second language acquisition principles and how these can be incorporated into learning activities that require two-way communicative exchanges between teachers and students as well as between students. (See Chapter 4 for a detailed discussion of the Second Language Acquisition Process).

Knowledge of Students' Developmental Language Practices

Mainstream teachers need to have shared knowledge of language acquisition techniques as well as those interactional classroom activities which promote language development. Teachers should be able to deliver an instructional program that provides abundant and diverse opportunities for speaking, listening, reading, and writing, along with scaffolding to help guide students through the learning process. Students' cumulative records, information included in home language surveys, compilations of students' essays, as well as data provided in the standardized tests provide teachers with information about their students' language development, language strengths, and needs. New Levine (1993) suggests that knowledgeable mainstream teachers incorporate second language strategies in their classrooms which promote understanding of concepts and language development. These strategies are summarized in Figure 10.1

Familiarity with Students' Native Language and Cultural Background

Teachers' knowledge and appreciation of students' cultural and linguistic diversity and their attention to students' progress in all-English instruction become important factors of teachers' effectiveness in the classroom. Culture plays a big part in how teachers teach and how they can affect students in either a positive or negative way. Experiences in understanding the second language acquisition process, and learning the cultural backgrounds of students will facilitate teachers' interactions with their students' learning experience. This competency includes an understanding of the political, historical, economic, social, and cultural backgrounds of students in the classrooms. Teachers need to be excellent at human relations skills, particularly in the area of culturally sensitive behaviors. Competent teachers understand that positive self-concept and positive identification with one's culture is the basis of academic success. The cultures students bring to schools should not be considered 'deficit models'. Black English, for example, is not an inferior variant of standard English. Teachers need to promote friendly, polite, and supportive interactions among themselves and their students, and between the students themselves. Establishing a climate of diversity may be shown by the ability of mainstream teachers to:

- Use the classroom as an arena for learning about prejudice and intolerance.
- Understand how to set and establish clear norms of acceptable behavior regarding prejudice and respect.
- Be aware of ways to teach respect, trust, and responsibility while holding high expectations for all students.

It is important to be familiar with a variety of materials and literature from diverse cultures with a focus on issues of intolerance, immigration, cultural variety, and differing historical perspectives. Direct contact with the culture fosters sensitivity which is a result of understanding the culture of the school/community population through direct experience. Cultural tolerance and awareness are integrated into daily classroom life.

Familiarity with Learning and Cognitive Styles

Learning styles refer to individuals' consistent and rather enduring preferences of intellectual functioning and personality. Cognitive styles is a term used to refer to

Figure 10.1 Second language instructional practices

- Writing and orally reviewing with students the lesson's objective.
- Writing legibly (in print at first) on the blackboard.
- Using classroom routines and patterned language for transitions.
- Modeling step-by-step procedures prior to student activities.
- Presenting information both verbally and visually.
- Summarizing frequently: visually (on charts) and auditorily.
- Rephrasing teacher language to promote clarity and understanding.
- Providing active listening activities for students who are pre-verbal.
- Demonstrating new vocabulary with objects and actions and new concepts through hands-on experiments and activities.
- Incorporating students' role plays, science experiments, pantomimes, construction activities, total physical response routines, illustrations and other hands-on activities to demonstrate language and content concepts.
- Using authentic materials such as objects, newspapers articles and magazines, catalogs, maps, and application forms.
- Using graphic organizers such as graphs, time lines, Venn diagrams, tree diagrams, semantic mapping and charts to provide visual and non-verbal information and to help students in the organization of written paragraphs and reports.
- Developing jazz chants and songs to support the acquisition of the target language and concept.
- Identifying key vocabulary which students will need to know in order to develop content concepts.
- Identifying key vocabulary that signals the transition in written texts and that is important to understanding concepts.
- Incorporating interactional routines in lessons that will allow students to use the target language in context.
- Locating and adapting text material that is appropriate for students' language level.
- Incorporating complex grammar and vocabulary into content lessons in a way that will enable students to understand and use the target language.

New Levine, 1993: 1, 5.

Figure 10.2 Learning styles

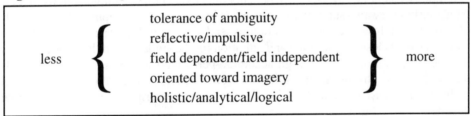

the manner in which people perceive, conceptualize, organize, and recall information. Each person is considered to have a more or less consistent mode of cognitive functioning (see Chapter 3). Examples of learning style can be seen in Figure 10.2.

Students' culturally specific learning styles are important considerations for classroom instruction. For example, Native American children are used to learning by carefully watching elders, not through direct instruction as is the common practice in United States classrooms. Students from Asian and Middle Eastern cultures, where schools often operate in accordance with a very strict transmission model (large classes and teachers controlling all interaction) will need to adjust and gradually adapt to an integrated classroom environment. Students from traditionally, cooperative, peer oriented cultures, such as the Hispanic culture, might have difficulties with several aspects of the transmission model of teaching, such as being expected not to help one another and singled out for responses.

Besides respecting and learning about the cultures of the students, teachers need to develop their own repertoires of teaching styles so that they can make adaptations in their classroom rules, procedures, and groupings to accommodate language minority student's needs. Teachers' awareness of their teaching styles will contribute to accepting students' varied learning styles by providing a variety of strategies using a wide repertoire of learning modes.

Effective Classroom Management

Teachers' ability to organize and manage the classroom as an efficient learning environment, to diagnose students' learning skills, and to prescribe appropriate learning activities that promote high student success are constantly related to students' achievement (Brophy & Good, 1974; Tikunoff & Ward, 1991). Rather than thinking of management techniques as a list of 'do's' and 'don'ts' that can be observed or not observed, good classroom management should be seen as the result of the academic tasks which children are engaged in (Doyle, 1991). Teachers need an understanding of how classroom settings (both social and physical) can be arranged to support a variety of instructional strategies.

High Expectations for their Students

Teachers' attitudes toward their students is a very important variable in effective teaching, and it has been related to teachers' expectations of their students (Brophy

& Good, 1974). Having high expectations of students seem to be characteristic of exemplary teachers. Effective teachers not only expect high achievement from their students but they also support attempts made by students. As Brophy & Good (1974) demonstrated, lower teacher expectations lead directly to lower academic perform-ance as well as less teacher time and attention for the students. On the contrary, high teacher expectations lead to high academic performance. Brophy & Good (1974) have shown a strong relationship between teachers' expectations, their actual behavior in classrooms, and students' subsequent performance in class. Effective teachers:

- Believe that all students can learn.
- Believe that students can be influenced.
- See themselves as facilitators of learning.
- Have high expectations of students learning.
- Respect and use the varied lifestyles of students.

Teachers must have high expectations of students. If teachers think that students do not have ability, they will find ways to avoid engaging students in the task (a perception of lack of abilities) rather than exposing them to these tasks. Students read certain teachers cues such as too much praise for a relatively easy task, too much pity for a slow student, too much help in doing a task as indications that the teacher considers recipients of these cues to be low-ability learners (Graham & Weiner, 1993). It is not surprising that teachers who demonstrate a genuine respect and appreciation for these students tend to respect and appreciate them as individu-als. Exemplary teachers respect students' feelings, emotions, and appreciations; they consider students as people with a right to their own views and feelings. More importantly, they are used to allowing children to be themselves and can even accommodate them without the fear of losing control. Effective teachers challenge students through provocative tasks and provide them with the mechanisms to become achievers of those tasks.

Facilitators of Parental Involvement

Teachers need to demonstrate the ability to draw parents of LEP students into classroom-related activities, thus tapping into their knowledge to enhance the instruction of linguistically and culturally diverse students. When parent–school partnerships are formed, parents often develop a sense of efficacy that communicates itself to students with positive academic consequences, especially in the case of language minority. Involving family members in the teaching process can benefit students, families, and the school community in general. Most parents of language minority students have high expectations for their children, and they want to be involved in promoting their academic success (Carrasquillo & London, 1993). Lack of parental involvement may be attributed to (a) work interference, (b) lack of confidence, (c) lack of English language skills, and (d) lack of understanding of the home–school partnership. Interaction between parents and school can enhance understanding of school practices and school culture in addition to promoting learning activities in the home.

Learning about the family's experiences prior to and since their arrival in the United States, their religious beliefs and practices, parenting practices, and roles ascribed to family members and close friends can also help the teacher plan collaborative activities with family members. Without information from the parents, many assumptions may be made about the students that do not reflect the parents' perspective. Parents can provide important information about the students' status and behavior in the family and in the community, as well as information about the students' educational strengths and weaknesses.

For any number of reasons, some parents will not be able to spend time in the classroom. Therefore, information about the students and the class must be sent home on a regular basis. Some students talk about what they do when things are going well in school. Parents are surprised and delighted when they receive a call about something special their children are doing in school. Teachers should inform parents about events and the accomplishments of their children. For example, a class newsletter is a good means of informing parents about what is going on in the classroom. The newsletter should include information about weekly events, samples of students' hand written work, and recommendations for reading and writing activities that parents can do with their children.

Including parents from diverse linguistic and cultural environments in the instructional component will help to: (a) build rapport with parents through adequate communication, (b) assist parents or other interested members of the community to understand the school curriculum, (c) solicit parental help in developing the instructional program, (d) gain parental support in implementing the program, (e) clarify conflicting values and goals, and (f) provide literacy training in the school so that parents can tutor children in the native language.

In summary, close cooperation and sincere and caring performance between parents, schools, and especially teachers can serve to improve LEP students psychological and academic performance (Carrasquillo & London, 1993). Such a cooperative atmosphere creates an environment that is conducive not only to children learning more but also to parents, teachers, and administrators working together as part of a comprehensive delivery system for the betterment of all.

Concluding Remarks

Teachers' competencies have been widely listed and discussed in the literature. The next step that needs to be outlined is how, as educators, we may be sure that these abilities are transformed into effective practices in the majority of classrooms. One means may be to start measuring teachers' competencies in delivering instruction. This can be brought about by observing teachers' abilities or competencies during instruction. Tikunoff & Ward (1991) list two ways in which this observations can be implemented:

(1) Illustrating ways in which a teacher applies his/her abilities from planning through initial instruction, to mid-point modification/adaptation of instruction, to completion of the unit.
(2) Demonstrating students' use of their increasing English language development and academic knowledge and skills across different phases and levels of the instructional process.

These two points need further attention and discussion for implementation.

CREATING APPROPRIATE LANGUAGE AND LEARNING ENVIRONMENTS FOR LEP STUDENTS

One of the key components necessary for successful classrooms and successful language minority students is the need to create the kind of classroom environment that will facilitate both language development and content learning (Hamayan, 1990; Milk, Mercado & Sapiens, 1992; Squire, 1987). Effective classrooms provide: (a) instructional activities that are systematically organized, (b) rules which prevail during each classroom activity which are content-sensitive and implicitly conveyed, (c) students' diversity in understanding and following classroom rules, (d) cooperative principles which organize conversation and are used to organize classroom interactions, and (e) teachers and students' negotiation of rules to help each other in following accepted rules and regulations. Teachers have the capacity to create an optimal learning environment. The literature on effective classroom management and organization states that effective instruction involves the instruction of students primarily in small groups with intermittent assistance by the teacher (Tikunoff, 1985). The teacher's role is to provide an instructional initiation. Students who are accustomed to working with others in accomplishing tasks, collaborating on projects, and generally working together are comfortable in cooperative classrooms in which these activities are rewarded. Although teachers need to elicit students' responses, these are kept to the minimum. Language facility, written as well as oral, develops primarily through personally meaningful active uses of language in the service of genuine human intentions including the intention to learn (i.e. build a representation of the world).

Teachers and schools can best influence students' language development by facilitating their intentional use of language, both oral and written, for a wide range of personal, social, and academic purposes, rather than by drilling students in predetermined information about language. Students' language plays a significant part in virtually all mental activity and school learning, and this language use not only promotes better learning but linguistic and cognitive development as well. Therefore, the language environment of the school classroom needs to be natural to allow students to participate in meaningful and purposeful language acts and events, because it is within the context of significant language use that learning occurs. Teachers should encourage students to take control of the discourse by inviting peer interaction, through which higher order cognitive and linguistic levels can be developed.

The interactive classroom is most easily organized by structured teachers. The teachers deliver information, but spend less time telling their students what to do, and more time helping them realize options and make decisions about their work. They want their students to learn as much as possible without relying on the teacher. The independence they foster in their students is reflective of a major difference between a product classroom and a process classroom — a change in the balance of control. In a process classroom, learners have considerable control of their learning as they make decisions on topic, audience, and final product. Teachers' roles change, as they allow their students to teach them. Teachers may know more than their students, but teachers have much to learn about their students' topics and reading and writing strategies. Teachers become one of the learners and share the operation of the classroom with other learners. Weaver (1988) proposes a classroom environment in which there is a promotion of language and literacy. In these classrooms:

(1) The learner is active, formulating hypotheses by transacting the environment.
(2) The teacher is the facilitator, creating an environment and structuring activities that provide the learner with opportunities to direct his or her own learning.
(3) Learners' errors reflect their current stage of development and provide teachers with information that will assist them in planning appropriate learning activities.
(4) Emphasis is on process, with the result that better products are produced.

Teachers establish an environment in which students come to understand their learning process as they work toward final products. The promotion of positive and interdependent interactions between teachers and students and between language minority student peers is an important instructional objective. Language development is facilitated by extensive interactions among native and non-native speakers. When teachers use supportive social and instructional interactions in equal amounts with both minority and majority language students, both groups perform better academically (Kerman, 1980). Teachers participate in genuine dialogue with students and facilitate rather than control students learning. This approach encourages the development of higher-level cognitive skills rather than just factual recall information.

DEVELOPING REFLECTIVE PRACTITIONERS

Since Dewey, teachers' educators have been concerned with how to prepare reflective teachers who have the capability and orientation to make informed and intelligent decisions about what to do, when to do it, and why it should be done. Effective teaching involves a sustained reflective process, which the teacher either initiates or enters into willingly as part of a collaborative enterprise (Langer & Colton, 1994; Milk, Mercado & Sapiens, 1992; Schon, 1987). Reflective decision makers are intrinsically motivated to analyze a situation, set goals, plan and monitor actions, and evaluate results as they work closely with others. Teachers learn to do new things not solely because they 'now have new information', but because they have become engaged in an active, introspective process through which they are, in some manner, transformed (Milk, Mercado & Sapiens, 1992). As a result of this transformation, teachers are better able to sustain the willingness and ability to effect change in their classrooms (Langer & Colton, 1994; Schon, 1987). Change will only occur if teachers themselves change what they are doing in the classroom. Practitioners need to become engaged in a process of 'reflective practice'. To make decisions, individuals draw on their knowledge base. As they experience the results of their decisions, new meanings are constructed to replace or enhance parts of the knowledge base. Langer & Colton (1994) propose a framework (see Figure 10.3) for developing teacher reflection that includes two main variables: *constructing knowledge and meaning* and *professional knowledge base*.

Reflective teachers need to have a framework to construct *knowledge* and *meaning*. This is what Langer & Colton (1994) call a *cycle of inquiry*. Cycle of inquiry is the meaning making process that teachers develop through specific experiences. These experiences are integrated into the teachers' knowledge base to construct new meanings; and meaning replaces or enhances part of the teachers knowledge base. The professional knowledge base is the information that teachers bring to the classroom/school experience that needs to be assessed and considered in interpreting experiences and making decisions. The knowledge base of teachers includes information about *content, students, pedagogy, school/classroom context, and personal values/attitudes*. Teachers may demonstrate a diversity of knowledge

Figure 10.3 Framework for developing teacher reflection. Model developed by G. Langer and A.B. Colton (1994: 3)

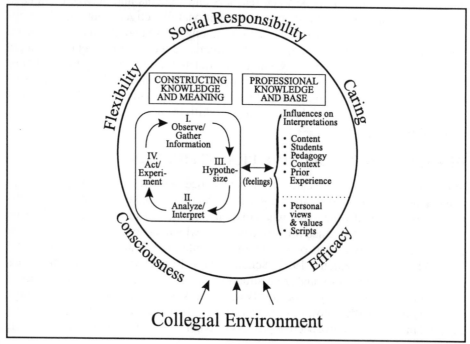

base depending on personal characteristics and prior experiences. In their development of teacher reflection model, Langer and Colton indicate that desirable reflective decision making depends on five attributes: efficacy, consciousness, flexibility, social responsibility, and caring.

Efficacy refers to the belief that one's effort can make a difference, that desirable outcomes are not just a result of luck. A high efficacy teacher realizes that an activity was successful because of careful planning, and knows that similar care will pay off for the future. *Consciousness* refers to the process of teachers' own thinking through the experience. *Flexibility*, using Langer & Colton's (1994) own words, refers to being able 'to put ourselves in another's shoes' to take on that person's point of view. It is the ability of an individual to accommodate to another's wishes or changing conditions. It is the readiness to accommodate or to change in accord with the wishes of another colleague or individual. *Social responsibility* is closely related to critical reflection and includes consideration of the ethical and moral aspects of participating in a social system. Langer and Colton indicate that socially responsible educators consider how their attitudes regarding race, gender, ethnicity, and class may affect their actions. Teachers should strive for justice and fairness in school. *Caring* relates to the trust and respect involved in the development of a collegial environment. Effective teachers need to develop positive relationships with students and colleagues in a collegial environment.

Staff development must be adapted to reflect students' demographic, cultural, and linguistic realities. Staff development must involve more than addressing a discrete set of competencies. It means engaging teachers in a process wherein they see themselves as learners involved in discovering how students learn and reflecting on how they can create optimal environments for their students in their classrooms (Milk, Mercado & Sapiens, 1992). The literature on effective teaching (Langer & Colton, 1994; Milk, Mercado & Sapiens, 1992; Schon, 1987) lists strategies for developing reflective thinking. Figure 10.4 lists most of the recommended strategies. The format use in grouping these strategies is the one presented by Langer & Colton (1994: 4).

Figure 10.4 Strategies for promoting reflective thinking

Individual Activities	Pair/small Activities	Group Activities
Personal Histories	Cognitive Coaching	Cases
Video/Audio Self-Assessment	Peer Supervisor	Discussions Writing
Journal Writing	Problem Framing	Problem Framing
Portfolios	Action Research	Action Research
Observation Peer	Interactive Journaling	Role-Playing

School staff development should provide for the monitoring of activities at the school and district level to ensure quality of training provided, and to increase the level of implementation of successful instructional practices and supportive learning environments. This staff development should use a reflective, cooperative model approach in which teachers, supervisors, and administrators participate together and learn as a team.

CONCLUSION

Attributes of teachers who are considered 'effective' in teaching LEP students include teachers who are highly experienced and have highly developed communication skills. They are teachers who think and reflect about their teaching, and are able to communicate their own instructional philosophies. These teachers work hard to understand the community, families, and students whom they serve. These teachers also work hard in incorporating into the curriculum attributes of their students' cultural and linguistic background.

Reflective teaching provides an opportunity for mainstream teachers to think about what they do and why — assessing past actions, current situations, and intended outcomes. Schools need to provide structured opportunities for teachers to reflect in ways that they find helpful in understanding their classroom experiences with all students, but especially those experiences related to the quality of teaching delivered to the culturally and linguistically diverse student population represented in the classroom.

References

Abrams, R. (1993) Language in the social studies classroom. Unpublished manuscript.

Austin, V. (1994) Language development in the social studies. Unpublished manuscript.

Baker, C. (1993) *Foundations of Bilingual Education and Bilingualism*. Clevedon: Multilingual Matters.

Baruth, L.G. and Manning, M.L. (1992) *Multicultural Education of Children and Adolescents. Needham Heights, MA: Allyn & Bacon.*

Beck, I. and McKeown, M.G. (1991) Research directions: Social Studies texts are hard to understand: Mediating some of the difficulties. *Language Arts* 68, 482–489.

Bossert, S.T. (1993) Cooperative activities in the classroom. In L. Darling-Hammond (ed.) *Review of Research in Education (pp. 225–250). Washington, DC: American Educational Research Association.*

Brophy, J.E. (1979) Teachers behaviors and student learning. *Educational Leadership* 37 (1), 33–38.

Brophy, J.E. and Good, T.L. (1974) *Teacher–Student Relationships, Causes and Consequences.* New York: Holt, Rinehart and Winston.

Brown, H.D. (1991) TESOL at twenty-five: What are the issues? *TESOL Quarterly* 25 (2), 245–260.

Burke, F.G. (1990) *Public Education: Who's in Charge?* New York: Praeger.

Burns, M. (1992) *About Teaching Mathematics: AK-8 Resource.* Sausalito, CA: Math Solutions Publications.

Canales, J. (1990) Assessment of language proficiency: Informing policy and practices. Unpublished manuscript.

Carrasquillo, A. (1991) *Hispanic Children and Youth in the United States: A Resource Guide.* New York: Garland.

Carrasquillo, A. (1994) *Teaching English as a Second Language: A Resource Guide.* New York: Garland.

Carrasquillo, A. and London, C. (1993) *Parents and Schools.* New York: Garland.

Carrell, P. (1989) Metacognitive awareness and second language reading. *Modern Language Reading* 73 (2), 121–134.

Carroll, J. and Sapor, S.C. (1959) *Modern Language Aptitude Test (MLAT)*. New York: Psychological Corporation.

Cazden, G. (1986) ESL teachers as language advocates for children: In P. Rigg and S. Enright (eds) *Children and ESL: Integrating Perspectives* (pp. 9–21). Washington, DC: Teachers of English to Speakers of Other Languages.

Cecil, N. and Lauritzen, P. (1994) *Literacy and the Arts for the Integrated Classroom*. New York: Longman.

Chamot, A.U. and O'Malley, J.M. (1986) *A Cognitive Academic Language Learning Approach: An ESL Content-based Curriculum*. Wheaton, MA: National Clearinghouse for Bilingual Education.

Chamot, A.U. and O'Malley, J.M. (1994) Instructional approaches and teaching procedures. In K. Spangenberg-Urbschat and R. Pritchard (eds) *Kids Come in All Languages: Reading Instruction for ESL Students* (82–107). Newark, DE: International Reading Association.

Chaudron, C. (1988) *Second Language Classrooms: Research on Teaching and Learning*. New York: Cambridge University Press.

Christina, B. (1992) *An In-service Training Course Designed to Increase Teachers' Strategies for Working Effectively with Second Language Learners in the Elementary School Mainstream Classroom*. Miami, FL: Nova University. (ERIC Document Reproduction Service No. ED 349 865).

Clark, E. and Barron, B.J.S. (1988) A thrower-button or a button-thrower? Children's judgment of grammatical and ungrammatical compound nouns. *Linguistics* 26, 3–19.

Clark, E. and Hetch, B.F. (1983) Comprehension, production, and language acquisition. *Annual Review of Psychology* 34, 325–349.

Clark, C.M. and Peterson, P.L. (1986) Teachers' thought processes. In M.C. Wittrock (ed.) *Handbook of Research on Teaching* (pp. 255–296). New York: Macmillan.

Cochran, C. (1989) *Strategies for Involving LEP Students in the All-English-Medium Classroom: A Cooperative Learning Approach*. Silver Springs, MD: Clearinghouse for Bilingual Education

Collier, V.P. (1987) Age and rate of acquisition of second language for academic purposes. *TESOL Quarterly* 21, 617–641.

Collier, V.P. (1992) A synthesis of studies examining long-term language minority students data on academic achievement. *Bilingual Education Research Journal* 16, 187–212.

Council of Chief State School Officers (1992) *Recommendation for Improving the Assessment and Monitoring of Students with Limited English Proficiency*. Washington, DC: Author.

Crandall, J. (ed.) (1987) *ESL Through Content Areas Instruction: Mathematics, Science, Social Studies*. Englewood Cliffs, NJ: Prentice-Hall Regents.

Crawford, A.N. (1993) Literature: Integrated language arts, and the language minority child: A focus on meaning. In A. Carrasquillo and C. Hedley (eds) *Whole Language and the Bilingual Learner* (pp.61–75). Norwood, NJ: Ablex.

Cuevas, G.J. (1981, April) SLAMS: A second language approach to mathematics learning. Paper presented at the annual meeting of the National Council of Teachers of Mathematics, Toronto.

Cummins, J. (1980) Teaching English through content-area activities. In P. Rigg and V. Allen (eds) *When They Don't Speak English* (pp. 139–151). Urbana, IL: National Council of Teachers of English.

Cummins, J. (1981) The role of primary language development in promoting educational success for language minority students. In California State Department of Education (ed.) *Schooling and Language Minority Students: A Theoretical Rationale* (3–49). Los Angeles, CA: California State University.

Cummins, J. (1984) *Bilingualism and Special Education: Issues in Assessment and Pedagogy.* San Diego, CA: College-Hill Press.

Cummins, J. (1989) *Empowering Minority Students.* Sacramento, CA: California Association for Bilingual Education.

Cummins, J. (1994) The acquisition of English as a second language. In K. Spangenberg-Urbschat and R. Pritchard (eds) *Kids Come in All Languages: Reading and Instruction of ESL Students* (36–62). Newark, DE: International Reading Association.

Dale, T. and Cuevas, G.J. (1987) Integrating language and mathematics learning. In J. Crandall (ed.) *ESL Through Content-area Instruction* (pp. 9–54). Englewood Cliffs, NJ: Prentice-Hall Regents.

DeGeorge, G.P. (1988) Assessment and placement of language minority students: Procedures for mainstreaming. *Equity and Excellence* 23 (4), 44–56.

Delgado-Gaitan, C. (1994) Russian refugee families: Accommodating aspirations through education, *Anthropology and Education* 25, 137–155.

DeMott, D. (1985) Exploring classroom interaction. *Educational Horizons* 63, 150–153.

Dewey, J. (1938) *Experience and Education.* New York: Macmillan.

Dickinson, D.C. (1987) Oral language, literacy skills and response to literature. In J.R. Esquire (ed.) *The Dynamics of Language Learning* (pp. 147–183). Urbana, IL: Clearinghouse on Reading and Communication Skills.

Doyle, W. (1991) Classroom tasks: The core of learning from teaching. In M. Knapp and P. Shields (eds) *Better Schooling for the Children of Poverty* (pp. 235–256). Berkeley, CA: McCutchon Publishing Corporation.

Dunkel, P. (1986) Developing listening fluency in L2: Theoretical principles and pedagogical considerations. *Modern Language Journal* 70 (2), 99–106.

Dunkel, P. (1993) The assessment of an L2 listening comprehension construct: A tentative model for test specification and development. *Modern Language Journal* 77 (2), 180–191.

Edmonds, R.R. (1979) Effective schools for the urban poor. *Educational Leadership* 37, 15–27.

Ellis, R. (1990) *Understanding Second Language Acquisition*. Oxford: Oxford University Press.

Enright, D.S. and McCloskey, M.L. (1988) *Integrating English: Developing English Language and Literacy in the Multilingual Classroom*. Reading, MA: Addison-Wesley.

Ervin-Tripp, M. (1974) Is second language learning like the first? *TESOL Quarterly* 8 (2), 111–127.

Faltis, C. (1993) *Joinfostering: Adapting Teaching Strategies for the Multilingual Classroom*. New York: Merrill Macmillan.

Fathman, A.K., Quinn, M.E. and Kessler, C. (1992) *Teaching Science to English Learners, Grades 4–8*. Washington, DC: National Clearinghouse for Bilingual Education.

Fishman, J.A. (1971) *Advances in the Sociology of Language*. The Hague: Mouton.

Flood J. and Lapp D. (1987) Reading and writing relationships: Assumptions and directions. In J.R. Squire (ed.) *The Dynamics of Language Learning* (pp. 9–26). Urbana, IL: Clearinghouse on Reading and Communication Skills.

Freeman, D.E. and Freeman, Y.S. (1991) Whole language lessons to promote social action. *Social Education* 55 (1), 29–32, 66.

Garcia, E.E. (1993) Language, culture and education. In L. Darling-Hammond (ed.) *Review of Research in Education* (pp. 51–98). Washington, DC: American Educational Research Association.

Gardner, R. (1980) On the validity of affective variables in second language acquisition: Conceptual contextual and statistical considerations. *Language Learning* 30, 255–270.

Gardner, R. (1985) *Social Psychology and Second Language Learning: The Role of Attitudes and Motivation*. Great Britain: Edward Arnold.

Gardner, R. and Lambert, W. (1972) *Attitudes and Motivation in Second Language Learning*. Rowley, MA: Newbury House.

Goldenberg, C. (1990) Research directions: Beginning literacy instruction for Spanish-speaking children. *Language Arts* 67 (6), 590–598.

Goldman, S. and Trueba, H. (eds) (1987) *Becoming Literate in English as a Second Language: Advances in Research and Theory*. Norwood, NJ: Ablex.

Gollnick, D.M. and Chinn, P.C. (1994) *Multicultural Education in a Pluralistic Society*. New York: Macmillan.

Goodlad, J.I. (1990) *Teachers for our Nation's Schools*. San Francisco, CA: Jossey-Bass.

Graham, S. and Weiner, B. (1993) Attributable application in the classroom. In T. Tomlison (ed.) *Motivating Students to Learn* (pp. 179–196). Berkeley, CA: McCutchon Publishing Corporation.

Graves, D. (1983) *Writing: Teachers and Children at Work*. Portsmouth, NH: Heinemann.

Graves, D. (1990) *Discover Your Own Literacy*. Portsmouth, NH: Heinemann.

Graves, W. (1991) Current developments in second language reading research. *TESOL Quarterly* 25 (3), 375–405.

Gray, P. (1993, Fall) Teach your children well. *Time,* pp. 69–71.

Halliday, M.A.K. (1977) *Explorations in the Functions of Language.* New York: Esevier North-Holland.

Hamayan, E.V. (1990) Preparing mainstream classroom teachers to teach potentially English proficient students. In *Proceedings of the First Research Symposium on Limited English Proficient Students' Issues* (pp. 1–21). Washington, DC: Office of Bilingual Education and Minority Language Affairs.

Hamayan, E.V. and Perlman, R. (1990) *Helping Language Minority Students After They Exit From Bilingual/ESL Programs: A Handbook for Teachers.* Washington, DC: National Clearinghouse for Bilingual Education.

Hansen, J. (1987) *When Writers Read.* Portsmouth, NH: Heinemann.

Hawkey, R. (1982) An investigation of interrelationships between cognitive-affective and social factors and language learning. Unpublished doctoral dissertation, University of London, England.

Heimlich, J.E. and Pittelman, S.D. (1986) *Semantic Mapping: Classroom Applications.* Newark, DE: International Reading Association.

Hickman, J. and Cullinan, B. (eds) (1989) *Children's Literature in the Classroom: Weaving Charlotte's Web.* Needham Heights, MA: Christopher-Gordon.

Hicks, K. (1994) Shared book experience with adults. *Journal of Reading* 37 (5), 422–423.

Hillerich, R. (1985) *Teaching Children to Write K-8.* Englewood Cliffs, NJ: Prentice-Hall.

Hoge, R., Smith, E. and Hanson, S. (1990) School experiences predicting changes in self-esteem of sixth- and seventh-grade students. *Journal of Educational Psychology* 82, 117–127.

Holt, D., Chips, B. and Wallace, D. (1992) *Cooperative Learning in the Secondary School: Maximizing Language Acquisition, Academic Achievement, and Social Development.* Washington, DC: National Clearinghouse for Bilingual Education.

Johnson, D.W., Johnson, R.T. and Holubec, E. (1988) *Cooperation in the Classroom.* Edina, MN: Interaction Book Company.

Johnson, D.W., Johnson, R.T. and Holubec, E. (1991) *Circles of Learning: Cooperation in the Classroom.* Edina, MN: Interaction Book Company.

Jordan, C. and Joesting, A.K. (1983) Patterns of classroom interaction with Pacific Island children: The importance of cultural differences. In M. Chu-Chang (ed.) *Asian- and Pacific-American Perspectives in Bilingual Education* (pp. 216–242). New York: Teachers College Press.

Kelly, P. (1990) Guiding young students' response to literature. *The Reading Teacher* 43 (7), 464–470.

Kerman, S. (1980) *Teacher Expectations and Student Achievement.* Downey, CA: Office of Los Angeles County Superintendent of School.

Kess, J.F. (1992) *Psychology, Linguistics and the Study of Natural Language.* Amsterdam, PA: John Benjamin.

Kessler, C. and Quinn, M.E. (1987) ESL and science learning. In J. Crandall (ed.)

ESL Through Content-area Instruction: Mathematics, Science, Social Studies. Englewood Cliffs, N.J: Prentice-Hall Regents.

Krashen, S. (1981a) Aptitude, and attitude in relation to second language acquisition and learning. In K.C. Diller (ed.) *Individual Differences and Universals in Language Learning Aptitude* (pp. 155–175). Rowley, MA: Newbury House.

Krashen, S. (1981b) *Second Language Acquisition.* Oxford, England: Pergamon.

Krashen, S. (1982) Accounting for child/adult differences in second language rate and attainment. In S. Krashen, R.C., Scarcella and M.H. Long (eds) *Issues in Second Language Research* (pp. 161–172). Rowley, MA: Newbury House.

Krashen, S. and Biber, D. (1988) *On Course: Bilingual Education's Education Success in California.* CA: California Association for Bilingual Education.

Krashen, S., Long, M.A. and Scarcella, R.C. (1979) Age, rate and eventual attainment in second language acquisition. *TESOL Quarterly* 13 (4), 573–82.

Kuccer, S.B. (1987) The cognitive bases of reading and writing. In J.R. Esquire (ed.) *The Dynamics of Language Learning* (pp. 27–51). Urbana, IL: Clearinghouse on Reading and Communication Skills.

Langer, G.M. and Colton, A.B. (1994) Reflective decision making: The cornerstone of school reform. *Journal of Staff Development* 15 (1), 1–7.

Langer, J.A. (1984) Examining background knowledge and text comprehension. *Reading Research Quarterly* 4 (4), 463–481.

Lara, J. (1994) Demographic overview: Changes in student enrollment in American schools. In K. Spangenberg-Urbschat and R. Pritchard (eds) *Kids Come in All Languages: Reading Instruction for ESL Students* (pp. 9–21). Newark: DE: International Reading Association.

Lewis, P. (1990) Language experience approach for ESL students. *Adult Learning* 1 (5), 27.

Lieven, E. (1984) Interactional style and children's language learning. *Topics in Language Disorders* 4 (4), 15–23.

Lucas, T., Henze, R. and Donato, R. (1990) Promoting the success of Latino language minority students: An exploratory study of six high schools. *Harvard Educational Review* 60 (1), 315–340.

Magocsi, P.R. (1989) *The Russian Americans.* New York: Chelsea House Publishers.

María, K. (1989) Developing disadvantaged children's background knowledge interactively. *Reading Teacher* 42 (4), 296–300.

McKay, S. and Wong, C. (eds) (1988) *Language Diversity: Problem or Resource?* New York: Newbury House.

McLaughlin, B. (1992) *Myths and Misconceptions about Second Language Learning: What Every Teacher Needs to Unlearn.* Santa Cruz, CA: National Center for Research on Cultural Diversity and Second Language Learning.

Milk, R., Mercado, C. and Sapiens, A.C. (1992) *Re-thinking the Education of Teachers of Language-minority Children: Developing Reflective Teachers for Changing Schools.* Washington, DC: National Clearinghouse for Bilingual Education.

Mohan, B.A. (1986) *Language and Content*. Reading, MA: Addison-Wesley.

Morrow, M.L. (1993) Promoting voluntary interest in literature: A program that works. In A. Carrasquillo and C. Hedley (eds) *Whole Language and the Bilingual Learner* (pp.76–86). Norwood, NJ: Ablex.

Myers, M. (1987) The shared structure of oral and written language and the implications on teaching writing, reading, and literature. In J.R. Squire (ed.) *The Dynamics of Language Learning* (pp. 121–146.). Urbana, IL: Clearinghouse on Reading and Communication Skills.

National Center for Education Statistics. (1993) *The Condition of Education*. Washington, DC: United States Government Printing Office.

National Center for Effective Schools. (1994, Spring) Language, culture and identity. *Focus in Change* 14, 1–2.

National Clearinghouse for Bilingual Education. (1993–94) Clinton administration outlines plan for coordination between Title I and Title VII. *Forum* 17 (2), 1, 4–5

National Commission on Excellence in Education. (1983) *A Nation at Risk: The Imperative for Educational Reform*. Washington, DC: United States Government Printing Office.

National Council for the Social Studies Position Statement (1989) Social Studies for early childhood and elementary school children preparing for the 21st century: A report from NCSS Task Force on Early childhood/elementary social studies. *Social Education* 53 (1) 14–23.

National Council of la Raza (1993) *Poverty Project Newsletter* 5 (1), 7.

National Council of Teachers of Mathematics. (1989) *Curriculum and Evaluation Standards for School Mathematics*. Reston, VA: Author.

Nevin, M. (1992) A language approach to mathematics. *Arithmetic Teacher* 46 (3), 142–146.

New Levine, L. (1993) Sharing the wealth: The collaboration of ESL and mainstream teachers. *Idiom* 23 (3), 1, 5.

New York City Board of Education. (1993) *Facts and Figures*. New York: New York City Board of Education.

New York State Education Department. (1987) *Learning about Haitians in New York State*. Albany: Author.

Newman, J. (1985) *Whole Language Theory in Use*. Portsmouth, NH: Heinemann.

O'Hare, W.P. and Felt, J.C. (1991) *Asian Americans: America's Fastest Growing Minority Group*. Washington, DC: Population Reference Bureau.

Ovando, C. (1989) Language diversity and education. In J. Banks and C.M. Banks (eds) *Multicultural Education: Issues and Perspectives* (pp. 208–228). Needham Heights, MA: Allyn & Beacon.

Ovando, C. and Collier, V. (1989) *Bilingual and ESL Classrooms: Teaching in Multicultural Contexts*. New York: McGraw-Hill.

Parker, W.C. (1989) How to help students learn history and geography. *Educational Leadership* 47 (3), 39–44.

Peterson, M. (1983) The Indo-Chinese refugee child in Iowa: Talking with teachers. *Contemporary Education* 54, 126–129.

Piaget, J. (1952) *The Language and Thought of the Child*. London: Routledge & Kegan Paul.

Pinleurs, P. (1966) *Pinleur Language Aptitude Battery*. New York: Harcourt Brace Jovanovich.

Ramirez, J.D. (1992) Executive Summary. *Bilingual Education Research Journal* 16 (1&2), 1–62.

Ravitch, D. (1988) From history to social studies: Dilemmas and problems. In B.R. Gifford (ed.) *History in the Schools, What Shall we Teach?* (pp. 145–169). New York: Macmillan.

Rhodes, L. and Dudley-Marling, C. (1988) *Readers and Writers with a Difference*. Portsmouth, NH: Heinemann.

Riddlemoser, N. (1987) *Working with Limited English Proficient Students in the Regular Classroom*. Washington, DC: ERIC Clearinghouse on Languages and Linguistics. (ERIC Document Reproduction Service No. ED 289 368)

Rigg, P. and Allen, V.A. (eds) (1989) *When They Don't All Speak English: Integrating the ESL Student into the Regular Classroom*. Urbana, IL: National Council of Teachers of English.

Rivers, W.N. (1988) *Communicating Naturally in a Second Language: Theory and Practice in Language Teaching*. New York: Cambridge University Press.

Romero, M. (1991) Transitional bilingual education: An instructional perspective. In A. Carrasquillo (ed.) *Bilingual Education: Using Languages for Success* (pp. 51–80). New York: New York State Association for Bilingual Education.

Ross, R. and Kurtz, R. (1993) Making manipulatives work: A strategy for success. *Arithmetic Teacher* 40 (5), 254–257.

Routman, R. (1988) *Transitions from Literature to Literacy*. Portsmouth, NJ: Heinemann.

Rowan, T. and Bourne, B. (1994) *Thinking like Mathematics*. Porstmouth, NH: Heinemann.

Rubin, J. (1994) A review of second language listening comprehension research. *Modern Language Journal* 78 (2), 199–221.

Rutherford, F.J. (1989) *Project 2061: Science for All Americans*. Washington, DC: American Association for the Advancement of Science.

Sapp, G. (1992) Science literacy: A discussion and information-based definition. *College and Research Libraries* 53 (1), 21–30.

Schallert, D.L. (1987) Thought and language, content and structure in language communication. In J.R. Squire (ed.) *The Dynamics of Language Learning* (pp. 65–75). Urbana, IL: Clearinghouse on Reading and Communication Skills.

Schifini, A. (1994) Language, literacy and content instruction: Strategies for teachers. In K. Spangeberg-Urbschat and R. Pritchard (eds) *Kids Come in All Languages: Reading Instruction for ESL Students* (pp. 158–179). Newark, DE: International Reading Association.

Schon, D. (1987) *Educating the Reflective Practitioner*. New York: Basic Books.

Short, D.J. (1991) *Integrating Language and Content Instruction: Strategies and Techniques*. Washington, DC: National Clearinghouse for Bilingual Education.

Short, D.J. (1993) Assessing integrated language and content instruction. *TESOL Quarterly* 27 (4), 627–656.

Short, D.J. (1994) The challenge of social studies for limited English proficient students. *Social Education* 58 (1), 36–38.

Short, D.J. and Spanos, G. (1989, November) *Teaching mathematics to limited English proficient students. ERIC Digest*, 1–2.

Silverstein, S. (1974) *Where the Sidewalk Ends*. New York: Harper and Row.

Singer, H. (1981) Instruction in reading acquisition. In O. Tzeng and H. Singer (eds) *Perception of Print* (pp. 291–311). Hillsdale, NJ: Lawrence Erlbaum.

Slavin, R.E. (1981) Synthesis of research on cooperative learning. *Educational Leadership* 38, 655–660.

Slavin, R.E. (1990) *Cooperative Learning: Theory, Research, and Practice*. Englewood Cliffs, NJ: Prentice-Hall.

Slavin, R.E. and Karweit, N. (1985) Effects of whole class, ability grouped, and individualized instruction on mathematics achievement. *American Educational Research Journal* 22, 351–367.

Sleeter, C. and Grant, C.A. (1993) *Making Choices for Multicultural Education*. New York: Maxwell Macmillan International.

Smith, F. (1993) Content learning: A third reason for using literature in teaching reading. *Reading Research and Instruction* 32 (3), 64–71.

Spangenberg-Urbschat, K. and Pritchard R. (eds) (1994) *Kids Come in All Languages: Reading Instruction for ESL Students*. Newark, DE: International Reading Association.

Squire, J.R. (1987) *The Dynamics of Language Learning*. Urbana: IL: ERIC Clearinghouse on Reading and Communication Skills.

Stahl, S.A. and Vancil, S.J. (1986) Discussion on what makes semantic maps work in vocabulary instruction. *The Reading Teacher* 40, 62–67.

Steen, L.A. (1991) Reaching for science literacy. *Change* 23 (4), 11–19.

Stenmark, J.K. (ed.) (1991) Mathematics Assessment: Myths, Models, Good Questions and Practical Suggestions. Reston, VA: National Council of Teachers of Mathematics.

Stern, H. (1983) *Fundamental Aspects of Language Teaching*. Oxford: Oxford University Press.

Strong, M. (1983) Social styles and the second language acquisition of Spanish speaking kindergarten. *TESOL Quarterly* 17 (2), 241–258.

Sutman, F., Allen, V.F. and Shoemaker, F. (1986) *Learning English Through Science: A Guide to Collaboration for Science Teachers, English Teachers and Teachers of English as a Second Language*. Washington, DC: National Science Teachers Association.

Terrell, T.D. (1981) The natural approach in bilingual education. In California State Department of Education (ed.) *Schooling and Language Minority Students: A*

Theoretical Framework (pp. 117–146). Los Angeles, CA: California State University.

Tikunoff, W.J. (1985) *Applying Significant Bilingual Instructional Features in the Classroom*. Roslyn, VA: National Clearinghouse for Bilingual Education.

Tikunoff, W.J. and Ward, B.A. (1991) Competencies of teachers of ethnolinguistically diverse students groups. Paper presented at the annual meeting of the American Educational Research Association, Chicago, Illinois.

Trueba, H.T. (1987) *Success or Failure? Learning and the Language Minority Student*. Cambridge, MA: Newbury House Publishers.

Trueba, H.T. (1989) *Raising Silent Voices: Educating Linguistic Minorities for the 21st Century*. New York: Newbury House.

United States Bureau of the Census. (1992) *Current Population Reports — Population Projections by Age, Sex, and Hispanic Origin: 1992 to 2050. Washington, DC: United States Government Printing Office.*

United States Bureau of the Census. (1993, May) *Population Profile of the United States*. Washington, DC: United States Government Printing Office.

United States Department of Education. (1993a) *Descriptive Study of Services to Limited English Proficient Students*. Washington, DC: Planning and Evaluation Service.

United States Department of Education. (1993b) Descriptive study of services to limited English proficient students: Analysis and highlights. Mimeographed.

United States Public Law 100-297. (April 28, 1988) *Bilingual Education Act. Title VII Bilingual Education Programs*. Washington, DC: United States Government Printing Office.

Urzua, C. (1980) A language-learning environment for all children. *Language Arts* 57 (1), 38–44.

Van Allen, R. and Allen, C. (1970) *Language Experience in Reading*. Chicago, IL: Encyclopedia Britannica Press.

Vygotsky, L. (1962) *Thought and Language* (E. Hangman and G. Vaker, Trans.). Cambridge, MA: MIT Press. (Original work published 1934).

Waggoner, D. (1993) The growth of multilingualism and the need for bilingual education: What do we know so far? *Bilingual Research Journal* 17 (1&2) 11–12.

Waggoner, D. (1994) Language minority school-age population now totals 9.9 million. *The NABE News* 1, 24–25.

Wasney, T. and Wilde, J. (1987) *Bilingual Program Report 1986–87*. Los Angeles: Los Angeles Unified School District Research and Evaluation Branch. (ERIC Document Reproduction Service ED 335 942)

Wax, M.L. (1971) *American Indians: Unity and Diversity*. Englewood Cliffs, NJ: Prentice-Hall.

Weaver, C. (1988) *Reading Process and Practice*. Portsmouth, NH: Heinemann.

Wells, G. (1986) *The Meaning Makers: Children Learning Language and Using Language to Learn*. Portsmouth, NH: Heinemann.

Williams, J.D. and Capizzi-Snipper, G. (1990) *Literacy and Bilingualism*. New York: Longman.

Wittrock, M.C. (ed.) (1986) *Handbook of Research on Teaching*. New York: Macmillan.

Wittrock, M.C. (1987) Constructing useful theories of teaching English from recent research on the cognitive processes of language. In J.E. Squire (ed.) *The Dynamics of Language* (pp. 371–380). Urban, IL: Clearinghouse on Reading and Communication Skills.

Wong-Fillmore, L. (1991a) Language and cultural issues in the early education of language minority children. In S. Kagan (ed.) *The Care and Education of America's Young Children: Obstacles and Opportunities. Ninetieth Yearbook of the National Society for the Study of Education, Part II* (pp. 30–49). Chicago, IL: University of Chicago Press.

Wong-Fillmore, L. (1991b) Second language learning in children: A model of language learning in social context. In E. Balystok (ed.) *Language Processing in Bilingual Children* (pp. 49–69). Cambridge, MA: Cambridge University Press.

Yao, E.L. (1985) Adjustment needs of Asian immigrant children. *Elementary School Guidance and Counseling* 19 (2), 222–227.

This page is out dated...... Please
refer to next page.

Index

Subjects

Authors

This page is out dated...... Please refer to next page.

This page is out dated...... Please refer to next page.

ERRATUM

Angela L. Carrasquillo and Vivian Rodríguez: Language Minority Students in the Mainstream Classroom.

The Index printed in the book should be replaced by the version below. The authors and publishers apologise for any inconvenience caused to readers of this book by the errors in the original version.

Index

Subjects

American Indian, 43, 44
Aptitude, 63
Arab student, 47, 49
Assessment, 31-36
— multiple criteria, 32
— naturalistic instruments, 33, 34
— standardized tests, 34
Asian students, 41, 43
Attitude, 63

BICS (Basic interpersonal communicative skills), 26, 27
Bilingual education, 66-69
— definition, 66
— programs, 69
Bilingualism, 65-68
— balanced, 65
— dominant, 65
— additive, 65
— subtractive, 65

CALP (cognitive-academic language proficiency), 26, 27
Children's literature, 53
Classroom environment, 12, 13, 168, 169
Classroom managment, 165
Cognitive styles, 62, 163, 164
Concept development, 131, 132
Cooperative learning, 118-120
Culture, 51, 52

Discovery learning, 128, 129

English as a second language, 69-72
— definition, 69, 70
— ESL in bilingual education, 72
— free standing, 71
— intensive, 71
— programs, 71, 72
— pull-out, 72
Ethnic diversity, 31-39

Grade level classroom, xiii

Haitian students, 44, 45
Hispanic students, 39-41

Individual differences, 62

Journal writing, 102

Language acquisition, 57, 58, 76-78
Language diversity, 49-51
Language experience approach, 95, 96
Language minority students, xii, xiii, 12, 20, 24, 27, 30, 38, 39, 49, 50, 62, 65, 74, 79, 85, 88, 118, 159, 166, 168
Language proficiency, 60-62
— English language proficiency, 60, 61, 111
Latino, 39
Learning style, 64, 163, 165
Limited-English proficient students, 163-165
Listening comprehension, 81, 82
Literacy, 88, 96, 97

184

Authors